DIGITAL Creativity

Techniques for Digital Media and the Internet

BRUCE WANDS

John Wiley & Sons, Inc.

Cover and interior design: Winslow Colwell/Wind Design

Published by John Wiley & Sons, Inc., New York.

Published simultaneously in Canada.

Library of Congress Cataloging-in-Publication Data:

Wands, Bruce.

   Digital creativity : techniques for digital media and the Internet / Bruce Wands.

        p. cm.

  ISBN 0-471-39057-7 (pbk.)

  1. Multimedia systems. 2. Web sites—Design. I. Title.

QA76.575 .W38 2002

006.7—dc21   2001017856

Printed in the United States of America.

10 9 8 7 6 5 4 3 2 1

This book is dedicated to my students, past, present, and future, and to my family for encouraging me to dedicate my life to art, music, creativity, and teaching.

CONTENTS

Preface xiii

Who Should Read this Book xiii   The Purpose of this Book xiv
What this Book is Not xv   How this Book is Organized xv3

Acknowledgments xvii

Chapter One The History of Digital Media 1
Then and Now: The Predigital Traditions
and Inventions That Have Spawned New Media

Oral History 2   Abacus and Mathematics 2
Cave Drawings and Paintings 3   Written Language 3
Books 4   The Printing Press 4   Photographs 4
Telephone 5   Electricity 5   Typewriter 6
Motion Pictures 6   Radio 7   Television 7
Early Computer Graphics 8   The Development of Workstations 9
The Development of Personal Computers 10
The CD-ROM Era 14   The Internet Era 15   Games 16
Summary 17   Bibliography 19   Exercises 19

Interview: Christiane Paul 20
New Media Curator for the Whitney Museum of American Art

Chapter Two The Basics of Digital Media...................... 27
Input 28   Analog-to-Digital Converters 30
Audio Input 30   Video Input 30   Processing 31
Central Processing Unit 32   Motherboard 32   Bus 32
Memory 32   Disk Drives 33   Ports 33
Modems 34   Cable Modem 34   DSL 35
Personal Digital Assistants 35   Software 35
Operating Systems 35   Software Applications 36
Painting and Drawing 36   2D Animation 37
3D Animation 38   Video Editing and Compositing 38
Internet 39   Programming 39   Output 40
The Computer Image 40   Color Palettes 42
The Web-Safe Palette 42   Video 42
Audio CD, CD-ROM, and DVD 42   Printers 43
System Configuration 43

Case Study: Wands Studio 46

Summary 49   Bibliography 49   Exercises 49

Chapter Three Creativity.. 51

What is Creativity? 52   The Four "I"s 52
Brainstorming 57   Practical Creative Techniques 58
Digital Methods 59   Libraries and Bookstores 62
Drawing and Sketching 63   Photography/Video 64
Summary 68   Bibliography 68   Exercises 69

Interview: Isaac Kerlow 70
Director of Digital Talent for the Walt Disney Company

Interview: Barbara Nessim 76
Chair of Illustration, Parsons School of Design

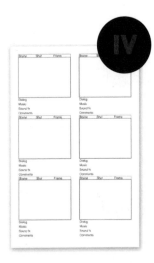

Chapter Four The Production Pipeline.......................... 81

Preproduction 82   Idea/Concept 83
Research/Sketching 84   Script 85   Storyboard 85
Navigation and Flow Chart 86   Animatic 87
Working Prototype 87   Final Preproduction Materials 88
Production 88   Postproduction 89
Manufacturing and Distribution 89   Production Environments 89
Scheduling 90   Budgets 92   The Production Team 92
Producer 92   Director 93   Artists 93
Designers 93   Video 93   Audio 94
Computer Animation 94   Web Production 94
Programmers 95   Systems Administrators 95
Summary 95   Bibliography 97   Exercises 97

Interview: Steven Heller 98
Art Director for *The New York Times Book Review*

Chapter Five Design and Typography.............................. 101

Design 102   Form Follows Function 104
Principles of Design 104   Color 104
New Design Considerations 106   Introduction to Typography 107
Fundamentals of Typography 107   Typefaces 107
Type Size 108   Type Style 109   Spacing 109
Alignment 109   The Creative Use of Type 110
Layouts 110   Choosing a Typeface 110
Working with Type 111   Working with Type and Image 000
Letting Images or Graphics Tell the Story 112

Case study: SVA Subway Poster Design 113

Summary 116   Bibliography 117   Exercises 117

Interview: Bonnie Hammer 118
Design Production Manager for Zagat.com

Chapter Six Web Design and Production.........................121

The Team 122   Concept/Idea 123
Define Content and Gather Information/Resources 123
Information Architecture 124
Determining Software for the Web Site 124
Site design and Prototype 126   Metaphor and Visual Style 127
Creating and Preparing Content for the Web 128   HTML 129
HTML Text and Tags 129   Fonts 130
Color and Images 130   Image File Formats 131
Vector Formats, Macromedia Flash, and Adobe LiveMotion™ 132
Links 133   Sound and Video 133

Case Study: www.brucewands.com 134

Case Study: Voyage of Discovery, The National Trust 136

Case Study: Rich Borge, Illustrator, www.richborge.com 142

Case Study: Pamela Hobbs, Illustrator, www.pamorama.com 146

Summary 151   Bibliography 152   Exercises 152

Interview: Pamela Hobbs 153
Illustrator, www.pamorama.com

Chapter Seven Digital Photography..............................157

Photographic Production Process 159   The Digital Camera 162
Technical Issues 163   Exposure and Shutter Speed 166
Exposure 166   Camera Equipment 167   Tripod 167
Creative photography 168   Lighting 172
Table-Top Photography 175   Portrait Photography 176
Location Photography 177   The Digital Image 178
Scanning and Digitizing 178   Digital Image Processing 179
Output 180   Summary 180   Bibliography 181
Exercises 181

Interview: Matthew Schlanger 182
President and CEO of Black Hammer

Chapter Eight Video Production......................................189

The Video Production Process 190   The Analog Video Signal 190
Adjusting a Video Monitor and Signal 192   Analog Formats 192
Digital Formats 193   Video Production Techniques 193
Script 193   Camera Techniques 194   Lighting 195
Studio Lighting Techniques 196   Location Lighting Techniques 197
Audio 197   Shooting Video 197
Covering a Scene 198   Digitizing Video 198
Practical Concerns When Digitizing Footage 199   Editing 199
Video Output 202   Video for the Internet 202
Streaming Media 203   DVD 203

Digital Video Software ..... 204　　Future Trends in Digital Video 204
Summary ..... 205　　Bibliography ..... 206　　Exercises 206

Interview: G. H. Hovagimyian 207
Cross-Media Digital Artist

Interview: Antoinette LaFarge 210
Director, Museum of Forgery

Chapter Nine Audio 215

The Nature of Sound ..... 216　　Analog and Digital Audio Theory 216
Frequency Range ..... 216　　Dynamic Range 217
Sample Rates ..... 217　　Bit Depth ..... 217　　Formats 218
MIDI ..... 218　　Audio on the Internet 218
Audio Internet Formats ..... 218　　Digital Audio Production 220
Audio Preproduction ..... 220　　Audio Production 220
Locating Sounds/Music ..... 221　　Narrators 221
Sound Effects ..... 222　　Music ..... 222　　Choosing Music 223
The Recording Process ..... 224　　Types of Microphones 224
Choosing a Microphone ..... 224　　Location Sound 226
Mixing ..... 227　　Mastering ..... 228　　Duplicating 229

Case Study: Louisiana Moon by Bruce Wands 230

Summary ..... 232　　Bibliography ..... 232　　Exercises 232

Interview: Pat Johnson 233
Digital Artist, Writer

Interview: Cathy Benante 236
Computer Artist, Electronic Arts

Chapter Ten 2D Animation: Traditional into Digital 241

History ..... 242　　The Creative Process for 2D Animation 245
The Role of the Animation Director 246
Breaking Down a Script ..... 248　　Making Exposure Sheets 249
Image Sequencing ..... 250　　Limited Animation 251
Character Animation ..... 251　　The Fundamentals of Motion 251
The Process of Animation Drawing ..... 254　　Roughs 254
In-Betweens ..... 255　　Clean-ups ..... 255　　Inking and Painting 256
Animation Photography ..... 257　　Digital 2D Animation 259
2D Animation for the Internet 260
Creating an Animation for the Internet 261
Summary ..... 263　　Bibliography ..... 264　　Exercises 264

Interview: Andy Lackow 266
3D Illustrator

Interview: Victor Acevedo 269
Digital Artist

Chapter Eleven 3D Animation..**273**

The 3D Animation Process 274
The 3D World Space and Navigating Through It 274
The Pyramid of Vision 275   Transformations 277
3D Cameras 278   Twist or Roll 279
Point, Lines, and Curves 279   Modeling 281
3D Scanning 283   Surfaces 283   Shading Models 284
Surface Properties 285   Textures 286   Lighting 289
Lighting Techniques 290   Animation 290
Planning Animation 291   Timing and Exposure Sheets 291
Layout and Camera Composition 292   Character Animation 293
Design 293   Advanced Animation Techniques 293
Rendering 295   Summary 295   Bibliography 296
Exercises 296

Interview: Joseph Nechvatal, Ph.D. 297
Digital Artist

Interview: Zach Schlappi 301
Technical Director, Blue Sky Studios

Chapter Twelve Professional Issues.............................. **305**

Resume 306   Portfolio 306
Exhibiting Your Personal Creative Work 307
Maintaining a Personal Web Site 308
Employment 308   Professional Organizations 310
Health 310   Summary 311   Bibliography 313
Exercises 313

About the Author 315

Index 319

PREFACE

I chose *Digital Creativity* for the title of this book because the creative process has a lot more to do with the content than the tools. Although computers give artists creative options they never had before, the machines are not the source of the ideas. What I hope to achieve with this book is to give the reader an understanding of how to create in both traditional and digital ways. The content of this book came out of a class I created as chair of the Computer Art department at the School of Visual Arts called "The Principles and Practices of Computer Art," which later became a graduate course entitled "Professional Issues." This lecture class gives students insight into the creative process and professional practices as they relate to using computers in their work. Most students are knowledgeable about how to use the software, but they need more information on how to be more creative and what the professional approaches to creating new media are.

I started working with computer art in graduate school at Syracuse University in 1975, well before the invention of the IBM PC and the Macintosh. We progrsammed the computer using punch cards and created line drawings that took many minutes for the plotter to draw. However, I saw the potential and knew that computers would revolutionize the way creative people worked. I had coined the term *teleputer* to describe the union of television and the Internet. Now, more than 25 years later, we are finally seeing that happen with webcasting, Web TV™, and concurrent programming on the Internet and on television, such as political conventions and large sporting events like the U.S. Open and the Super Bowl. We are still in the midst of the digital revolution. The Internet is evolving and growing at a rapid rate, and we have several more years of development yet to see. It is a very exciting time for people using computers to create.

Who Should Read This Book

This book will be of use to anyone interested in the creative process as it applies to computers. The primary audience is undergraduate and graduate students studying computer art. However, it is also written for professionals who are making the transition to digital media and for the general public. The methods used in this book are a result of my 17 years of teaching undergraduate, graduate, and continuing education courses at the School of Visual Arts in New York and other institutions, such as the Hong Kong Arts Centre, as well as my experiences lecturing abroad in China, Japan, England, and Italy. I also draw on my professional experience as a digital artist, designer, and independent producer. There is tremendous curiosity about digital art and new media all over the globe. Hopefully, this book will give those interested in creating digital art a head start and a road map of production methods.

The Purpose of This Book

The purpose of this book is to provide a solid foundation and serve as a reference for those creating work for digital media and the Internet. Most traditional creative disciplines have added digital tools to the production process. Photographers now use digital cameras, videomakers use digital video cameras and nonlinear editing, illustrators use digital tools in addition to traditional methods, and fine artists are exploring the creative potential of the computer. New fields such as Web design, computer animation, and streaming media have emerged as a result of technological development.

The approach of this book will be from both a practical and theoretical point of view. Although digital tools are relatively new, the goal of producing the best possible work has not changed. Good design shows itself no matter what medium is used.

We'll start with a look at the history of new media and the Internet to give an idea of how this revolution came about. After that, we'll talk about the basics of digital media and then an entire chapter will be devoted to creativity. Although digital tools give the designer and artist an incredible array of creative options, the original idea and vision are still the most important part of new media design. A variety of techniques for coming up with creative ideas and producing the most original work will be described. Next, we'll discuss the digital production pipeline. This is the standard industry approach to the work flow of creating for digital media and the Internet. Although there are differences between disk-based media and media for the Web, we'll look at the total process from a standard business model point of view. Subsequent chapters will deal with the different areas of new media. These will include typography and Web design, photography, video, audio, 2D animation, 3D animation, and professional issues. Each chapter will outline the fundamental principles of designing for that particular medium and some important factors to consider when using digital media. It is hoped that the reader will begin to focus on the content and quality of their work, rather than the technical aspects.

What This Book Is Not

This book is not intended to be a software manual but rather an approach to using the software for the maximum creative result. In my research during the writing of this book, I found that 98% of the books in the digital section of bookstores are software manuals or books that contain mostly software instruction and very little theory. You will not learn software techniques from this book, but you will learn how to apply software knowledge to producing creative and professional work.

How This Book Is Organized

This book is intended to cover all aspects related to using digital media in the creative process. There are chapters on the history of digital media, the creative process, and the production process. The later chapters deal with individual topics in depth. Each chapter of this book is meant to be self-contained, so if you are interested only in digital audio, for example, the audio chapter will give you all the information you need. Obviously, there will be some overlap, since audio is used with video, images with Web sites, and so on.

Each chapter is organized to allow the reader to learn the creative process for that particular aspect of digital media production. It starts with a general introduction to the field followed by a discussion of the production process as it relates to that particular media. Technical issues are then covered in depth. After that, we look at the creative issues that relate to that particular media, followed by a section of techniques, tips, and the deconstruction of professional projects. Interviews with well-known professionals in a variety of new media fields have been included to give additional perspective.

For additional resources, point your web browser to:
  www.wiley.com/wands

ACKNOWLEDGMENTS

I would like to thank all those who helped me with the development of this book, in particular, Silas Rhodes for founding the School of Visual Arts. I would like to thank David Rhodes, President of the School of Visual Arts for his support over the years, and Anthony Rhodes, Executive Vice President, for his help with the development of the Computer Art Department and BFA Computer Art program at SVA. I would also like to thank my colleagues, coworkers, staff, faculty, and students at SVA for making this book possible, particularly those in the MFA Computer Art Department.

The staff at John Wiley & Sons deserve a big thank you for giving me the opportunity and assistance in publishing this book: Margaret Cummins, Kim Aleski, Jennifer Mazurkie, Winslow Colwell, and others. Sarah Jane Freyman for her excellent advice. Eileen McVicar, Yaron Cannetti, and Jeanine Boubli for help with the illustrations. All the people I interviewed and who donated their time, artwork, and knowledge to this book. The people I have worked with over the past eight years at the Hong Kong Arts Centre for their support of my approach to teaching computer art and animation. Everyone I have met on my international travels who broadened my view of culture, art, and creativity. Finally, to all my friends who let me disappear during the writing of this book: Your names are too numerous to mention, and for fear of leaving someone out, I know that I have already thanked each of you in person. You'll always have a special place in my heart.

Chapter One

The History of Digital Media

Then and Now: The Predigital Traditions and Inventions That Have Spawned New Media

Before taking a look at new media, it will be helpful to take a brief look at some of the major inventions throughout history that preceded it and influenced its development (see Figure 1.1). The Internet and computers are now such a part of daily life, that we often forget how recently they were developed and what we used to rely on for information and knowledge.

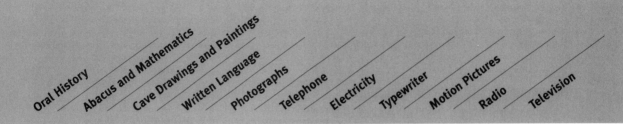

Oral History · Abacus and Mathematics · Cave Drawings and Paintings · Written Language · Photographs · Telephone · Electricity · Typewriter · Motion Pictures · Radio · Television

[1.1] This is a list of some major predigital inventions that affected the development of new media. Although we are entering a digital era, many are still widely used for human communication.

Oral History

Then: For countless millenia, before the advent of written and drawn history, most of our social information, customs, and history were passed down in the oral tradition. Storytelling was the primordial form of communication and handing down information and tradition. There were no permanent records of events, and early societies consisted of roaming bands of hunters and gatherers. Agricultural societies developed as people began to live in permanent locations. Trade began to develop between different regions. Along with the development of trade came cross-cultural exchange, and the economic and social benefits of dealing with others from faraway places. In contrast, societies like the Chinese protected themselves from conquering societies with the Great Wall. In both cases, written language, letters, and books developed as means for people to trade and communicate over long distances.

Now: Storytelling remains one of the most important and effective ways to communicate, even with modern technology. The motion picture is one of the most popular forms of entertainment. The quality of the storytelling is often a major factor in a film's success.

Abacus and Mathematics

Then: A simple calculation device invented by the Chinese to make counting easier and faster (see Figure 1.2). The concept is to have different rows stand for different levels of units. This approach to mathematics was the foundation of digital mathematics. In the early 1800s Charles Babbage designed an analytical calculation engine that was intended to perform calculations mechanically. Because of this and his other work related to the mechanization of mathematical calculations he is known as the Father of Computing.

DIGITAL | Creativity

Now: Digital numerical systems form the basis of how computers work. Everything is reduced to ones and zeros, allowing for extremely fast calculations and data handling.

Cave Drawings and Paintings

[1.2] This is an abacus. Counting is done by moving the beads along the rows.

Then: The cave drawings discovered in France are some of the earliest evidence of the power of the image. Many art history courses start with these drawings, and for good reason. They point to the power of the image and the desire of people to communicate with each other and to make a record of their cultural and personal history.

Now: Images are still a major part of how we communicate. Although photography allows us to reproduce an image exactly as we see it, drawings and paintings can give us a glimpse of things we cannot see, the creations of our imagination. An artist's rendition allows us to look back through history. We can enter fantasy worlds we never dreamed of through the imagination and skill of the artist. The need to escape from our daily reality was, and still is, served by those who can create visions other than those we see every day.

Written Language

Then: The Chinese language is thousands of years old and developed out of a pictorial tradition. It has been refined over the centuries and now contains about 7,000 characters. Words and concepts are made through the association of the characters used in the language. This also makes it difficult for the Chinese language to be adapted to a keyboard with a limited amount of characters. Egyptian hieroglyphics formed an early bridge between images and written language. The Greeks and Romans were very influential in the development of writing. The Roman alphabet is the basis of the English written language.

Now: The development of a standard character set allowed for greater numbers of people to communicate with each other. English is the main language used on the Internet, although there

are many other language options. More and more, digital communication via e-mail is becoming the standard. Handwritten and even typewritten letters are becoming less common. E-mail is now becoming a major form of communication among those digitally equipped.

Books

Then: Books were one of the first permanent records of events, traditions, and societies. The Egyptians used papyrus to record their writings. The Chinese are credited with the invention of paper, which was used to preserve sacred Buddhist texts. Early books were drawn and written by hand, and were thus very valuable. Most early books were created by monks. Texts that are thousands of years old have been discovered in Europe, the Near East, and Asia.

Now: Interestingly, Amazon.com was the first well-known e-commerce Web site. It sells books. It now has built-in artificial intelligence that tracks your book buying habits and recommends books that fall within your area of interest. It has become, in a sense, an enormous digital library that only needs your credit card number for you to purchase the books. New trends are evolving in publishing that will eventually put all books on-line, and you will be able to order the books on a print-to-order basis.

The Printing Press

Then: The invention of the printing press made books and other written material available to a much wider audience and began the era of mass communication. No longer were handmade books available only to a select few. The printing press allowed for hundreds and eventually millions of copies of Bibles, historical records, and so on to be distributed and read.

Now: Printing has made a significant move from high-cost commercial presses to local desktop printers in people's homes, which have the ability to print photographic-quality images. What cost hundreds of dollars to print just a few years ago can be printed inexpensively and selectively by end users.

Photographs

Then: Photography started in the 1800s with tintypes and glass negatives (see Figure 1.3). Black-and-white photography became a popular medium for newspapers and eventually for creative and personal photography. Color photography followed in the 1900s and became the standard for all kinds of image making, both commercial and personal. The four-color process used in printing is photographically based.

Now: New technology is moving printing and photography to a digital standard. The invention of megapixel cameras and the resulting higher resolution are fast making digital photography a standard professional medium. It is already in wide use on the Internet and in newspapers.

[1.3] This old Wands family photograph was printed on a glass negative.

Telephone

Then: Invented by Alexander Graham Bell in 1876, the telephone allowed the transmission of voice and music over wires. Long distance vocal communication became a reality.

Now: Telephones have become wireless and still hold a major place in communication technology. Digital phones can carry both digital and voice data. Personal digital assistants allow users to send e-mail and access the Internet.

Electricity

Then: Although it is difficult to believe, people used to go to Times Square in New York in the early evening to watch the electric lights be turned on. Thomas Edison invented the electric light in the late 1800s. Electricity allowed inventions like the stock ticker, telegraph, and radio to become widespread.

Now: Electricity forms the basis for much of modern society's daily routine. It pervades almost all of our normal daily lives. We ride to work on electric trains, work inside buildings lit with fluorescent lights, and spend much of the workday using computers. We go home and watch television, surf the net, or go to restaurants and music clubs to hear electric music. Restaurants with wood stoves and nonelectric music are a rarity. We go to sleep and wake up to an electric alarm clock and start the cycle all over again.

Typewriter

Then: The typewriter ushered in the era of individual printing. Personal and business communications could be typewritten much greater speed faster than they could be written longhand. The original QWERTY keyboard was invented to minimize collisions between keys that were frequently struck.

Now: Typewriters are slowly becoming obsolete, thanks to word processors, but the original QWERTY keyboard is still with us.

Motion Pictures

Then: Thomas Edison invented the motion picture camera in 1891, launching the era of movies as entertainment and documentaries. Early films were black-and-white until the color process was invented (see Figure 1.4). Early cameras were cranked by hand. The frame rates of old films were low, just fast enough to exploit the persistence of vision of the human eye, but slow enough to keep the cost down. The addition of sound moved the frame rate to 24 frames per second, where it stands today.

[1.4] Motion picture film was widely used until video became common. It is now mainly used for feature films, commercials, and short independent films. This is a photo of 16 mm film.

Now: Movies are a $7-billion-dollar business worldwide. It is a major form of entertainment. Over the past decade, large theaters began turning into multiplex theaters with smaller screens but more choices for the audience. Experiments with digital cinema are underway but remain extremely expensive. The cost of making multiple prints of the original film is still less than making theaters digital and distributing the films over the Internet. Considerable effort is being made to perfect video compression to allow full-screen movies to play in real time over networks.

DIGITAL | Creativity

Radio

Then: Radio was invented by Gugliemo Marconi in 1874, and he received an American patent in 1900. It was called the "wireless telegraph," and it could transit signals across distances without wires. One of the major milestones was when he sent a signal across the Atlantic Ocean in 1901. Lee DeForest continued the development of radio with the invention of the audio vacuum tube, which allowed for better signal transmission/reception and amplification. This was followed by Edwin Armstrong's invention of FM radio, which eliminated the static associated with AM radio. AM radio was based on the concept of amplitude modulation, where the radio signal is linked to the strength or amplitude of the signal (see Figure 1.5). FM radio is based on frequency modulation, where the signal is linked to the frequency with which it is transmitted.

Now: Radio continues to be a popular mass medium. Both AM and FM radio stations thrive. Programming is extremely diverse, ranging from talk shows and National Public Radio to popular music, to niche stations playing only jazz or specific genres of music. New developments include using the Internet to transmit radio programming. Listening is no longer restricted by geography.

[1.5] This is a photo of myself using a crystal radio I built in the 1950s.

Television

Then: The invention of television relied on the development of a cathode ray tube, or kinescope, as it was called by its inventor, Vladimir Zworkin. He applied for the patent in 1923 and first demonstrated it in 1929. Another individual who had a major role in the development of television was Philo Farnsworth. In 1927, he was the first person to transmit a television image. The image transmitted was a dollar sign. Television was showcased at the 1939 World's Fair in New York, and the TV era began. The first public television station was WQED-TV, which began broadcasting in Pittsburgh in 1954. Several years later, color television was developed. The early years of television were dominated by the three major networks, ABC, CBS and NBC. This was followed by the development of CATV, or cable television, which provided better reception to certain local areas and offered a wider range of programming.

Now: In the United States 98% of homes have at least one television. The number of hours a typical viewer watches television is staggering. Cable networks are now fully developed. Television stations are now broadcasting content over the Internet. Although it is neither full screen nor of high quality, many people see this as the trend for the future. Just as Amazon.com provides suggestions for books to read, future television systems will provide lists of programming suited to one's taste. The concept of prime time and watching television programs at a specific hour is changing. Video on demand will be the new paradigm of the digital broadcasting era.

Now that we have looked at some of the major inventions that formed the basis of the digital revolution, let's now take a closer look at the development of digital technology.

Early Computer Graphics

Computer graphics existed long before they were used to create digital media. The ability of the computer to handle increasing amounts of data and more sophisticated calculations made it a natural for creating graphic representations of mathematical formulae. Early computer graphics systems relied on programming to create images. Early plotters drew thin black lines on a piece of paper. Some of the other early images were made with ASCII character sets, with periods and commas representing light areas and number signs and asterisks representing the darker areas. These primitive methods of creating imagery relied on mainframe computers. Terminals were nothing more than a keyboard and a dot matrix printer. The idea of a video monitor was still new and kept in the control room out of access of remote users. This was during the mid-1970s, and the Internet had existed for quite a while as a text-only research network of government administration, the military, and universities. Access to the Internet was slow and cumbersome, but the seeds of the future were there. It was obvious that this new technology was going to evolve and grow into something more useful and more accessible to people other than scientists and programmers.

The early machines were known as mainframes. IBM held a near monopoly on computers in the early days. The IBM 360 was the most sophisticated machine at the time, and at Syracuse University, where I was a graduate student in the mid-1970s, it formed the basis around which the campus network was built. I was taking an Experimental Studios course and was using a language called Art

Speak (see figure 1.6). It was written in FORTRAN and gave a series of commands to the plotter to create complex mathematical drawings, reminiscent of the toy Spirograph. The time it took from handing in your stack of punch cards to seeing the printout was about $1/2$ to 3 hours.

Another sign that technology was about to make a leap was the arrival of video games. Previously, games like ping pong and foozeball were the main pastime for young people. Then a game called Space Invaders arrived. A silent group of characters slowly marched down the screen as players tried to eliminate all of them before they got to the bottom. This was an example of an early use of raster, or pixel-based, graphics. Close on the heels of Space Invaders came Asteroids. This game had a different look, and the player was now in the center of the screen with 360 degrees of rotation and the images were sharp and clear. It was the first vector-based game.

[1.6] I created this line drawing in 1976 using Art Speak. The dodecagon at the left center was sequentially modified to form the image.

The Development of Workstations

Large mainframe computers were very expensive and beyond the reach of most businesses. While development was continuing with these machines, General Electric was working on another graphics system, called Genigraphics. This system was used to make slides for business presentations. Until then, all of the artwork had been done by hand and then photographically double-exposed to add the type. Traditional methods of producing slides were expensive and time consuming. Genigraphics was a very high resolution system that became the standard for still computer graphics.

During the same period, a group of artist/programmers were working on a new computer graphics system called Synthavision. This software was based on government research concerning the behavior of radiation. The research was looking at how surfaces reflected or absorbed radiation from atomic bombs. The people developing Synthavision figured out a way to add color to these surfaces. Objects were built with primitives (i.e. rectangles, spheres, planes, etc.), and a new computer animation system was born. The early Disney movie *Tron* used this system.

Dolphin Productions, a well-known studio in the early 1980s, used digital and analog methods to create graphics. Digital Effects and several other companies that produced computer graphics were appearing. On the West Coast, John Whitney was experimenting with digitally controlled machines that created computer graphics.

Most of these early computer systems were large and cumbersome, and they required a lot of maintenance. Shortly after these systems were developed, a new generation of systems was born. They were called workstations. Companies like Via Video, the IMAGES system from the Computer Graphics Laboratory at NYIT, and Silicon Graphics began to produce very expensive workstations in the $75,000 to $100,000 range. Computers were just beginning to fall within the reach of the business and creative production communities. The Quantel Paint Box, one of the first video graphics systems capable of producing broadcast quality graphics, became available.

Systems like Via Video and IMAGES were still affordable only by large corporations, and these systems were used mainly to create slides for business presentations and graphics for corporate videos.

The Development of Personal Computers

In the early 1980s, intense research into developing smaller and more affordable computers was underway. In 1982, IBM introduced the IBM PC, a basic computer, capable of 16 colors and very poor audio. Early software was mostly business software like spreadsheets, word processing, and a business graphics package called Lotus Symphony, which included the spreadsheet Lotus 123 and a simple graphics package.

In parallel with this was the development of the Apple computer. The Apple II had graphics capability and the ability to display 256 colors as compared to IBM's 16. The early Macintosh computers were black and white (see Figure 1.7). The most significant feature

[1.7] This is my first Macintosh 512e, bought in 1985. It has 512k of RAM, an 800k internal disk, and an 800k external disk for a total of 1.6 MB of storage. This was state of the art at the time. I used MacPaint, MacDraw, MS Word, and Pagemaker software to produce design work for print and film. It still works!

DIGITAL | Creativity

of the Macintosh system was referred to then as "desktop publishing." Early graphic programs included MacPaint, a pixel-based program, and MacDraw, a vector-based program. Shortly thereafter, several page composition software packages emerged, including Pagemaker® and Ready Set Go, which later developed into QuarkXpress™. The first desktop publishing systems with a Macintosh, a scanner, and a LaserWriter cost about $10,000 and were extremely primitive by today's standards. However, this system caught the eye of forward-looking graphic design professionals. The profession was quickly divided into two camps. The most vocal of the two proclaimed the computer as a new revolutionary tool for design professional. The almost as vocal other camp decried that the computer was not capable of creating professional quality work, that the typography was poor and the images were low resolution. We all know the outcome, and as 16-, then 24-, then 32-bit color became available and typographic controls increased, more advertising agencies, design studios, corporate graphics departments, and individual designers jumped on the bandwagon.

The desktop revolution has come of age and won over the entire design community. At the present time, the great majority of magazines and books are produced using desktop publishing, or digital design as it is now called, software.

Imagery was not the only area that was undergoing a fundamental revolution. MIDI, the musical instrument digital interface, was invented in the mid-1980s, and it has revolutionized the recording and music industry, along with the development of digital audio and CD technology.

The original intention for the development of MIDI was to sell more synthesizers. If there were a way that keyboards could talk to each other, it would be in the interest of a musician to own several of them, so that they could create a wide range of sounds. Early music synthesizers like the MOOG and the ARP were analog. Sounds were created by turning knobs. The first digital synthesizer was the Casio CZ1000 (see Figure 1.8). The innovation of MIDI was that this was converted into a digital process. MIDI was run by a digital clock, which became the time keeper. Notes, or keys, were numbered 0 through 126, and given parameters like pitch, duration, note on, note off, velocity, and aftertouch. Because the clock ran at 384 cycles per second, MIDI was so sensitive that a digitally recorded performance played back with MIDI was indistinguishable by the human ear from the original performance. Not only was this revolutionary, but the

[1.8] This is the Casio CZ1000, the first digital synthesizer. It has a total of 16 preset sounds, 8 waveforms, and MIDI in and out. It was the first affordable MIDI synthesizer.

data needed for MIDI files was small and within the capabilities of low-cost computers. Very soon, MIDI sequencers and scoring software emerged, which allowed musicians to control a whole range of synthesizers and compose with digital control over tempo and harmony and gave them the ability to go in and fix mistakes by changing the MIDI data.

MIDI also became the scourge of recording studios. In the past, musicians had to play a song over and over again until they got it right. The were limitations on the number of tracks you could record on, and tape generated hiss. MIDI changed all that. Musicians now bought inexpensive sequencer systems for their home studios and perfected the performances with MIDI before going into a studio. Professional recording studios had to jump on the digital bandwagon to keep from going out of business. Slowly, digital was beginning to replace analog in the audio business. There is a saying in the industry, "audio precedes video." What is meant by that is that technological developments that happen in the audio business eventually work their way into the video business. The data-handling needs of audio are much smaller than those of video, so that as technology advances, the ability to handle video is increasing.

Standards started to emerge. The first IBM machines were VGA and used a video card called the Video Graphics Adapter, which had a resolution of 320 by 240. The next step up was SVGA, which had a higher resolution of 640 by 480 and the ability to have 256 colors.

During the mid to late 1980s, good quality video for computers was still very expensive, and the state-of-the-art video system at that time was the AT&T Targa Graphics board. These first came out in 16-bit color, and then evolved to 24-bit and 32-bit color. They also had the capability of storing a single video frame in the frame

DIGITAL | Creativity

buffer. Compared to the Quantel Paint Box, which at that time was well over $100,000, $3,000 for a TARGA board seemed a bargain and was what we would now call "prosumer." Along with the TARGA boards came a video board for the Macintosh, and other vendors began to create full-color systems for the Macintosh and the IBM. The race was on to see which computer would win the popularity contest. The Macintosh was popular with designers, artists, and academics. This was partly due to an aggressive campaign by Apple to get the computer on college campuses. The IBM was popular with corporations and businesses. For the time being, the Macintosh was the computer of choice for design professionals.

After the computer came of age as a graphic design tool and word processor, the computer industry needed something to sell more computers. Technology was also catching up with people's imaginations and the color, audio, and video capabilities of the machines were increasing by leaps and bounds.

Alongside this was the further development of the more expensive workstations. Silicon Graphics Incorporated developed machines with built-in rapid graphics calculation capabilities. Companies like Wavefront, Alias, and Softimage were developing 3D animation software. *Star Wars* ushered in a new era of special effects. Even before computer graphics had made its presence known, animators were attaching digitally controlled stepping motors to the Oxberry camera and creating digital photographic effects that had not been possible before. The star gate sequence in 2001 was an early example of this.

Along with these developments came the focus on multimedia. There was a call to develop a multimedia standard for computers so that there could be more compatibility. Not all software that was on the Macintosh worked on the IBM PC and vice versa. There were endless debates as to which platform was the more desirable and which machine should one buy. During the late 1980s the Macintosh had the edge on design and audio, and the IBM had the edge in the corporate community.

Another significant development during this period was the development of CD-ROM technology as a storage medium (see Figure 1.9). Before this, the only removable media available were floppy disks and Syquest drives that had storage capacity of about 1 MB and 44 MB or 88 MB, respectively. As image quality increased so did file size. The CD-ROM was capable of storing 650 MB. Since computers of that time were able to create and store text, images, audio, and video on their hard drives and CD-ROMS, a field emerged from this technology called Multimedia.

To many, this was the coming of age of digital technology because it was becoming affordable. For $5,000 one could purchase a machine with more capability that a $75,000 workstation that was three years old. This skyrocketing development in clock speeds and storage is still going on, with no real end in sight.

The CD-ROM Era

In the early 1990s the CD-ROM medium started to become widespread, spawning the development of interactivity. At the time the Internet was text only, but CD-ROMs could hold text, graphics, audio, and video. CD-ROMs were hailed as a new era in computers. There was also a major sales effort to promote these new uses of computers. The "multimedia standard" was born. The promise was huge. Computers could hold 250,000 pages of text on a CD-ROM disc, high-quality audio was now an option as evidenced by the success of the audio CD, and the early stages of digital video were becoming evident, with the rapid public acceptance of the Quicktime standard. Finally, CD-ROMs could be made interactive. Macromedia was one of the major players in the early days of CD-ROM authoring. Their professional-level software, Authorware, was cross-platform and very versatile. It was used for a lot of early interactive applications. Multimedia was now used for business presentations, making interactive books and converting films to the interactive format. There was a lot of research and development in the multimedia area.

However, a large problem began to develop: compatibility. Since most Macintosh systems were sold as complete units, with standard graphics and audio capabilities, CD-ROMs tended to work on most Macintosh machines, although they ran much slower on older machines. Also, Apple was the only manufacturer of Macintosh computers, and there were no clones. PCs had some serious problems with CD-ROMs. IBM manufactured their machines, and a host of clone manufacturers built competing machines using a wide variety of graphics boards and sound cards. There was very little standardization. As a result, commercial CD-ROMs did not work on all PC com-

[1.9] CD-ROM disks were the first storage medium to hold a significant amount of data. 650 MB of storage enabled the development of multimedia. These disks could store text, images, audio, and digital video.

puters. Sales of CD-ROMs were disappointing, and many companies scaled down their operations or closed altogether.

This was in the early 1990s, right when the Internet was getting ready to explode. The rapid growth of the Internet signaled the end of the CD-ROM era, and sales of CD-ROMs became smaller and smaller. People wondered why they should spend $40 for 650 MB of data on a CD-ROM when they could access gigabytes of data on the Internet for free. CD-ROMs are still widely used, mainly for software and content delivery. Many of the early compatibility problems have been solved.

The Internet Era

The Internet has caused a cultural and technical revolution both in the United States and abroad. We are in still in the early stages of this revolution, and although almost every television commercial lists a Web site and many of us spend countless hours on the Internet, we have yet to see the full impact of this revolution. Before we talk about what is happening now, let's take a look at the history of the Internet. We have traced the recent history of new media to the present, but Internet history goes back to the 1960s.

The Early Internet

The Internet was started in the 1960s as a way to link research institutions supported by the Advanced Research Projects Agency (ARPA). ARPAnet, as it was known, allowed various types of computers to talk with each other through the development of Internet Protocol (IP). It was a text-only system.

My first professional exposure to the Internet was as a Senior Information Scientist for Sandoz Pharmaceuticals in 1972. We used an Internet service provider that connected us to various on-line storage and retrieval systems. We could access the National Library of Medicine through a service called MEDLINE. The National Library of Education had a service called the Educational Resource Information Center (ERIC). Several other on-line resources were also available. The method used for on-line research was very similar to ones we use now. You would type in keywords and see how many matches you had. By carefully selecting the keywords, I would narrow down the choices to about 30 to 50 articles. I would then enter the print command and wait. The typical wait for response on the Internet in 1972 was 5 to 15 minutes. I would enter the command, return to my desk, and then wait until I heard the printer typing out my results. We joke now about how WWW stands for "World Wide Wait," but we

have come a long way in 30 years and still have a long way to go.

In the mid-1980s we started to see further development of the Internet through the establishment of NSFnet. This was a high-speed network created by the National Science Foundation with a speed of 1.5 Mbps.

One of the most significant developments that has allowed the Internet to develop into what it is today appeared in the early 1990s. The World Wide Web (WWW) was developed at the European Laboratory for Particle Physics (CERN).

In 1993, the National Center for Supercomputing Applications (NCSA) developed Mosaic, a graphical user interface for the Web. A few years later, Netscape and Internet Explorer were invented.

Although new developments continue to happen on the Internet on an almost daily basis, the rest is really history. The number of users on the Internet is still growing exponentially, and we are continuing to see new areas develop. Some rapidly developing areas are the increasing of access speed through cable modems and DSL. Streaming media now allows audio and video to be streamed over the Internet. Shortly, we will have full-screen video and high-quality audio available to people with broadband connections. One of the major organizations involved in this development is the World Wide Web Consortium (W3C), which collaborates with industry and is located at the Massachusetts Institute of Technology (MIT).

Games

The history of digital media would not be complete without an in-depth discussion of the development of video games. In some ways, this industry has been one of the driving factors of the digital revolution. One major manufacturer of early video games was Atari (see Figure 1.10). Recently, video games became a $7-billion-dollar industry worldwide, surpassing the film industry. The future of video games also looks promising from both a creative and technical perspective. To get the big picture, we'll take a closer look at the history of video games. Video games evolved along the same pathway as personal computers. One of the earliest video games was Pong. Played much like ping-pong, the "ball" moved back and forth across the screen, and the object was to keep it in play. As the game progressed, the ball started going faster and faster. It could be played either as a single player or dual player game. Another early game was Tank. This vector-based game moved through a 3D world made up of line drawings. The object was to destroy the other player.

[1.10] This is an early Atari video computer system. Games were played by inserting a cartridge into the slot and attaching the system to a television.

As video games evolved, they began to work more with 3D, and a significant development was the addition of textures to worlds and characters. This relied on the increasing speed of computers and additional memory to store the textures.

The next development in the video game revolution was the addition of sound. With more memory, sound could be stored and played back, adding realism and more impact to the game play.

CD-ROMs greatly affected what video games could be. With 650 MB of data available, the quality of the imagery and methods of game play could be greatly expanded. This is currently a limiting factor for games. We will see the development of using DVD technology for video games in the future due to their advanced storage capabilities.

Recent developments for video game development include networked games like Doom and Quake. As bandwidth increases on the Internet, global multi-user video games will develop. The creation of new game machines, like Sony Playstation 2, are pushing the envelope for game play.

Summary

This chapter presented a review of the development of technology and its creative use by artists. It started by looking at the early technology that predated the computer but foreshadowed its development. The key concept to remember is the use of technology for mass communication. The early systems were controlled by pro-

gramming, and artists had to have a broad knowledge of this in order to create images. The development of workstations in the early 1980s foreshadowed the widespread use of computers for creating digital media. Workstations like the IMAGES system and Via Video allowed for fairly sophisticated digital effects to be applied to still images. Within a few years, the presence of pixels and aliasing developed into the new "computer look" and became fashionable on MTV. The early MTV graphic style took advantage of this by using geometric patterns and shapes. In the mid-1980s the Macintosh and IBM PC set the standard for computers used for creative and business purposes. The falling cost of computers, combined with the development of the graphical user interface (GUI) made computers more accessible to more people. With the invention of the Macintosh computer and LaserWriter printer, the term *desktop publishing* was coined by Apple computers, and graphic designers began using this system for design. There was a lot of criticism of the early systems, particularly about the lack of sophisticated typographic controls. As the software developed and full color capability was added, many more designers began using computers. As technology advanced, personal computers were able to store and play back audio and video. In addition, new user-friendly programming languages like Lingo, the programming language of Macromedia Director, were being written. When all these elements were combined with the new storage medium of CD-ROM, the field of multimedia was born. Like many new technology-based disciplines, multimedia had a quick rise to popularity, followed by myriad technical and cross-platform problems. Approximately 20% of CD-ROMs produced were not compatible with all computers. During this period, the World Wide Web was invented and the Internet began to gain momentum. Along with this development, video games became much more sophisticated and began to have astronomical sales. Their development was directly related to the increasing speed of computers. The rapid rise of popularity of the Internet cut short the attention paid to multimedia. The Internet has been growing at an exponential rate and is continuing to do so. We are in the midst of the Internet revolution. Many digital design technologies have matured, such as imaging, 2D and 3D animation, but there is still a long way to go in the development of the Internet.

Michael Rush, *New Media in Late 20th Century Art,* Thames & Hudson, London, England, 1999. www.thameshudson.com

This is a good overview of new media art and the artists who create it. It includes chapters on media and performance, video art, video installation art, and digital art.

Nicholas Negroponte, *Being Digital,* Vintage Books, New York, NY, 1995. www.randomhouse.com/vintage

This was a *New York Times* bestseller and gives a unique view of the digital world from the perspective of the founding director of the MIT Media Lab.

Ray Kurzweil, *The Age of Spiritual Machines,* Penguin Books, New York, NY, 1999. www.penguinputnam.com

This is a comprehensive look at digital technology from a futuristic and well-informed perspective.

Marshall McLuhan, *Understanding Media,* MIT Press, Cambridge, MA, 1964. mitpress.mit.edu

This 1960s classic started the widespread examination of the effects of mass media on society. A must-read for anyone who wants to see how mass communication was viewed during its early days.

Marshall McLuhan and Bruce Powers, *The Global Village,* Oxford University Press, New York, NY, 1989. www.oup.co.uk

A good theoretical look at the effect of technology on society.

Bill Gates, *The Road Ahead,* Penguin Books, New York, NY, 1995. www.penguinputnam.com

A look at the past, present, and future of technology by one of the most influential men in the digital industry.

 1. Explore the connection between written language and pictorial history. Trace your cultural roots or those of a culture you are interested in, and collect a series of early images and writings. Use this research either to write a short paper on this period in history or to produce a series of images based on this time.

 2. Do an in-depth study of one of the important inventors of predigital or digital technology. Try to discover what led this person to making that invention. What was his or her educational and professional background? What social and cultural conditions prompted the inventions? Write a short biography of your subject and the effects of his or her invention. Speculate on what would have happened if the invention had not been made.

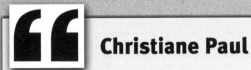

Christiane Paul

INTERVIEW

Adjunct Curator for New Media Arts, Whitney Museum of American Art

Publisher/editor, Intelligent Agent Magazine, www.intelligentagent.com

As the Adjunct Curator for New Media Arts at the Whitney Museum of American Art, Christiane Paul is one of the most influential people determining the future of digital art. Intelligentagent.com is a Web site that focuses on interactive media in the arts and education. It is a valuable resource and includes essays, reviews, art projects, archives, and links to virtual galleries, art projects, arts organizations, educational resources, and discussion groups. Christiane is the author of *Unreal City: A Hypertextual Guide to T. S. Eliot's "The Wasteland."* She holds a Ph.D. from Düsseldorf University.

When did you enter the digital realm?

I entered the realm of digital media in the early 1990s by starting to work with hypertext software (such as Storyspace). Apart from several smaller hypertext projects, I completed a hypertext guide to T. S. Eliot's poem "The Wasteland," which was published under the title *Unreal City* by Eastgate Systems (Watertown, Mass.). In 1995, I cofounded the magazine *Intelligent Agent,* which focuses on the use of new media in arts and education, since I felt that there was a need for a publication that would chronicle and present networked digital art and educational projects.

What was your background prior to your entry into the field of new media?

My background was in English literature with an emphasis on postmodern American fiction.

What made you decide to work with new media?

It was my background in postmodern and post-structuralist theory that led to my interest in hypertext and new media. On a lot of levels, hypertext and hypermedia seemed to illustrate and visualize the basic premises of poststructuralist theory: The networked, hypertextual environment is by nature nonlinear, nonhierarchical, and polyvocal; it favors a plurality of discourses and frees the reader/viewer from "domination" by the author/artist/creator. Readers and writers as well as artists and their audiences can collaborate in the process of remapping textual, visual, kinetic, and aural components.

What aspect of your background have you found most helpful in your transition to new media?

My background in theory and hypertext was extremely helpful in understanding the nature of the networked environment and the changed notions of the art work and the artist.

Who has influenced you most within the field of new media art?

As far as the history and theory of new media are concerned, Ted Nelson's *Computer Lib / Dream Machines* and Vannevar Bush's *As We May Think* have been influential texts. When it comes to new media art, I would mention the artists who have created work that I consider groundbreaking in various respects. In random order, these artists and art works are

• jodi.org, for turning the interface inside out. Jodi's site is a decidedly low-tech graphics battle that reminds us both of the standardization of the interface and the inherent beauty of its form elements and "sign language."
• Sawad Brook's "Prosthesis to a Well."
• Tom Ray's "Tierra," a network-wide biodiversity reserve for digital organisms built on the premise that evolution by natural selection is able to operate effectively in genetic languages based on the machine codes of digital computers.
• The installations of Christa Sommerer and Laurent Mignonneau, such as "A Volve," which often experiment with artificial lifeforms and create navigational interfaces that make the CPU disappear.
• Alternative Web browsers such as I/O/D's Webstalker and Maciej Wisniewski's Netomat.
• Mark Napier's potatoland.org, the Digital Landfill and the Web Shredder in particular.

What do you see as the important milestones in the development of new media?

Since new media is still in its infancy, future milestones are developed on a daily basis. As the important ones so far, I would cite the creation of the World Wide Web itself; the open source movement; agent software and A-life; alternative Web browsers; the recent victory of etoy over etoys may very well have been a milestone in illustrating a shift of power relations in the networked environment.

How have the use of new media and the use of the computer affected this process?

The most obvious effect on the creative process was that I started thinking in terms of mixed media—that is, possible combinations of navigable visuals, sound, and text as supposed to clearly defined categories. With new media and the use of the computer, there's an emphasis on process and an openness to continuous revisions and combinations instead of a focus on a finished result.

Technology is a rapidly changing and complex medium. Because of the diverse skill sets required to work in the field it is often necessary to collaborate. What effect does this have on the art?

The effect of collaboration is an openness to combining multiple points of view and to constant renegotiation. I believe that the collaborative process of creation is not too different from the result of the work, at least when it comes to interactive art works whose experience is dependent on the point of view of the audience and their renegotiation of the work's meaning.

New media incorporates the elements of video, sound, interactivity, and navigation. How has this affected the creative process?

Again, it has led to an increased openness of the process and to an emphasis on thinking in nonlinear terms—considering conditions of possibilities and multiple strands of a narrative (in the broadest sense). There is less control over the outcome of the work, which is experienced by the viewers in very different ways.

The artist/author is less of a controlling creator and more of a mediatory agent.

What advice would you offer to people entering the field of new media and technology?

To get a firm background in the history and cultural context of network technologies and communications in order to get a better idea of where new media is heading.

With all of the rapid developments in the technology, it is virtually impossible to know all of the software packages and have programming, video, and audio skills. How important is it for a new media artist to know "everything?"

I think it's important to know everything in terms of being informed about what hardware and software are being developed and how programming and network technologies are evolving. This doesn't mean that one has to learn all the tools, skills, and programming languages, but I believe that it's crucial to take a look at the big picture.

Where they should focus their attention?

They should focus on acquiring the skills that are absolutely necessary for the type of work they are doing and on building a network of collaborators who can assist with all the other tasks.

What is most lacking in the education of design and new media students?

An understanding of how design and new media have challenged and changed existing cultural concepts and a solid background in the history of these two realms. I believe that this knowledge and understanding is vital if one wants to be innovative and push the limits in this field.

How do you think the Web has changed traditional design?

Conceptually, the Web is a nonlinear, nonhierarchical network structure, and its characteristics have already tremendously influenced design. Design has become more and more network-oriented (in terms of visualizing a contextual network) and interactive, from smart houses to furniture that reacts to users and surroundings.

Where do you see Web design heading?

There certainly will be an abundance of design tools that will allow any user to create Web sites with a fairly sophisticated design. In terms of efficiency and database management at information-intensive sites, there probably will be increased use of dHTML and XML. Hopefully, there also will be more possibility for interaction on the users' end when it comes to allowing users to filter information and create their own informational resources.

How do you see the Web affecting other media, for example, print/news, traditional art, TV, movies, animation, galleries?

I think the Web has already tremendously influenced the design and content of print/news, TV, and other media. More and more magazines are using "Web design" such as frame structures for their layout or simulate a network structure and links. For example, through lines that point to subcategories and topics. The current TV program announcements of ABC simulate roll-overs (the little circle next to the time and program changes color as if you had moved the cursor over it). There is an increasing number of movies dealing either specifically with cyberspace and virtual worlds (such as *The Matrix* or Kronenberg's *eXistenz* or with the general idea of parallel (perceptual) worlds (such as *Being John Malkovitch*). Museums and galleries increasingly make use of the Web to inform the public about their shows and collections or to webcast events. They also start paying more and more attention to digital art and trying to integrate it into the museum system. Although the traditional art world is trying to integrate on-line art and there are more and more efforts to create virtual museums in conjunction with physical ones, there so far aren't many successful ways of collecting, selling, or even exhibiting digital art that is available on a network. In the on-line world, the (physical) gallery/museum context doesn't necessarily work as signifier of art status and the traditional art system may have to adapt to these parameters.

Where do you see the Internet heading?

On the one hand, the Web is certainly getting increasingly commercialized. While it was more or less a promotional tool for corporations in the beginning, e-business and commerce are now seriously taking off. I would predict that there will be a growing use of agent technology to identify and attract target audiences for commercial purposes.

On the other hand, the Web is still a free information space and will hopefully continue to maintain that quality and be able to rely on self-regulating mechanisms. I also hope that access to the Internet (from any part in the world) will improve. When it comes to art, there already is an "established" on-line art world with an array of prestigious galleries, critics and curators, acclaimed artists, and critical forums. (I wouldn't call it a ghetto, but this art world sometimes has an air of exclusivity, which is at least to some extent created by the players themselves). Hopefully, net artists will find ways to make their art commercially viable, be it through their work as content providers for other sites or through the sales of tools they create.

What are your favorite Web sites/URLs?

Mark Napier, "Web Shredder"
　　http://www.potatoland.org/shredder/

Digital Landfill
　　http://www.potatoland.org/landfill/

I/O/D, "WebStalker"
　　http://www.backspace.org/iod

Maciej Wisniewski, "Netomat"
　　http://www.netomat.net/

Jackpot
　　http://www.adaweb.com/context/jackpot

Christa Sommerer & Laurent Mignonneau, "Life Spacies"
　　http://www.ntticc.or.jp/~lifespacies

Sawad Brooks & Beth Stryker, "Lapses & Erasures"
　　http://www.thing.net/~sawad/erase/

Disseminet
　　http://disseminet.walkerart.org/

Victoria Vesna, Bodies, Inc
　　http://www.arts.ucsb.edu/bodiesinc/

Noah Wardrip-Fruin, "The Impermanence Agent"
　　go to http://www.plexus.org/omnizone/ click on "Works" and choose Noah Wardrip-Fruin

Fakeshop
　　http://www.fakeshop.com/

Jodi
  http://www.jodi.org

What is your take on the development of interactivity?

The notion of interactivity itself has changed quite a bit since the advent of new media. In the beginning, simple point-and-click navigation was considered interactive by many people, while it ultimately is nothing but a more sophisticated way of browsing. Interactivity should mean that users can assemble and reassemble information according to their needs and have an active influence on the display of information. Regarding artworks, interactivity can mean anything from choosing navigational routes through a work (and thus creating its meaning) to actively influencing the outcome of the work by adding to it and changing it.

Where do you see multimedia heading?

I'm sure that we are going to get more accustomed to a seamless combination of visuals/text/audio/video/animation. There are also going to be more tools for the creation of multimedia environments. Hopefully, these will be editing tools that allow users to incorporate as many media as possible and to create their own content and multiuser environments. In my opinion, multimedia tools won't be of much value if they don't allow for interactivity in a networked environment.

The ability to randomly access any portion of an animation, or work, is unique to multimedia and allows interactivity. How has this changed the creative process, and what are the special considerations that this creates?

The creative process in an interactive multimedia environment requires multidimensional thinking. One has to consider all the possible routes a user/viewer might take and their impact on the negotiation of the work's meaning. It's easy to lose interest in a work if there isn't some underlying narrative (be it a story or a navigational method) that pulls all the different possibilities together. One of the main challenges in the creative process is to negotiate openness and closure—to leave a work as open to interaction as possible while providing an underlying framework of content.

How do you compare the Internet with the gallery system as a venue for artists?

The Internet to a large extent allows artists to circumvent the traditional art system (with its venues, curators, collectors, and critics). In the on-line world, the (physical) gallery/museum context doesn't necessarily work as signifier of art status. Potentially, the Internet also allows access to a greater audience for an artist. When it comes to the commercial value of art, the status of on-line art is problematic. The value of art is, at least when it comes to the traditional model of the art and museum world, inextricably connected to economic value, and the scarcity = value model doesn't work when it comes to on-line art (it didn't work for photography or video, either, and one would expect that these art forms have led to modifications of the equation). Interactive art installations have a place in museums and galleries, but it gets more problematic when it comes to on-line pieces, particularly if they are time-based and open to interaction with the public.

What is the future of digital fine art?

I believe that digital fine art will easily be integrated into the traditional art system (and already has been to some extent). Digital fine art is still an object (even if it is as reproducible as photography) and thus can be commodified much more easily than net art.

What is the outlook for the future of digital media?

They will become increasingly incorporated into our lives on every level, from the entertainment industry and consumer products to household appliances. The interfaces we are used to today are probably going to change rapidly: The CPU will disappear, and we're probably going to rely more on touch screens, wireless technology, voice recognition, and various other methods of interface navigation.

What careers will be important?

Programmers, software developers, and designers will be very much in demand, and hopefully artists will more and more become content providers and developers on the market (if they desire to do that). It is already remarkable how many artists are in fact designing or developing multimedia content for corporations since their creative input pushing of limits often transcends the skills of a traditional designer.

What emerging technologies will become important?

I believe that there will be more and more focus on agent technology and multiuser environments.

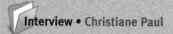

Chapter Two

The Basics of Digital Media

Like all creative tools, the better you get to know how your computer works, the better you will you will be able to make art with it. Being able to troubleshoot, configure, and optimize a system will save hours of lost time due to crashes, lost files, and other problems. The purpose of this chapter is to review and explain the basics of how computers work, how they are put together, and how they can best be adapted for digital media production. Simply put, the computer is a device that processes data. This data is first input, then processed, and then output.

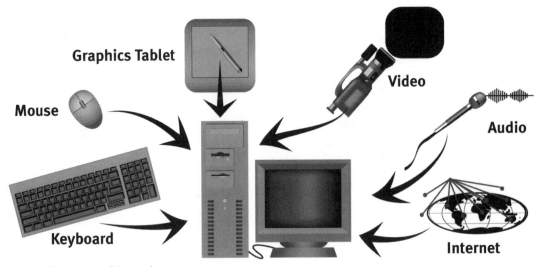

Graphics Tablet

Mouse

Video

Audio

Keyboard

Internet

[2.1] How different types of data can be brought into the computer.

[2.2] A standard keyboard for an Apple computer. Notice the QWERTY layout of the keys. It also has function keys at the top and a numeric keyboard at the right.

[2.3] A keyboard for an AVID digital video editing system. Look at the keys and notice how they have been assigned to different functions of the software.

Input

Input is the manner is which the data is entered into the computer (see Figure 2.1). The most frequently used input device is the keyboard. There are many different types of keyboards, and if you are going to spend significant time in front of a computer, it is a good idea to examine the various keyboard options. Two common ones are the standard QWERTY layout (see Figure 2.2) and the ergonomic layout, which is designed to create a minimum amount of stress on your hands. There are many sizes and shapes of keyboards, and they can work on different machines. Some keyboards have special keys. For example, the AVID keyboard, which has functions assigned to keys to speed the video editing process (see Figure 2.3 and Color Plate 1). Keyboards are not expensive, so it is a good idea to choose one that matches your hand size and work style.

The second most frequently used input device is the mouse. There are many kinds of mice, as well, but they generally break down into the one-, two-, and three-button models. The basic

DIGITAL | Creativity

metaphor for their use is the click and drag method. There are mechanical mice, which use a track ball that glides over a surface (see Figure 2.4). There are also optical and laser mice, which use a beam of light as a reference. This is again a matter of personal choice. There are also several alternative input devices, such as track balls, joy sticks, game controllers, and so on.

For drawing with the computer, the graphics tablet is an excellent idea. It allows you to draw and sketch in a way that is similar to drawing. The Wacom tablet is the most popular, and the tips have a pressure control stylus (see Figure 2.5). They come in a variety of sizes and shapes. They even have different types of styli, which emulate a pen or airbrush (see Figure 2.6). All of this is a matter of personal choice, but it is well worth the money to set yourself up with an input system that matches your hand size, work style, and personal preference.

Scanners are used to bring flat art and photographs into the computer. Scanners work by converting the image into digital form through a row of charge-coupled devices on the arm of the scanner as it moves over the art. The resolution of scanners varies with their quality, but 1440 dpi scanners are fairly inexpensive. Once an image has been scanned, it can be modified with an image processing program like Photoshop.

[2.4]
A mechanical mouse for an Apple computer sitting on a rare ILM mouse pad.

(left) [2.5] A WACOM graphics tablet. This is a 12 by 18-inch model. It came with a mouse and a pen.

(above) [2.6] A close-up view of the WACOM mouse and pen. Notice the five buttons on the mouse. It can be programmed for a variety of functions. The pen is also pressure sensitive.

Analog-to-Digital Converters

Mice, keyboards, pens, and digital data from networks and files create input data that is in digital form. Images, audio, and video need to be converted into digital data before they can be used and processed by the computer. This process is done with analog-to-digital converters (ADCs). Converters generally sample the signal coming in and convert it into digital data. For example, we can look at the sky during a sunset and see a smooth range of colors, from the fading yellow of the sun, to the gradated colors of the sky and clouds, to the overhead dark sky. When an image like this is sampled, it is divided into a number of discrete elements, both in terms of resolution (pixels) and colors. The image might then conform to a digital image standard by being 640 by 480 pixels in height and width and 256 colors. True photographic color is 24- or 32-bit samples using 16.7 million colors. At this level of quality, our eye cannot tell the difference between the original photograph and the digital image. The same thing happens with audio. The analog-to-digital converter for CD-quality audio uses 16-bit samples at a frequency of 44.1 kHz. This level of sampling is beyond our ability to tell the difference between the analog recording and the digital recording.

Audio Input

Audio input can happen in three ways. The first is through a built-in microphone or external microphone. Generally, microphones that come with computers are of low quality, and this type of input is recommended for memos, recording ideas, and other nonprofessional purposes. If you want to record high-quality voice into the computer, it is generally better to use a professional quality microphone, which is run through a mixer before it is plugged into the computer's audio input jack. The same applies to music.

Although removable media and CD-ROMs generally do not fall under input devices, many people use software to pull prerecorded audio from audio CDs and images from clip art CDs into the computer. This type of input should be mentioned here because of its widespread use.

Video Input

Input can either be through a camera or video cable. The same standards for audio apply to inexpensive video cameras. They are good as webcams and for recording low-quality video, but for professional uses, video should be shot in the highest quality possible and digitized into the best machine available. However, a simple setup, such as a digital video (DV) camcorder and Firewire can create very high-quality digital video. We should mention here that, currently, the DV standards for the Internet are still not full screen. However, DV, VHS, and other

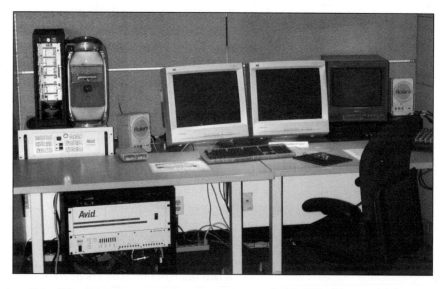

[2.7] An AVID editing system. It is a specialized system with three monitors: two RGB and a NTSC video monitor. There are also several hard drives to allow for sufficient storage. There is also an audio mixer and external speakers.

consumer and prosumer standards can be used for video for the Internet. Professional systems like the AVID are designed for professional quality video and are therefore much more expensive than the typical desktop video solution using Firewire (see Figure 2.7).

Firewire was developed to allow for the high-speed transfer of data between peripheral devices. It is most commonly used on DV camcorders for inputting and outputting video, but it is also used for many other devices, such as digital cameras, hard drives, and printers. Firewire allows for very high-speed data transfer rates and is 30 times faster than Universal Serial Bus (USB). Currently, Firewire can support up to 63 devices and cable lengths of up to 14 feet. It also allows you to plug it in without turning the computer off. It is also called IEEE 1394 or iLink.

Looking at this from the big picture, *input* refers to the bringing of data into the computer, whether from a keyboard, mouse or stylus, audio, video, or transmitted over cables.

Processing

This is what happens to the data once it has been entered into the computer. The main components of a computer include the central processing unit (CPU), the motherboard, and storage devices. The motherboard contains all the printed circuits that enable the CPU to talk to all the other components of the computer. The motherboard is connected to a monitor, mouse, and keyboard by direct connections or circuit boards (i.e., a video card).

Central Processing Unit (CPU)

The central processing unit is the "brain" of the computer. However, it is incapable of working unless it is turned on and loaded with the system and application software. We'll talk more about this later. The CPU is where the calculations and manipulation of data happen. CPUs are generally referred to by clock speed, brand, and generation. Current clock speeds are in the 500 to 800 MHz area. Ten years ago, clock speeds were in the 33 to 66 MHz range. We can expect to see clock speeds continue to increase in the future. Another way to get more speed out of a computer is to have multiple processors. Dual processor machines are becoming more common, and high-end computers can have 4, 8, 16, or more processors working together.

The two main manufacturers of computer CPUs are Intel and Motorola. Intel CPUs evolved through the 286, 386, 486, the Pentium I, II, and III machines. Motorola CPUs are 80260, 403, Power PC, G3, and G4.

Motherboard

The motherboard is the main circuit board on the computer where everything resides and/or gets plugged in. The CPU is on the motherboard, as is the memory, system bus, and connections for the disk drive, expansion cards, video card, audio card, hard disk, peripherals, and so on.

Bus

The bus is the pathway through which the data travels around the computer. The bus connects the CPU with the hard drive, video cards, audio cards, ports, input devices, and so on. Buses have speeds, just as motherboards do. Several buses have been developed over the years, starting with ISA, EISA, and Video Local Bus. Currently we are using the PCI bus technology. Bus speeds evolve with processor speeds and are intimately linked to the speed of a computer. If a really fast CPU is installed in a machine with a slow bus, the speed of the computer is limited by the bus speed.

Memory

RAM is the random access memory that exists on the motherboard. Most computers come with 64 or 128 MB of RAM. For better performance, especially with digital media computers, it is recommended that at least 256 MB is installed. For high-end 3D computers, very large images, or video, 512 or more RAM will be helpful. The general rule for RAM is to buy as much as you can afford.

Disk Drives

There are many different kinds of disk drives. Most computers have a single hard disk. This is where the operating system and application software resides and where the data files are stored. The cost per megabyte has been dropping with time and hard disks are getting larger and larger. Now 18 and 36 GB drives are common.

There is also removable media, such as floppy disks (see Figure 2.8), CD-ROM, removable hard drives, DVD, and so on. Floppy disks are inexpensive and hold about 1 MB of data. They are starting to be used less frequently because of increasing file size. Zip drives are very widely used. The original zip disk had a capacity of 100 MB, and now a 250-MB format is available (see Figure 2.9). They are relatively inexpensive, stable, and many people have them. CD-ROM has become a standard format for the delivery of software, video games, and other types of data. The cost of CD recorders has dropped and many machines now come with them built in. The cost of CD media has also fallen dramatically. CDs are stable and easy to store and carry. The popularity of audio CDs has made them also a very popular form of data storage. In the future, DVD will become a major form of data storage. DVD writers are currently very expensive but prices will fall just as prices for CD-ROM writers have fallen. DVD has the advantage of storing very large amounts of data. As DVD players become more popular, we will see an increase in the use of DVD writers and disks for data storage.

[2.8] A high-density floppy disk. It can store 1.4 MB of data.

[2.9] A 100 MB Zip disk. With increasing file sizes, Zip disks are becoming very common.

Ports

Ports are ways that data can travel into and out of the computer. There are three main types of ports on today's computers. Parallel ports are generally used for printers, and the data flows over several wires in a parallel manner. Serial ports can be used for a variety of devices, such as mice, keyboards, and printers. Serial ports allow data to flow sequentially and have fewer wires. The newest standard is Universal Serial Bus (USB), a very fast system. Many different kinds of devices can be connected to a USB port. USB ports also support a wide range of peripheral devices, and one of their greatest advantages is that they are "hot swappable." This means that you do not have to turn the computer off before connecting or dis-

[2.10] An external US Robotics modem for a Macintosh computer.

connecting a USB device. Most computer manufacturers are adopting the USB port because of its speed and ease of use.

Another widely used port is an Ethernet port. Ethernet is a networking system that allows machines to communicate with each other and exchange data and files. There are several flavors of Ethernet. 10 Base T is the least expensive and most common. 100 Base T is much faster and is quickly becoming a standard port in many computers. An extremely fast connection is gigabit Ethernet, which allows for a million bits per second of transfer speed.

Modems

Modems are the pieces of hardware that allow computers to talk to each other over a network. Every computer connected to the Internet uses either a modem or a network card (see Figure 2.10). Modems have different speeds. This is what is referred to as *bandwidth*. The wider, or faster, the bandwidth, the faster the computer operates. 56K is currently the most common modem speed.

Cable Modem

Cable modems work on systems that are basically a wide area network. Cable modems operate at significantly higher speeds than telephone modems (see Figure 2.11). They cost more, but the time

[2.11] A cable modem made by Motorola for Comcast @Home. This modem is capable of very high-speed navigation on the Internet.

DIGITAL | Creativity

saved with these modems pays for their cost. The greatest advantage of cable modems are their very fast data rates. One disadvantage of the cable modem is that it is based on a shared network strategy; that is, the more people who are using the network, the slower the computer will work.

DSL

Digital subscriber lines (DSL) are also becoming prevalent. They operate at various speeds, and you pay for the speed you want. One of the advantages of the DSL system is that it is totally digital. What you pay for in speed is exactly what you get, and there is never any variance.

Personal Digital Assistants

Personal digital assistants (PDAs) are portable computing devices (see Figure 2.12). They are not used for digital media production, but they need to be mentioned in this book. They are a great way to manage your time and to keep in touch with clients, and so on. You can store to-do lists, schedules, appointments, and other information. Some PDAs allow wireless connectivity to the Internet, allowing users to check e-mail, look at the stock market, and even get maps. PDAs are also starting to use color. In the future, we will see continued development of PDAs as portable computing devises.

[2.12] A PDA from China. It has an English-Chinese translation system and a pen. One can draw a Chinese character and the system will translate it into English. It also has the other functions of a PDA, such as appointments, memo list, phone numbers, calculator, etc.

Software

Software is the means by which things get done on a computer. Two basic elements are needed: the operating system and the software application. The operating system is the basic set of instructions that tells the computer what hardware components it is made of and, in essence, what it can do. Software applications allow specific tasks to be done.

Operating Systems

The operating system is the set of software that is loaded into the computer when it is turned on. There are also instructions that reside in the computer when it is turned off. The instructions that the operating system gives to the computer are to bring it up to

[2.13] A screen grab from Adobe Photoshop. Photoshop is a bit-mapped software that is used for working with photographic and other pixel-based images.

speed so that software programs can be used. Several operating systems are currently in use. They have varying degrees of compatibility and are moving toward being more compatible in the future. In the early days of personal computing, it was to the manufacturer's advantage to be exclusive. For example, the Macintosh computer was the first to have a graphical user interface (GUI), and this was its major sales feature. Early IBM and clone computers used the text-based Disk Operating System (DOS). To compete with the Macintosh, the Windows operating system was developed by Microsoft. Now, with the development of the Internet and cross-platform software, the differences between operating systems are more of a hindrance than a marketing advantage. The two main operating systems are the Macintosh OS™ and Microsoft™ Windows™, but there are many other operating systems, such as Linux, Irix, and Unix. Linux is becoming very widespread due to its open architecture, low price, and stability. For many Web servers, it is the operating system of choice. It is important to have a good knowledge of the operating system of the computer you are using. Operations such as file transfers, copying, renaming, deleting, color palettes, and changing the resolution of your monitor are functions of the operating system. Once the operating system has been loaded, other software programs can be installed on the machine.

Software Applications

We will talk about various software applications in detail in the later chapters. This section will give a brief overview of applications that are used for digital media design and production.

Painting and Drawing

This group of software packages is used to create, edit, and manipulate images. There are two types of painting and drawing programs. The first group works with bit-mapped images, or images composed of pixels. The second group is vector-based. These programs create images by using curves, lines, and shapes, which are drawn by using mathematical operations. There are advantages and disadvantages to each type of program. Bit-mapped programs, like Adobe Photoshop™, are good for dealing with photographic images, scanned images, and illustrations (see Figure 2.13). Images are composed of pixels of a particular resolution and bit depth.

A *pixel* refers to a picture element, or the smallest component of an image. It can be thought of as a square dot on the screen. Images on the computer are composed of thousands of pixels, each one assigned a particular location on the screen and color. Typical screen resolution for a computer image on your monitor would be 640 by 480. As mentioned earlier, the bit depth, or the number of bits assigned to each pixel, determines the color of the pixel. Screen location is generally done with x and y values. For example, 0,0 might be at the top left of the image, 320,240 in the middle, and 640,480 at the lower right corner.

The second type of painting and drawing software is vector based. The two most popular software packages using this type of system are Adobe Illustrator™ and Macromedia

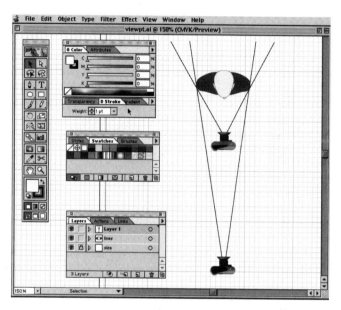

[2.14] A screen grab from Adobe Illustrator. This is a vector-based software. Although the tool palette may look the same, the software operates very differently from Photoshop. It relies of mathematical formulas, rather than pixels to form images.

Freehand™ (see Figure 2.14). These software packages define shapes through mathematical equations, rather than by using pixels. In doing so, they can be changed in a variety of ways without losing the precision of the mathematical curves. This is often referred to as *resolution-independent software*. For example, a very small vector graphic can be scaled to many times its original size and retain its smooth edges. A low-resolution bit-mapped image, on the other hand, will start to show its pixels if it is enlarged too much. Resolution independence is one of the strengths of this category of software. Also, the file sizes of vector-based images tend to be smaller than bit-mapped images. We will see continued development of this type of software in relationship to the Internet based on this fact, as well as combining bit-mapped and vector-based functions into a single software package.

2D Animation

This type of software allows one to create animation on the computer. It is similar to painting and drawing software in that there are bit-mapped and vector-based animation programs. Bit-mapped programs use a series of still images to form the basis of the animation. They also have built-in controls to allow for "inbetweening," or allowing the computer to create the motion by calculating the images that fall in between the start and end position of the animation. Macromedia Director™, Adobe Premiere™, and Metacreations Painter™ are three popular 2D animation software programs. There are also high-end packages like US Animation™ and Animo™ that are used for television and feature films.

3D Animation

Three-dimensional animation has made considerable progress in the last few years. Packages that once were extremely expensive and only affordable by the major film studios are now available for personal computers. Three-dimensional animation allows users to create a mathematical world within which animation can be created. Feature films, video games, and TV commercials are the places you see 3D animation most often. The learning curve for this type of software is fairly complex. In order to create an image, you must first create a 3D mathematical model of the object, and then assign surface properties like color, and texture to it. After this has been done, a scene is created by placing the model in an environment with a camera and lights. Animation is then done by keyframing the object in various positions. After an extended period of refining and testing, the images are then rendered into 2D images by the computer and output to digital video files, videotape, or film. Two examples of high-end software packages that have been adapted to personal computers are Alias/Wavefront Maya™ and Softimage XSI™. Other popular packages include Discreet 3D Studio MAX™ and Lightwave™.

Video Editing and Compositing

Because of the large amount of data needed for video, early video editing programs for personal computers worked mainly with smaller digital video formats like Quicktime. The most popular of these is Adobe Premiere™. With the rapid increase in computer speed, low cost of RAM and hard drives, and the development of Firewire and USB, it is now possible and affordable to edit video on a personal computer. One of the first systems invented was called the AVID, and it is still the standard for the broadcast industry. A complete AVID system is expensive and beyond the reach of most small studios. However, new software, like Apple's Final Cut Pro™ includes many of the editing features of an AVID system but costs much less. It is slower and does not include all of AVID's features, but the capabilities of software like this are impressive.

Another category of this software is compositing and special effects software. One of the most popular packages is Adobe After Effects™. This software has can work with a wide range of files and is popular with large professional studios as well as smaller ones. High-end compositing systems like Discreet Inferno™ and Flame™ are very expensive and the realm of Hollywood and broadcast environments. Software like Shake™, Combustion™, and After Effects can produce many of the same effects of the high-end software. Again, they are slower but are much less expensive. Many studios use these packages in addition to or in place of the high-end systems. Compositing and special effects software allow you to combine live action, 2D animation, and 3D animation to create all kinds of special effects on these images.

Internet

A tremendous amount of software has been written to deal with the creation of Web sites. HTML is still the standard for creating sites, but many packages have evolved that eliminate having to write code from scratch. There are simple HTML editors like BB Edit™, and a whole range of more sophisticated Web site creation software like Adobe GoLive™ and Macromedia Dreamweaver™. Macromedia Flash is a vector-based software that is used to create Web sites and animation for the Web. Additionally, programs like Adobe Image Ready™, Macromedia Fireworks™, and several others support creating images for the Web. We can expect to see this category of software evolve over the next several years as Internet standards change and different software companies compete for dominance in this area.

Programming

Programming languages are used to create software packages. Most software packages come with a tool set, and you have to work within the limitations of the software. Considering the sophistication of the software available, it is rare that one needs to be a programmer. However, programmers are among the most desired and highest

paid individuals in the field today. This is because programmers are essential in many situations. One of the fields that they are in most demand is the Internet. Given the rapid changes in the Internet, programmers can create applications for the Internet that give their companies a competitive edge. Feature film and special effects studios also use programmers extensively to create effects that no one has seen before. The Hollywood film industry is highly competitive, and while off-the-shelf software packages are common, big-budget feature films always strive to create something new that will give the audience a reason to go see the film. Some of the languages that Web programmers use are HTML, XML, Java, and Javascript. The C and C++ programming languages are in wide use by video game, computer graphics, and special effects programmers.

Output

It is easy to see that the type of output we can get from a computer can be very broad, including images, video, CD-ROMs, DVDs, Web sites, and software applications (see Figure 2.15).

The Computer Image

When an image is displayed on a computer screen, what really happens? What are its components, and why does it look the way it does? Working from the monitor inwards, the size and type of monitor is the first consideration.

Monitors come in a standard range of sizes. Larger monitors are more expensive. One of the most common monitor configurations is 17 inches, measured diagonally. The older standard was 15 inches, and there are still millions of computers with 15-inch monitors.

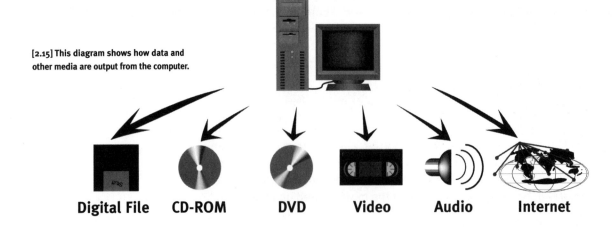

[2.15] This diagram shows how data and other media are output from the computer.

Digital File   **CD-ROM**   **DVD**   **Video**   **Audio**   **Internet**

Large monitors range in size from 19 to 21 inches. Other specialized monitors have unique layouts for print or digital video work. The new generation of monitors is the flat screen LCD variety.

Video cards drive monitors. The video card determines the resolution of the image and how fast the information is fed to the monitor. Video RAM speeds up the display of the image and allows for higher-resolution images to be displayed. Resolution is determined by the number of pixels that make up the image. Standard resolutions are 640 by 480, 1024 by 800, etc. (see Figure 2.16). The more pixels or resolution an image has, the sharper and more realistic it will appear.

In addition to the resolution, color depth is an important component of the image. Three different types of color depth are black and white, 256 colors, and 16.7 million colors. Another way to describe the color depth is by using bits. The number of bits that are assigned to a pixel will give it the color possibilities. Two-bit color is black or white. Eight-bit color gives a range of 256 colors, and 24-bit color gives a possible range of colors of 16.7 million and is photographic in quality. This is based on different levels of red, green, and blue. For example, 8 x 8 x 8 = 256.

While color depth is used to determine the number of colors created, the color systems used in computers are important to understand. The additive color system is defined as colors that are combined using light; for example, monitors and video. When this happens, red and green make yellow, green and blue make cyan, red and blue make magenta, and all three together make white, as shown in Color Plate 2. Print uses the subtractive color model, which means that colors are created by adding dyes and pigments together. Color Plate 3 shows how this model works. In print, there is a slightly different terminology. The inks are called cyan, magenta, yellow, and black—or CMYK. In this model, all colors add together to make black.

For videotape, color bars are used as a standard, as shown in Color Plate 4. Whenever professional video is shot, 60 seconds of color bars are recorded at the beginning of the tape as a color reference. In the editing process, different reels of tape are adjusted in the studio by referencing them to the studio's color bars, or "house bars." Color bars are also used as a reference to adjust how a video monitor looks. Another way of defining the color of light is to use the color temperature, as shown in Color Plate 5. Measured in degrees Kelvin, 3200 degrees is photographic white. Sunlight is slightly blue and is 5500 degrees Kelvin. A standard light bulb emits a warmer yellow color and is measured at 2800 degrees Kelvin.

640 by 480
800 by 600
1024 by 768
2048 by 1532

[2.16] These are standard computer monitor resolutions. As the speed and memory of a computer increases, you can take advantage of higher resolutions.

Color Palettes

Video cards work with software. They communicate to the computer via a driver. The software driver tells the computer what the video card is capable of. Both system software and application software have a wide range of ways to handle color (see Color Plates 6–9). The Macintosh uses a system palette with 256 colors. Computers are capable of a wide range of color display. The fewer colors used in the palette, the less data the images have. Because 256-color images are fairly small in size, they can be displayed quickly on the machine. Images with thousands or millions of colors require more data, but look more realistic.

The Web-Safe Palette

The Web-safe color palette is the group of colors that looks the same on Web-connected computers. They are pure colors and do not use dithering, a method of combining different colors to get a wider color range. There are 216 colors in the Web-safe palette, the 40 remaining colors being used by the Windows operating system (see Color Plates 10 and 11–13). Web colors are done using the hexadecimal system; that is, 00=0, 33=51, 66=102, CC=204 and FF=255. For example, purple would be 6600CC in hex and 102, 0, 204 in RGB. In order for a Web site to look the same on all computers, it must use this palette.

Video

Video can be output from the computer in a variety of ways. Digital video files, such as Quicktime or AVI, can play on a wide variety of machines and over the Internet. Another format for Internet video is RealNetworks, a streaming video format that does not have to be downloaded before it can play. Video can also be output directly from the computer onto videotape.

Audio CD, CD-ROM, and DVD

Audio CD, CD-ROM, and DVD disks can be produced by using disk writers. These have come down considerably in price over the past few years and are an inexpensive way to store data and make disks. DVD writers are still expensive, and this medium is its early stages. Because DVD disks can hold a large amount of data, it would be safe to assume that DVD drives will become much more common.

Printers

One of the oldest forms of computer output is paper prints. Recent developments in technology have brought color printers down to as low as $100. There are several types of printers. The early dot matrix, or impact, printers are becoming more difficult to find. These printers worked much like a typewriter with a ribbon and print head that had a mechanical matrix that matched the pixels on the screen. They have been replaced by laser printers and ink jet printers. Laser printers use lasers and a heat transfer process to create images. Black-and-white laser printers are very good and affordable, but color laser printers are more expensive and require more complex technology. Ink jet printers are the most common kind of printer. They work with ink cartridges that are digitally controlled and are relatively inexpensive. Some of the most popular brands of ink jet printers are Epson and Hewlett-Packard. By using archival inks and paper, artists can create high-quality images. Recent developments allow ink jet printers to use pigments instead of dyes. This allows for prints to be much more archival. Ink jet printers are also extensively used in design and publishing.

System Configuration

To configure a system means to assemble a computer system designed for a specific purpose. It may be a simple home computer, a Web design computer, digital audio system, or digital video system. System configuration includes specifying both the computer components needed and the software needed. When designing a system, you need to look at costs and functionality required. Many computer companies allow customers on Web sites to configure a range of machines tailored for specific purposes and costs.

When you configure a system, the first thing you consider is what the system is going to be used for and what the budget is. Home computers are generally bought preconfigured and cost the least. High-end professional systems are generally designed by the buyer and are relatively expensive.

There are two schools of thought when it comes to putting a system together. One is that you buy the latest, most expensive computer. The reasoning is that your system will be state of the art and that you will get the longest life out of the computer. The down side to this approach is that the currently available software may not have been rewritten to take advantage of the new hardware. New

systems also tend to have "growing pains," or compatibility problems with hardware and software. These problems are generally worked out within 6 to 12 months after the new machines are released.

The second approach is to buy a system that is one level down. The reasoning here is that it is considerably less expensive, and it will also be compatible with all current software and hardware. The difference in speed between the slightly older machine is usually 10%, which is not a major compromise. There are exceptions, though. For instance, the Macintosh G4 platform is considerably faster than the G3 platform.

When putting together a Macintosh system, these are several factors to consider. Macintosh machines are generally reasonably priced, so I would recommend getting the fastest, most expensive system you can afford. When looking at RAM, I would try to get 512 MB if you can afford it, but 256 MB is adequate for most uses. It is handy to have 512 MB when you are working with several programs at once, very large images, or video editing. For input, I recommend finding a keyboard that fits your hands and suits personal preferences. Keyboards are inexpensive and come in a wide range of configurations, as do mice. You will be spending a lot of time in front of your machine, so the keyboard and mouse setup should be one that agrees with your working style. You may want to consider a Wacom tablet, especially if you are going to do photo retouching. They come in several sizes and price ranges. Most artists feel that the mouse is not a good tool for drawing.

Regarding monitors, buy the largest monitor you can afford, preferably 17 inches or larger. Currently, 17-inch monitors are relative inexpensive, and there is a big price jump when you look at 19- or 21-inch monitors. However, if you use software that has a lot of windows (e.g., ProTools, Macromedia Director, Photoshop, etc.) screen real estate becomes very valuable. I use a Sony 19-inch monitor and am very happy with it. If you have to spend a lot of time moving windows around on the screen so that you can see what you are working on, you are wasting time. Macintosh machines can accommodate multiple monitors easily. This is another option.

You will also need a scanner. Scanners come in a range of prices, and you get what you pay for. If you are going to use it a lot, buy a really good scanner. You will get better quality images, and they tend to work faster.

You will also need a printer. Ink jet printers have come down in price considerably over the past few years. For a few hundred dollars, you can get a really good printer. Epson and Hewlett Packard are two of the most popular brands. I have both and am happy with them. You may want to consider the all-in-one approach as well. Hewlett Packard's Office Jet series has a scanner, copier, printer, and fax machine in one box. It is also a good idea to have a CD writer. They are inexpensive and provide for a good method of backup and a way to transport your data. Most computers have CD drives, and this is an advantage when sending work to clients.

The recommendations for PC systems are generally the same. I have a Sony VAIO system and am very happy with it. It came configured with a 500 Mhz processor, 128 MB of RAM, a 20-GB hard drive, and capabilities for digital video, audio, and a built-in CD writer. For high-end PC systems, dual-processor Windows NT systems are most common.

The mouse, keyboard, computer, monitor, scanner, and printer are the basic elements of a computer system. You'll also need a modem to connect to the Internet. You may also need a digital camera, digital video camera, external disk drives for additional flexibility, USB or Ethernet hubs if you have more than one computer, and so on.

As a consultant, I advise professionals to buy systems they can pay off in one year. One year is the usual lifespan for machines, and two years is considered a good life for a production machine. After two years, new machines are significantly faster, and software releases are tailored for the newer machines.

The most common software packages used by the professionals I work with are Adobe Photoshop, Illustrator, Image Ready, After Effects, Premiere, Macromedia Director, Dreamweaver™, Flash, Terran Media Cleaner Pro™, Apple Final Cut™, Alias Wavefront Maya, Softimge XSI, Discreet 3D Studio MAX, Lightwave, Microsoft Word™, Netscape™, Internet Explorer™, and BB Edit™. Commonly used utilities include Norton Utilities™, Adobe Acrobat™, and Stuffit Deluxe™. Software choice is a combination of professional standards and personal preferences. Many software packages perform similar functions but are produced by different companies. The preceding is the result of my professional, personal, and teaching experience. I suggest you try out a number of competing packages and make your own decision.

CASE STUDY

Wands Studio

I started my freelance career and Wands Studio in 1980 as a traditional animator, designer, and photographer. I created all of my artwork by hand. Having studied computer graphics in graduate school and worked as a Computer Animator for Spectacolor in New York, I knew that I would eventually have a digital studio. However, in 1980, the IBM and Macintosh computer had not yet been invented, and computers were very expensive and limited in what they could do. My first studio consisted of all the elements of a traditional art studio: a drawing table, pencils, pens, brushes, ink, mechanical drawing tools, and photographic equipment. As an independent producer, I would use other professional studios on an as-needed basis. For example, if I needed animation photography done, I would pay a cameraman who owned an Oxberry camera to shoot it or go to a video studio and pay them an hourly rate to do the editing.

This is the way most creative professionals worked at the time. In 1985, I bought my first Macintosh system. I bought a Macintosh 512e, Imagewriter II printer, and an external floppy disk drive. I had 512 K of RAM and 1.6 MB of storage. This was state of the art in 1985. The total cost of the system was about $2,500. Over the next several years, the computer paid for itself several times over. The computer allowed me to have word processing, typesetting, and advanced mechanical drawing capabilities. Since most of my work at the time was corporate animation and design, I could use the computer to do a lot of what I used to do by hand. I could also make changes much more quickly. I was also saving a considerable amount of money on typesetting costs. Because of this cost savings, I expanded the type and amount of work my studio took in.

Taking a look at Wands Studio today, I now have expanded my capabilities to coincide with the new advances in creative digital technology (see Figure 2.17). Given my busy academic career as chair of SVA's MFA Computer Art program and director of the New York Digital Salon, I do not do as much commercial freelance work as I have in the past. Much of my commercial work now focuses on consulting, teaching workshops, and lecturing. In my studio, I am now focusing on marketing my creative work, which includes writing, poetry, composing, licensing and performing music, photography, and digital art.

In 2001, Wands Studio now consists of a digital studio designed for audio recording, digital imaging and photography, inter-

[2.17] This view of Wands Studio shows the Macintosh G3 computer, synthesizer modules, CD writer, and audio gear.

active media production, and Web design. The recording studio is built around Digidesign ProTools software (see Color Plate 14). I have a Macintosh G3 with 320 MB of RAM, a Seagate 10,000 RPM, 19-gigabyte hard drive with an Ultra SCSI III connection to the computer. This allows for 32-track real-time recording. The MIDI interface is a MOTU Express XT. I also have a Sony 500 PS 19-inch monitor and a CD writer that uses Masterlist CD software. Outboard audio gear includes a Mackie SR24-4 audio mixer, DBX 2215 dual 15-band equalizer, patch bay, Roland JV 1010, 1080 synthesizer module, Oberheim Matrix 1000 synthesizer module, Lexicon MPX100, Deltalab Effectron II and Digitech DSP 128 echo and reverb units, Roland HandSonic HPD 15, and Kramer Pitchrider 7000 guitar-to-MIDI converter. Tape decks include a Tascam DA-30 Mk II DAT and Tascam 302 dual cassette recorder. Microphones include a Neuman TLM 103 and Audio Technica 4050CM5 and several Shure SM 57 and 58 mikes. Monitor speakers include Yamaha NS 10M and Auratone speakers. I also have an assortment of guitars, basses, and amplifiers, including my pride and joy, a 1964 Fender precision bass, vintage Fender Bassman amplifier, and Ampeg SVT all tube amplifier with eight 10–inch speakers.

The above setup is often referred to as a "project studio" (see Figure 2.18). Although I do not have as much gear as a large professional record-

[2.18] A closer look at the audio gear. On the left is a guitar-to-MIDI converter, Oberhein Matrix 1000, echo unit, and preamp. The mixer is a Mackie 24-4. A DAT and dual cassette decks are on top. On the right are a dual 15-band equalizer, patch bay, and Digidesign AD converter. The speakers are Auratones and Yamaha NS-10M.

ing studio, I have everything I need to produce, write, record, mix, and master audio CDs and interactive CD-ROMs using Macromedia Director. Although I do use commercial studios for overdubs, recording sessions, and other things, 90% of my production work occurs in this studio. Without the advances in digital technology, having a 32-track digital recording studio would have been cost prohibitive ten years ago.

In addition to the recording studio, I also have a Sony R545DS VAIO computer and an Apple G3 Powerbook computer. I have a Wacom tablet for drawing, a Nikon CoolPix 990 for digital photography, a Sony PC10 miniDV camera for digital video, and a Nikon 35-mm traditional photographic system with several lenses. Printers include a Hewlett Packard OfficeJet R80, scanner, printer, fax machine color copier, Hewlett Packard DeskJet 855Cse, and an Epson 1160 printer that is capable of 13- by 44–inch prints. There is also a UMAX Astra 1220s scanner. The systems are connected by an Ethernet network that is connected to a cable modem and USB hubs for peripheral devices. This allows me to take advantage of both the Macintosh and PC platforms, use the printers from different machines, transfer files between machines, and have multiple access points to the Internet. Finally, I use a Macintosh iMac DV computer to exhibit my digital art.

My primary software used includes Digidesign ProTools, Masterlist CD, Adobe Photoshop, Illustrator, GoLive™, Image Ready™, Premiere™, Macromedia Director, Flash, Dreamweaver, Apple Final Cut Pro, Microsoft Word, Metacreations Painter™, Media Cleaner Pro, Quark Xpress™, Netscape, and several other software packages and utilities. I use Alias Wavefront Maya and other high-end software packages at commercial production facilities.

My objective here is not to list what I spend my hard-earned money on or to impress the reader. It is meant to show how a professional digital studio is designed and configured. This studio was built over many years and carefully focused around audio, imaging, photography, design, and interactive media. I still have all of my traditional art tools and supplies. I have the capability to create digital media from concept to finished product. This is the goal of all professional digital studios, and the software, hardware, and other tools I chose for my studio are the result of many years of experience, consulting with other professionals, and careful research. Hopefully, this will help you when you begin to build your digital studio. It is now the norm for professional digital artists to have a personal studio in addition to the access they have at their workplace. With the increased reliance on the Internet, more and more people are beginning to telecommute and to work from their home studios.

Summary

It is very important to understand how the tools that you use for digital production work. This chapter described the basic hardware and software components of the computer, including CPU, RAM, hard disk, monitor, scanner, and printer. Various operating systems and software packages were also mentioned. How information gets into and out of the computer was explained. The basic process of configuring a system was also described. Wands Studio was used as an example of how to design and build a digital studio for digital media production.

Ron White, *How Computers Work,* Que Corporation, Indianapolis, IN, 1999. www.mcp.com/que

This book will give you all that you need to understand how your computer works.

Ruth Maran, *Teach Yourself Computers and the Internet Visually,* IDG Books, New York, NY, 1998. www.idgbooks.com

If you learn better visually, this book is a good choice.

Terrence Mason, *CG 101: A Computer Graphics Industry Reference,* New Riders, Indianapolis, IN, 1999. www.newriders.com

This book is an excellent reference book, with definitions of all the important terms used in digital media production.

Preston Gralla, *How The Internet Works,* Que Corporation, Indianapolis, IN, 1999. www.mcp.com/que

A good look at the technical side of the Internet.

1. **On a sheet of paper, design and configure two computer systems for a particular purpose, one being an economical system and the other having no price limit. Examples of the uses of the system might be Web production, digital audio, or 3D animation. List the components needed and then check different manufacturers on-line to get prices for these systems. Compare the two systems in terms of price and performance. Make a plan to build the larger system by expanding the smaller system by adding components in $500 to $1,000 increments.**

2. **Research different software packages and see how many you can locate that perform similar functions. For example, research how many 2D drawing software, 3D animation software, or video editing software packages there are. Compare the packages for price, number of features, and ease of use. Read reviews in different on-line magazines, talk to users, and try them yourself, if possible. Order the list in terms of what you feel are the best software packages for your own needs.**

Chapter Three

Creativity

This chapter will give the reader a deeper understanding and appreciation of the creative process. There will be an extended discussion of the definition of creativity. Once the foundation of the creative process has been laid, ways of enhancing one's creativity and specific techniques for coming up with creative ideas will be presented. A look at digital media from a creative viewpoint will give the reader new insight into the marriage between the creative and technical. This will be further elucidated with a discussion on design theory and how designers approach their craft.

What Is Creativity?

Creativity is an elusive state of mind. It often strikes us when we are someplace other than our studio. For artists, it is one of the moments in time that is most sought after. Webster defines *creativity* as "creative ability; artistic or intellectual inventiveness." Other words used in further research of this definition describe the process as "skillfully executed" or "esthetically satisfying." The definitions tend to be somewhat circular. When asked what creativity was, a recruiter from a large West Coast studio remarked, "We can't tell you what it is, but we know it when we see it." I found this definition actually the most satisfying. There is definitely an element of skill and craft involved in the creative process. One must be the master of one's tools in order to allow inspiration to flow smoothly. What follows is a series of methods to help enhance your creativity and to put yourself in a situation where you can maximize your creative thought process and not fall victim to a creative mental block (see Figure 3.1).

[3.1] The dilemma of the artist in search of that ever-elusive creative idea.

The Four "I"s

Whenever I talk about creativity, I always use the example of the four "I"s (see Figure 3.2). The proper use of these four words will always yield a solution for any creative problem. They are listed in the preferred order in which to use them. Although they are discussed as separate topics, more often than not, you will use a combination of the four "I"s to refine creative ideas.

Inspiration

Inspiration is the easiest and yet most difficult to use and master. Inspiration strikes at odd times, and when it does it provides a very clear picture of what you are seeking. One way to describe inspiration is as an idea strikes you. All of a sudden, there is an understanding and clarity of thought. There are the familiar stories of composers hearing music in their dreams or people seeing paintings or the future in their dreams. For inspiration to work, you must

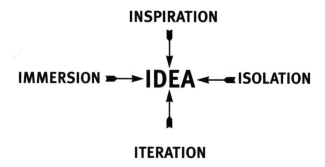

INSPIRATION

IMMERSION → IDEA ← ISOLATION

ITERATION

[3.2] The four "I"s. I have used and taught this method for many years. It has always yielded results.

be ready for it. You should have a notebook or a pad and pencil near you at all times. If you are riding on the subway or in bed asleep when the idea strikes, you must be able to write it down or record it immediately. If you think you can wait until you get home or later in the day, you are wrong. I have had many really good ideas that faded by the time I was in a place to write them down. I carry a notebook and sketchbook with me at all times. If I can, I also have a digital camera or digital video camera. Small portable digital audio recorders are now available that are inexpensive and easy to carry. Some are so small you can use them as a key chain. There are several other ways to encourage inspiration, and they will be discussed in more detail next.

Immersion

The immersion method relies on doing adequate research. The principle behind the immersion method is to surround yourself with as much information and material as you can that is related to the particular idea you are trying to develop. In your studio, you should have a large bulletin board where you can post your sketches, ideas, research, and other items related to your particular idea. As you pass by these items every day, they will begin to sink into your subconscious and help generate the ideas that you are seeking. Also, by looking at the way that other artists have treated a particular idea, you can begin to define your own unique way of looking at something. Immersion has been made much easier by the Internet. In the past, it would require a trip to the library and the photocopier. Now, by the proper use of search engines, you can easily get hundreds of pages of text, images, audio, and video clips relating to any topic.

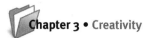

[3.3] Meditation is a great way to allow ideas to come into your mind.

One of the main principles of immersion is the development of keywords. We will discuss this more later, but every idea should begin with a central core or theme, an idea that can be expressed in a few words or sentences. For example, "I would like to do an animation about a college student's search for identity." Or, "my one-person show is based on the conflicts that arise between technology and everyday life." By defining something in a few words, you focus the idea. A focused idea is much easier to communicate than a vague one. Once a focused idea has been identified, it can then be expanded and developed. By keeping the focused idea at the core, you have something upon which to build a dramatic structure or series of images.

Isolation

The isolation method is the opposite of immersion. Isolation works by clearing your mind of everything and allowing the idea to enter. This can be done in your studio or at another location. Using the isolation method is almost like meditating (see Figure 3.3). The idea is to calm and to clear your mind. The easiest way to do this is to sit in a comfortable chair or to lie down on a bed. Dim the lights, and then start by focusing on finding the idea. Let your mind wander and do the work itself. Don't try to force it. Every time you find yourself wandering too far away from the idea, bring your mind back to the center. Tricks for meditation are to look at a candle flame or the smoke coming off of an incense stick. If you do not have a focal point, your mind will tend to wander, and you will start thinking. If you concentrate on a flame or a column of smoke, you are keeping your senses focused and allowing your mind to work on its own, rather than you controlling it.

Another way to approach the isolation method is to remove yourself from everything associated with your research or idea. Take a walk on the beach or in the woods. If you live in a city, take a walk around the block. By exposing your mind to stimuli that are radically different from the idea that you are seeking, you are giving your mind a chance to work and formulate the ideas. Once it has done this, the idea will surface. Always make sure you have a small pad and pencil with you, so that you have a way to record any ideas hit you.

Sleep is an extreme form of the isolation method, and for many

DIGITAL | Creativity

artists and composers, one of the best. It is always a good idea to have a blank piece of paper and a pencil next to your bed. A lot of ideas come in dreams or when you are just falling asleep or just waking up. Psychologists call this the "alpha state" because there is an increased number of alpha waves in your brainwave pattern. The alpha state is often associated with the creative state of mind. One trick is to set your alarm for an hour or so before you actually have to get up. If you do this, you will have a chance to doze, and dozing is an alpha state of mind. Another approach is to go to bed a little earlier than you might want to. If you go to bed when you are really tired, you will fall asleep immediately. If you go to bed and relax for a while before falling asleep, you are also encouraging the alpha state.

Iteration

When the above methods have failed to produce satisfactory results, the old reliable method is iteration. Iteration in this context means to create a variation on something that previously exists. There are some potential problems with this method, and we need to address them first. The most important element of creativity is to come up with a unique idea that is completely your own. Iteration starts with a previously existing idea. Copying an idea is not creative and can be unlawful. Imitation may be viewed as a form of flattery, but it is definitely not creative. Copyright is a way to legally protect your and other people's intellectual property and relates specifically to this method of creativity. If you use copyrighted material, you are placing your personal and financial integrity in jeopardy. When using this method, please be very careful to avoid this pitfall.

Now that we have put iteration into its proper perspective, let's see how it can be used effectively. The best way to approach iteration is to look for universal themes and ideas. Universal themes cannot be copyrighted and have appeared in countless stories, films, books, and other media for thousands of years. This is part of the reason that makes them so successful. They are ingrained in our cultural tradition. They touch on basic human needs and desires. We have all heard the phrase that deep down inside, we are all the same. For example, a love story or a person's search for identity are all universal themes that can be adapted to your particular idea without risking copyright infringement.

The following illustrations are adapted from Joseph Campbell's book *The Hero with a Thousand Faces* (see Figure 3.4). He analyzed myths and stories from cultures all around the world. He found that certain universal themes permeated all cultures. The general thrust

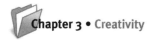

Return · Realization · Departure · Understanding/Victory · Conflict/Struggle

[3.4] This is my adaption of Joseph Campbell's ideas regarding the mythic journey of the hero. I highly recommend reading his books.

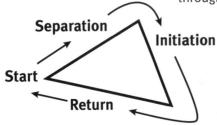

Separation · Initiation · Start · Return

[3.5] This is another adaption of Joseph Campbell's ideas in a simpler form.

of Campbell's ideas is that the hero starts out on a journey for a variety of reasons. Early into this journey, the hero then goes through a test of some sort, either encountering an adversary or other personal struggle. He goes through this test by achieving a victory or reward of some sort. After the test he reaches a new level of awareness. He brings this knowledge and awareness back to his original starting point, and his world is now restored and/or changed for the better. A variation is to use three elements in your story: separation, initiation, and return (see Figure 3.5).

This story structure has been used by major Hollywood studios for years. During a storytelling conference at a major Los Angeles studio, one seasoned writer confided to me that other approaches to storytelling had been tried and that the movies had not been successful. They have always returned to the method described by Joseph Campbell. I would highly recommend using this story structure approach as an exercise when you begin working on a narrative.

One way to work with iteration is to peel back the layers of external conditions and look into the cyclical nature of things. For example, every story has a beginning, middle, and end (see Figure 3.6). A more elaborate way to approach a story is to have a beginning, followed by a period of tension/conflict. This leads to a conflict/resolution, followed by the ending of the story (see Figure 3.7). Every day starts with a sunrise, followed by midday, then sunset, then night (see Figure 3.8). Try to place your idea in this context or time frame. The typical daily pattern is to awake, begin a period of activity, eat or rest during the middle of the day, have another period of activity, eat, and then rest and finally go to sleep. Lives work in a similar manner. We begin life as a child. We learn, grow, and experience life. We mature, become adults, apply what we have learned in our youth to build a life for ourselves. Then we have a family, or in some way pass on what we have learned to those who are coming after us (see Figure 3.9). Structuring your story in this way makes it easy for others to relate to. For artists, musicians, and creative people, our work is what we pass on. In some strange way, the creative outpouring of a soul provides some sort of immortality to an individual. Something of the artist stays behind. Anyway, we are getting a little off the subject, but iteration is a way to make subtle and personal changes to universal themes and human conditions and thus make them our own.

Brainstorming

All of the above methods have been discussed in terms of the individual, but they can also be used by groups. This process is called brainstorming (see Figure 3.10). Brainstorming is one of the most effective means of coming up with creative ideas because it introduces different points of view into a discussion. Brainstorming can be done with any size group (see Figure 3.11). Because so much of digital media production is a team effort, this method is very common in today's studios.

The typical brainstorming session is usually moderated by a single individual to keep the discussion on track. Some sort of agenda is usually handed out, so that the discussion can focus on selected ideas or concepts. The room also should have a large board of some sort and plenty of paper and pencils, so that ideas can be written down and talked about. Brainstorming sessions are usually done several times with the results of each meeting summarized and handed out. The individuals in the meeting then take the summary with them and think it over before the next meeting.

Beginning - Middle - End

[3.6] In the most basic form, a story has these three elements. Write them down on three pieces of paper and begin to list events under each category. This will help you get started.

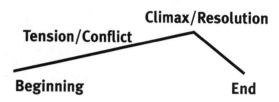

[3.7] This is a more traditional approach to building a story structure.

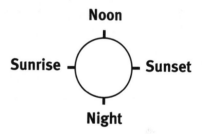

[3.8] This is the structure of a typical day. Take it, write comments around each part of the day, and write a story based on a day in the life of someone, either an imaginary person or yourself.

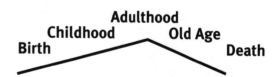

[3.9] A life cycle is another approach to a narrative. Take a person you have known and weave a story based upon their life. Another approach is to read someone's autobiography or biography and build a story around that.

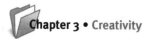

[3.10] The best way to brainstorm is to fill your head with all sorts of thoughts and let them interact. Write your ideas down on a piece of paper or record them on audio or video tape.

[3.11] Sometimes you feel like your head's going to explode when you're trying to get an idea. Have patience and keep trying.
© Pamela Hobbs, pam@pamorama.com

Practical Creative Techniques

Before any extended discussion of creativity can begin, it is absolutely essential that you have the means to record your ideas. There are countless times when I have had a good idea fly into my head, only to let it fly out again. One of the most important parts of being a creative person is to begin to capture your ideas, so that you can give them further thought and development. The best way to do this is to always carry a sketchbook or notebook.

The Sketchbook

A sketchbook or idea book should always be close at hand for an artist. This gives you a way to write down your ideas or to quickly sketch them out while the iron is hot (see Figure 3.12). As mentioned before, the creative state of mind is fleeting and needs to be taken advantage of while it is there. There are many kinds of sketchbooks, but a small one that easily fits into a coat pocket or book bag is best. Use it all the time. Use it to write down your ideas (see Figure 3.13). It is always a good idea to write down the date and time of your entries as well.

The Studio

It is important to have a specific place where you do your creative work. This can be a studio or simply a corner of a room where you work. By having a specific location, you begin to associate that location with creative ideas. This association will continue to develop and the more you work in that space, the more creative you will become. This plays off the traditional idea of the artist in his studio. Although we are in a digital age, this space should also include some sort of desktop or drawing area, where you can write, sketch, and use traditional media, as well as the computer.

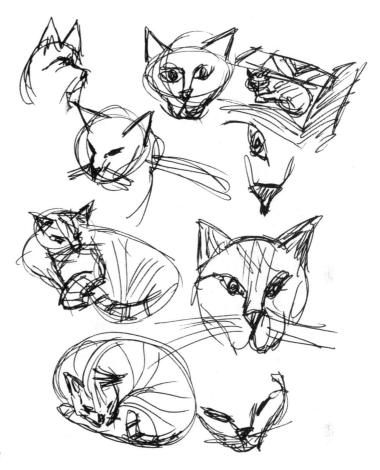

[3.12] You don't have to be the world's greatest illustrator to sketch. I made these sketches over a five- to ten-minute period while watching my cat settle down for a nap. The more you sketch, the easier it will be. Try to sketch several times a week.

Digital Methods

With the advent of personal digital assistants (PDAs), it is becoming possible to carry around something that can record video and audio, as well as allowing one to write and sketch ideas into. Although not absolutely necessary, they can be of tremendous help. One example

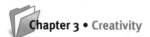

> MARCH 25, 1976   3:45 AM   SYRACUSE
>
> CARRY-OVERS: YET TO BE DONE.
>
> CURRENT PROJECTS: MUSIC
>   POETRY
>   COMPUTERS
>   FILMS
>   WRITING + RESEARCH
>
> ① CREATIVE FILM   10   — BIBLIOGRAPHY
>   GRAPHICS |
>   15 SELECTED
> ② ART + POETRY, MUSIC   — BIBLIOGRAPHY,
>   AND COMPUTERS   LEONARDO
>
>   ITV SERIES
> ③ HOE CREATIVE ENERGY   ④ CREATIVE   20
>   WORKSHOPS: MUSIC,   BROADCASTING
>   POETRY, MEDITATION,
>   WRITING, ARTISTIC,   ⑤ COMPUTERS AND   10
>   NUTRITION,   MASS COMMUNICATION

[3.13] Writing down your ideas is good practice. I found this page in a notebook of mine from graduate school in 1976. Looking at the categories, I realized that I have been on the same path since then. It is reassuring to know my interests have not changed. In fact, I am now in charge of an annual issue of Leonardo for the New York Digital Salon. Writing down your ideas and goals can help you focus and make them happen.

of this is the Palm Pilot, which allows one to have a to-do or idea list and also to draw. They are still fairly expensive and mostly back and white. However, with the race of technology still well under way, we can expect to see low-cost, full-color, high-resolution PDAs within the next few years.

Another useful piece of portable digital technology is a small digital video camera, such as those made by Sony and Panasonic. The PC100 is slightly larger and heavier than a pack of cigarettes but not by much. I have an older PC10 and bring it along on all the trips I take. It can record video, stills, and stereo sound. If an idea strikes, I can speak or sing into the recorder and have a decent permanent record of the session. I can also use it to take relatively high-quality video, still images, and audio recordings. Although relatively expensive, these small digital video cameras are now being used in a number of production companies for preliminary shooting and in

DIGITAL | Creativity

some cases final shots on video that are transferred to film. They are also great to sketch out video ideas and locations, before bringing a crew in for the final shoot. With the popularity of short films on the Internet, these cameras are perfectly fine for shooting video intended for the Internet. As mentioned earlier, there are other devices, such as small digital audio recorders that can fit on a key chain.

The point of using portable means to record ideas and images is that an idea is simply that: an intellectual concept that has no existence in the real world. The purpose of carrying a sketch pad, note book, personal digital assistant, or small digital video camera is to give you the means to record your ideas and to begin to make them real. One you have taken this initial step, you can bring them back to your studio and develop them further into a piece of work.

This is actually the foundation of my creative approach. I use motorcycles as the literal and figurative vehicle for my ideas (see Figure 3.14). I find that the rhythm of the road helps me to come up with ideas for songs. I ride until I have a fairly coherent musical idea worked out, pull over to the side of the road and sing it into my digital video camera. I use the video camera to gather sound effects and environmental sounds. I also carry a digital still camera with me, so if I see something interesting I will stop and photograph or videotape it. After I have gathered this raw material, I return to my studio and refine the images, sounds, and recordings into finished creative work.

[3.14] I use my motorcycle to give me time to think and create. I carry my Sony PC10 video camera with me and when an idea strikes, or I see something I want to photograph or videotape, I pull over and use the camera either as an audio recorder, still digital camera, or video camera. I then bring these thoughts, images, and tapes back to my studio and work with them on my computer.

The Disciplined Creative Process

Now that we have talked about getting into the habit of writing and sketching your ideas, let's talk about how to formalize this process.

Professional artists working in a variety of media must be creative on a daily basis and on demand. They cannot wait for the mood to strike them and are often under deadlines to produce creative and innovative work on very short notice.

Following are several techniques used by a variety of studios for the development of ideas.

Research

One of the primary methods used for the development of ideas in studios is research. This method is tried and true and always yields results. Start by gathering all the information you can on a particular topic or idea. Compile it into a production sourcebook. Then, circulate the material to all people involved in the project, have them study the material, and develop it into a coherent creative product.

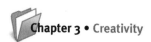

Let's take a closer look at this approach and use an example. Suppose you are making a Web site about taking a motorcycle trip from New York to the Catskill Mountains for a weekend trip. In the production book you will want to have information about the routes taken, restaurants to go to, places to stay, historic sites, and scenic routes.

Keywords

The first thing to do in your research is to define the keywords that relate to your project. Keywords begin to isolate the specific details regarding your project and form a virtual road map for you to follow. Libraries and Internet search engines rely on keywords to classify books, files, Web sites, and so on. In this case, the keywords would include *motorcycles, New York, Catskill Mountains,* and *history.*

Internet Search Engines

A few years ago, the first stop on a research journey would have been the library or artist's morgue in your studio. Today, it is the Internet. Go to several search engines and locate Web sites that relate to your project. The proper use of search engines will yield good results. Print out images, text files, and other information that relate to your project.

When working with search engines, take the time to learn how to use them properly. Learn the logic of search engines and how to expand and limit the search. Get really good at picking keywords.

Also, use a variety of search engines (see Figure 3.15). There are dozens of search engines and many important search techniques. The most popular search engines are Yahoo®, Excite℠, Alta Vista™, HotBot, Infoseek, and Lycos®. The major browsers like Netscape™, AOL, and MSN have their own search engines. Other popular search engines are Ask Jeeves™, GoTo™, Google™, and WebCrawler™.

Libraries and Bookstores

The library is still another stop on your research journey. Use your keywords to search the subject index of the library. Go to the stacks and browse through the books. Photocopy relevant images and text passages for your project. Take a look at the *Reader's Guide to Periodical Literature,* too. Magazines tend to have more up-to-date information than books. Many libraries also have picture and slide collections and other reference material.

Bookstores are also a good place to do research. Locate a bookstore in your area that allows you to sit and look through the books.

Yahoo
Excite
AltaVista
HotBot
Infoseek
Lycos
Ask Jeeves
GoTo
Google
WebCrawler

[3.15] There are many search engines on the Web. These are just a few. Spend an afternoon and locate several more. Make bookmarks for them to use for future reference.

DIGITAL | Creativity

Used bookstores are also very helpful, because they are less expensive and they often have a more extensive collection of books than bookstores that carry only new books. Depending on your budget, purchase the books that are relevant to your project.

Drawing and Sketching

The importance of drawing for the creative individual cannot be emphasized enough. Artists are visual creatures. We do not see everything in words. To be able to think creatively, it is extremely important to know how to draw. Knowing how to draw does not mean being able to render an exact likeness of an image. It means being able to take your ideas into a pictorial form. Drawings have the power to communicate in a very powerful way. Even though we are learning about digital media production in this book, the importance of drawing cannot be overemphasized.

[3.16] This sketch was done directly on the computer by Troi Jackson as a background for one of my poems. The poem has not been written yet.

First of all, please realize that drawing is about a lot more than being able to put an image down on paper. The most important benefit of drawing is that it changes the way you see. You look at things differently after you learn how to draw. You look at form, composition, where the light is coming from, how the shadows fall, and many more details than you ordinarily would. This is called artistic sensitivity. You are now a more visually aware person. This heightened awareness will reflect itself in your work and dramatically improve the quality of your digital work. The pencil is a very easy piece of technology to master, and you can start to concentrate on content much more quickly than you can when working with a new software program. Many digital illustrators make a quick pencil sketch, which they then scan into the computer as the foundation for an illustration. Some illustrators sketch directly on the computer, as Troi Jackson did with this sketch using the TARGA TIPS™ software (see Figure 3.16 and Color Plate 15). Pam Hobbs uses a combination of a brush and the computer to do her illustrations (see Figure 3.17).

[3.17] Pam Hobbs made this illustration of the crystal ball that is full of ideas, or is it "eye-deas"? © Pamela Hobbs pam@pamorama.com

If you cannot draw, learn how. Everyone can draw to some extent, and drawing improves with practice. Quick sketches are not finished illustrations, but they do give meaning and form to your ideas.

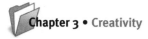

Practice makes perfect, and by carrying a sketchbook with you at all times, you can take a few minutes here and there to draw things you think of or see. Someone who works at a major studio once told me, "Everyone has a thousand bad drawings in them. The sooner you get them out of you, the sooner you can start to enjoy your drawings."

Photography/Video

As mentioned before, photography and video play an important part in your research. Using our last example, you could take a trip up to the Catskill Mountains, stop and take photographs, make notes, and shoot video to gather as much information about your project as possible. In the film and video world, this is called scouting the location. The poem in Figure 3.18 and Color Plate 16 was done by combining a 2D computer image with a poem I wrote some

[3.18] This poem was written years before the background illustration was done by Troi Jackson. It is always a good idea to go through your older work once in a while and see how it relates to your newer creative work.

SPIRIT
SPIRIT TO GUIDE YOU
SPIRIT TO LOVE YOU
SPIRIT IS UNDER, AROUND AND ABOVE YOU.
IT WILL ANSWER, YOU NEED NOT CALL,
THE ANSWER IS IN WHAT YOU DO.
AND IF YOU FALL, YOU NEED NOT CALL,
FOR HELP IS ALREADY ON THE WAY.
ON WAVES OF LIGHT, THAT FLOW AND GLISTEN,
THAT GLIMMER AND SHINE,
AND WILL FINALLY LIGHT YOUR SOUL.

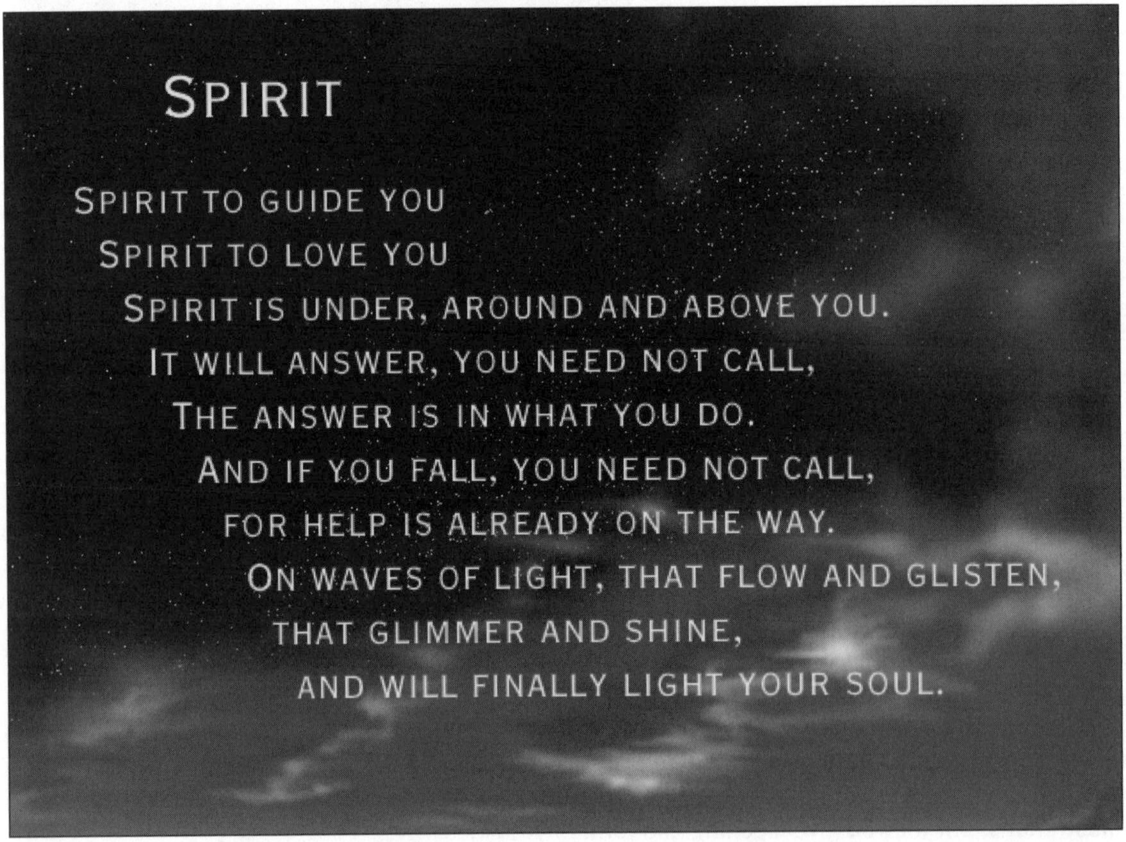

©1999 Andy Lackow

years before. Andy Lackow created the illustration in Figure 3.19 with 3D software. The illustration in Figure 3.20 and Color Plate 18 of Silas Rhodes, founder of the School of Visual Arts, was begun with a scanned photo and then expanded upon in Adobe Photoshop. Finally, even sculpture can be "sketched out" using 3D

[3.19] Andy Lackow made this illustration using a 3D modeling program. Sometimes our mind's eye does feel like a machine. See Color Plate 80 for the final image. © Andy Lackow.

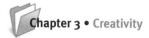

[3.20] This illustration was made by combining photography and techniques in Photoshop. The blending of media often brings unique and creative results. Please refer to Color Plate 18 for the final result.

software and then created in physical form, as shown in the following "before and after" examples by David Morris (see Figures 3.21–3.24). The point is, use all means at your disposal to create and refine your ideas. Don't rely on the computer.

[3.21–3.24] This series of examples shows the before and after of a sculpture by David Morris. The before was done in a 3D modeling system, and the after is the sculpture in physical form. This method is helpful for sculptors, since they do not have to go through the time-consuming process of creating models before making the final work. David works interactively with both 3D software and physical models and sculptures. Courtesy of David Curt Morris.

Summary

In this chapter we explored the realm of creativity from the theoretical to the practical. Creativity is what drives art, and it is an extremely important talent that one must continuously nurture and develop. Several ways to enhance your creativity were mentioned, including research, keeping sketchbooks, and the four "I"s: inspiration, immersion, isolation, and iteration. Brainstorming was also mentioned as one of the more effective techniques for developing ideas. In the professional studio environment, brainstorming is a standard practice, as is an extended form of research, usually referred to as the preproduction or development stage of a project. For Hollywood feature films, this stage can last as long as two years before a film is given the green light to go into production. If you are a freelancer, you may need to put this process into high gear when a client comes in with a high-paying project that needs to be done yesterday. Work with all of the suggestions in this chapter. If you are working on a project and reach a stalemate, reread the chapter and apply some of the techniques to your project.

BIBLIOGRAPHY

This bibliography has a wide range of topics. Zettl's book is an excellent media textbook. The other books look at creativity from a variety of viewpoints, including interviews, drawing techniques, written language development, philosophy, and spirituality. Other recommended reading includes interviews and autobiographies of artists and creative people.

It is hoped that this list will help the reader begin a process of self-discovery and self-expression through their own chosen readings, research, and creative development.

Herbert Zettl, *Sight, Sound, Motion: Applied Media Aesthetics,* Wadsworth, Belmont, CA, 1999. www.wadsworth.com

This book is a comprehensive approach to the development of a media aesthetic. It looks very closely at the use of light, space, time/motion, and sound as they apply to media production. Although theoretical in approach, this book will make a significant contribution to the quality of your work and your approach to it.

Judy Martin, *Sketching School,* Quarto Publishing, 1991.

An excellent approach to the sketching process. There are a large number of good examples and helpful step-by-step exercises to improve your drawing and approach to sketching.

Jack Hamm, *Drawing Scenery: Landscapes and Seascapes,* Perigee Books, New York, NY, 1972. www.penguinputnam.com

This is a good book about learning how to draw. Jack Hamm has written several other good drawing books, including *Drawing the Head and Figure* and *Still-Life Drawing and Painting.*

Wayne Enstice and Paul Rubin, *Jazz Spoken Here,* Da Capo Press, New York, NY, 1994. www.dacapopress.com

This book consists of conversations with 22 jazz musicians. Understanding what makes musicians play music may shed light on what makes artists create art.

Julia Cameron, *The Artist's Way: A Spiritual Path to Higher Creativity,* Jeremy Tarcher/Perigee Books, New York, NY, 1992. www.penguinputnam.com

A great look at the spiritual underpinnings of the creative process. This book is filled with quotes and inspiration techniques to help you develop your own creativity.

Paramahansa Yogananda, *Man's Eternal Quest,* Self-Realization Fellowship, Los Angeles, CA, 1975. www.yogananda-srf.org

A collection of transcriptions of talks by the author of *The Autobiography of a Yogi.* There are many other collections of his writings, including a poetry book entitled *Songs of the Soul.*

T. Lobsang Rampa, *You Forever,* Samuel Weiser Inc., York Beach, ME, 1990. www.weiserbooks.com

One of several interesting books by a Tibetan monk.

EXERCISES

1. **Get a sketchbook and carry it with your all the time for one week. Write down your ideas and do at least five sketches of images and ideas you have had during the week. Using those ideas, create a finished piece of work.**

2. **Pick a subject that you are interested in and research it thoroughly. Go on the Internet and find at least 25 Web sites related to your area of interest. Go to the library and make a list of 25 books that are about your idea. Collect 50 photocopies of images and text passages that relate to your idea. Summarize your research in a short document or production notebook.**

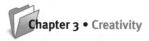

Isaac V. Kerlow

Independent Artist
Director, Digital Production and Talent
for The Walt Disney Company

Isaac Victor Kerlow is an artist who pioneered the use of computer graphics technology in visual projects. He is also the author of several books, including the widely-referenced second edition of *The Art of 3D Computer Animation and Imaging* published by John Wiley & Sons. Isaac is currently Director of Digital Production and Talent at The Walt Disney Company. During the mid-1990s Isaac led the group of digital artists and animators who developed and produced CD-ROM, on-line, and platform games at Disney Interactive. Before joining Disney, Isaac spent a decade at the Pratt Institute in New York, where he was a tenured professor and the founding chairman of the Department of Computer Graphics and Interactive Media.

When did you enter the digital realm?

I started working as a computer artist in the early 1980s at a time when the art world snubbed computer technology and also a time when most digital technology barely worked.

My pioneering efforts in this field were recently recognized in the Pioneers of Computer Art SIGGRAPH 1998 Show and the 1999 HDTV documentary *The Story of Computer Graphics.*

What was your background prior to your entry into the field of new media?

I started as a self-taught artist, dropped out of undergraduate studies in Sociology, and went to art school in Barcelona and New York. I started working mostly on paintings and prints while working as a graphic designer and illustrator in a variety of interesting projects and companies.

What made you decide to work with new media?

When I was a kid I was fascinated with the idea that machines could be smarter than humans. As an art student I particularly liked that you could animate drawings and simulated three-dimensional objects. I have always liked to experiment with new media and I leaped as soon as I had the opportunity to work with digital technology.

What aspect of your background have you found most helpful in your transition to new media?

My devotion to craft and my focus on concept. I have always believed that mastering the details of a particular craft are a condition for becoming a great artist. Because of this, I dedicated countless hours to learning the new programs and computer systems, especially at a time when user's manuals were sparse and not very user-friendly.

What do you see as the important milestones in the development of new media?

The better understanding of what to do, artistically speaking, with digital technology, the lowering in prices of both hardware and software systems, and the amazing increase in computing power that we have experienced in the last 10 years. For example, the processing speed of a Silicon Graphics 4D/70 GT workstation, a power horse used for commercial production in the late 1980s (GT stands for Graphics Turbo), was 70 MHz, while today's average personal computers run at speeds that range between 300 and 500 MHz. Many more artists now than a decade ago have the opportunity to work with digital technology.

Describe your creative process. How do you begin a new media project?

I usually start by collecting and organizing my ideas in a notebook that doubles as sketchbook and scrapbook. Defining the project is one of the most fun aspects of working as an artist, and unfortunately the larger public rarely gets to see documents from this stage of the work. I spend a good amount of time clarifying the central theme, and I continue to polish and refine the secondary ideas and the images used to express them. Working with new media requires a fair amount of planning, or preproduction, as it is called in the world of commercial art production. There is no way around that, and it took some getting used to—when I started working with digital media, I was used to the immediacy and simplicity of pencil and paper. Once enough of the planning is done I usually tape or pin images, ideas, flowcharts, and timelines on an empty wall and go over

everything. This helps to see what you have and how it is coming together. The flowcharts help me clarify the mechanics of the process and the flow of files from one program to another. Independent digital artists often become their own project managers.

How have the use of new media and the use of the computer affected this process?

When I used to work exclusively with traditional tools, my creative and my production processes were often simpler than they are today. Preproduction for a drawing is usually much simpler than preproduction for an interactive installation. However preproduction for some forms of traditional artwork like printmaking, sculpture or film have always been extensive.

What are the major constraints you have encountered in working with new technology?

It seems like you don't always get enough computing power, storage space, and output resolution. Our imaginations usually work faster than reality, and this can sometimes be frustrating, especially when we lack enough computing power or storage space or output resolution. I guess digital artists have to learn how to be creative within these types of constraints because no matter how well-funded or well-staffed your project might be there is always going to be something that you can't do because of finite resources. Another constraint in working with new technology occurs with people who don't really understand what is doable within the limitations and what is not. That breeds having unrealistic expectations and generally an attitude that takes away from a smooth production.

Technology is a rapidly changing and complex medium. Because of the diverse skill sets required to work in the field it is often necessary to collaborate. What effect does this have on the creative process?

Collaboration might be a shocking concept to traditional painters or poets who are used to and often need to be totally self-sufficient and independent throughout the creative process. But collaboration has always been the norm in some of the traditional fine arts (e.g., the sculptor and the foundry, the visual artist and the printmaking shop) and in most of the performing arts (e.g., theatre companies, orchestras, dance troupes, film crews. Collaborating with others is an integral part of digital creation, whether the goal is to get technical support, develop a custom software program, create sound for an installation, or do nonlinear editing for an animated piece.

New media incorporates the elements of video, sound, interactivity, and navigation. How has this affected your creative process?

Digital media offers new options that were not available with predigital media, and I think that many artists have welcomed and taken advantage of having an enhanced toolbox. Certain types of work, like interactive installations, for example, were so difficult and impractical to create in the predigital world that few artists bothered with them. Today we see many wonderful examples of interactive artwork because the digital environment facilitates its creation. Computer software makes it easy for artists to try multiple versions of a single idea and to add multiple layers of image, sound, interactivity, and motion. But digital media can also remove creators from the physicality of their

work. This is particularly visible with many digital artists who are just starting their careers, and they don't always consider the details of delivering the completed work until the end of the process—it's almost an afterthought.

Many artists still work with traditional media and then translate it into a digital format. What implications does this have on your creative process?

I personally think that it is great and artistically legitimate to use the different tricks of the trade for creating and delivering our message. Traditional media and digital media each have their unique strengths, such as the delicacy of a line drawn with charcoal on paper or the capability of creating multiple layers. In some cases mixing digital with nondigital media can yield unique results; much of my artwork has been created that way. Many artists are comfortable using just digital tools, and that is fine, too. I think that when both nondigital media and digital tools are available, choosing to mix them is a matter of personal and artistic preference.

What are you working on now?

Currently I work as Director of Digital Production at The Walt Disney Company. In this role I advise production teams on how best to integrate the new digital technologies and media into their production pipelines. Whether it is motion capture or digital video production, I help with the strategic research for and with the teams and contribute to providing them with an optimal production pipeline.

Describe your most recent fine arts/personal project.

I am currently in the development stage of an independent movie that I plan to shoot on a combination of film and high-definition digital video. I am visualizing some of the art direction with a combination of photography and 3D CGI. I plan to do the visual effects digitally with desktop computer systems, and some of the animatics for the live action and the animated sequences are also being laid out with the computer. Of course before preproduction starts I need to take care of two small details: complete the script and secure the financing. Details, details. . . .

What software and hardware do you use?

I have used so many different types of hardware and software that I don't keep track anymore. In a way this question is like asking a painter what brand of paint he or she uses, and I am not sure that it always helps to better evaluate and appreciate somebody's work. I work with PCs and Apple computers; I used to work with SGIs when they offered a competitive advantage, but that is less and less the case. As for software I like to mix the high-end with the low-end. Some of the expensive software packages allow you to do unique things, but the same is true of the inexpensive software programs. I almost always mix 3D with 2D and bring it all together with a compositing/editing type of program (see Color Plates 18–21).

What advice would you offer to people entering the field of new media and technology?

Be curious, patient, and persistent all at the same time if that is possible. You will need curiosity to discover which features of software might be useful to you. Patience will help you put up with the intermittent tediousness of working with machines and the great challenge of working with other members of a creative team. Persistence might contribute to successfully completing your projects and implementing your visions.

With all of the rapid developments in the technology, it is virtually impossible to know all of the software packages and have all the programming, video, and audio skills. How important is it for a new media artist to know everything?

I think that it can be useful for a digital artist to understand the basics of most of the mainstream types of software because that knowledge can make you more astute when tackling a complex project. It is important to spend enough time with different programs to familiarize oneself with them, but eventually you end up mastering one or two types of software based on the kind of work that you do. The software for each of the different artistic areas touched by digital technology is so different that it would be very difficult for a single individual to master them all.

Where should they focus their attention?

The years spent in art school are the perfect time to experiment with different software programs, and hopefully to specialize in the ones that match the areas of personal interest and talent. Finding the "right" combination of software packages that works for each one of us is similar to deciding what major and what minor we want to pursue while in art school. For example, someone interested in sculptural types of things will probably gravitate toward 3D modeling software and might eventually become a specialist in that area. People entering the field of new media should also take the time to learn what has already been done in their fields by viewing and studying existing works.

What is most lacking in the education of new media students?

In my opinion the ideal education of a new media student should have a balance between the conceptual and the technical. Unfortunately many new media programs are heavily weighted to one side or the other. This split is sometimes seen in art programs that teach their students mostly craft and technique (how to use the program) while ignoring the conceptual and historical knowledge that is so important to artistic creation. The inverse situation is equally limiting: art schools and universities where professors focus almost exclusively on theory and critical thinking while relegating craft and technique to the lab assistants.

What are the important elements of a new media portfolio?

First and foremost, a new media portfolio should present the artistic point of view and quality of work of the individual. More than anything else, what I look for in a reel or portfolio is the unique artistic sensibility and technical abilities that might make the individual unique. Second, some of the best samples of work should be placed at the beginning or early in the portfolio or reel in order to capture the attention of the reviewer. Third, a new media portfolio or reel should be presented in a way that benefits the type of work in question. For example, if the work is about interactivity, then it may be contained as interactive software in a Web site or on CD-ROM so the reviewer can experience the interaction in its intended medium. If the work is about image quality, high-resolution printouts might be most appropriate. If the work is about high-end computer animation, videotape is probably the best medium. Special care should be taken when new media portfolios require the reviewer to install software. Installation instructions and procedures should be as clear and foolproof as possible. Last but not least, the portfolio or reel should have contact information both at the beginning and at the end.

How do you think the Web has changed traditional design?

The Web offers several new creative possibilities that were not available a few years back, and its explosive growth is both exciting and promising. To me the most unique feature of the Web from the artistic point of view is the ability to deliver your work through a huge network, potentially to a large audience. The interactive nature of the Web is also a distinctive factor. Years from now multiplayer games and activities might be the genre that defines the artwork typical of the Web. We are witnessing the growing pains of this new medium and environment. Still, with the exception of a few brilliant pioneering works, most Web-based artistic creations are hampered by crude technique, narrow bandwidth, cross-platform incompatibility, or a lack of imagination. But things are changing quickly.

Where do you see video moving in the future?

Digital video technology is evolving rapidly. What we can do today with video was impossible to do just a few years back. I expect that trend to continue. I also believe that future generations of moviemakers will be as familiar (or more familiar) with digital video as they are with traditional media. That might also play a role in the future growth of video.

What do you think about webcasting?

Most of the recent webcasting has been about proving that the technology works, and in that sense it has been somewhat limited on the creative level. With the exception of a few lucky individuals who have very fast access to the Web, the image quality that most people see today in a webcast is fairly low both in terms of pixel resolution and number of frames per second. The time and technical expertise required to properly set up a webcast on the receiving end can sometimes also be quite significant. In that sense, I think television is still a superior medium for live broadcasts. By the end of this decade many of the limitations faced by webcasting will probably disappear.

The ability to randomly access any portion of an animation, or work, is unique to multimedia and allows interactivity. How has this changed your creative process, and what are the special considerations that this creates?

Multimedia is all about giving the user, traditionally called the viewer or spectator, an active role in the art piece. The idea of having the audience participate in the work is not unique to digital media, but in theory, at least, this participation is easy to implement in a multimedia project. Unfortunately many multimedia pieces fall short of this promise because they fail to recognize that interactivity is a lot more than having an individual click a mouse or touch a screen. Interactivity is about engaging the audience in the ideas that drive the work. Examples of this interactivity can be found in some participatory theatre plays, dancing, children's games, and plain conversation between two individuals. My goal would be to bring some of the freshness and spontaneity of these types of interaction into the digital domain.

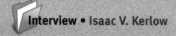

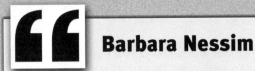

Barbara Nessim

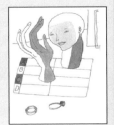

INTERVIEW

**Illustrator, Artist, Nessim and Associates
Chair of Illustration, Parsons School of Design**

Barbara Nessim is an internationally known artist and educator whose paintings and drawings are part of numerous public and private collections and have been shown in museums and galleries worldwide. Her work is in the permanent collection of the Museum of Modern Art in Sweden, the Smithsonian Institute, and the Hungarian National Gallery in Budapest. Nessim's work was also exhibited in the Kunst Museum in Düsseldorf and the Louvre in Paris. She has had her editorial illustrations published in *Rolling Stone, Time, Newsweek,* and *The New York Times.* In July 1992, she was appointed Chair of the Illustration Department at Parsons School of Design in New York.

What was your background prior to your entry into the field of new media?

I was and still am an illustrator and an artist working in a variety of media such as oil, watercolor, acrylic, etching, and bookmaking, (see Color Plates 22 and 23).

© Barbara Nessim 2000.

© Barbara Nessim 2000.

What made you decide to work with new media?

In 1980 I was invited by Peter Spackman, who was then affiliated with MIT, to go up and take part in Muriel Cooper's Visual Language Workshop, a graduate program pairing artists with programmers to develop visual computing. I found the invitation fascinating, but because of time, work, and geographical constraints, I could not take advantage of the offer. What it did do was to motivate me to find a computer in New York and pursue teaching myself how to use it. In 1980 Time Incorporated invited me to be their Artist in Residence. There I taught myself how to use the IPS 2 by Norpak computer. This was a computer manufactured in Canada, and the project that TVIS was working on was a networking experiment that was a precursor to the Internet as we know it today.

Who has influenced you most within the field of new media art?

Being one of the first in my field I had to be self-motivated and innovative, looking to my own work as inspiration.

Describe your creative process.

Since I am always thinking of creative ways to express myself, I have been keeping sketchbooks since 1960 to record these thoughts (see Color Plates 24 and 25). These books provide inspiration that I constantly refer to when I start new projects.

How do you begin a new media project?

Ideas build. They come to me at the oddest moments, usually when I'm daydreaming in the shower or right before I am going to sleep or when I am just waking up. I always have a pencil and paper by my bed to capture these thoughts. When something stays with me long enough and keeps reoccurring and building, then I formally put these ideas into motion.

What are the major constraints you have encountered in working with new technology?

The learning curve in constantly trying to keep up with the ever-changing hardware and software and the expense it all incurs. The meshing of creative ideas and the ability to technically carry them out.

With all of the rapid developments in the technology, it is virtually impossible to know all of the software packages and have all of the programming, video, and audio skills. How important is it for a new media artist to know everything?

You cannot possibly know everything. What is important is to acquaint yourself with people who know things you don't. That's where collaboration comes in. If you choose your collaborators wisely, the result is usually an extremely creative experience that allows a project to grow in ways you never dreamed of.

How has digital technology affected illustration?

The illustration business has changed dramatically over the past few years. An illustrator must know how to use a computer even if it is just to scan their work in and e-mail it to the art director. The computer has allowed illustrators to do more than just the art. The illustrator now has the ability to do a complete job and include type in the overall design. For example, an illustrator can design and illustrate a complete book jacket.

Many artists still work with traditional media and then translate it into a digital format. What implications does this have on your creative process?

I use all ways to employ the computer. It all depends on the project. The project usually dictates how I incorporate the use of the computer. For example, with the flag project, I input the drawings with a digitizing tablet and printed out black-and-white line drawings on archival paper and later hand painted them. At that point in time, in 1991 when I was creating these images, archival color and large sizes were not available.

What are you working on now?

I am continuing to work on my RAM minibooks and want to put them on my nessim.com Web site. It will be under Books on the Run. I am also re-vamping and redesigning my barbaranessim.com Web site.

GPS (global positioning satellite) technology is very interesting to me, and I am currently thinking about a project using this new technology. I am working with the artist Tony Longson on this and the Books on the Run project.

Please describe the creative process as it relates to this project.

Thinking about it at odd moments. Jotting down ideas as they surface. Learning about the technology. Thinking about it at odd moments. Jotting down ideas as they surface. Learning about the technology. Thinking about it at odd moments. Jotting down ideas as they surface. Learning about the technology.

How has this changed your creative process, and what are the special considerations that this creates?

My randomly accessed interactive minibook is a perfect example of how technology has affected my work and expanded my creative process. Without going into too much detail, a person who attends one of my gallery shows can create a minibook with 14 randomly accessed drawings and take it home with them. Each minibook is a unique work of art, and it is free to them.

Describe your most recent fine arts/personal project.

My ongoing personal sketchbooks (now at number 80) are the most important works in my life, along with the ones I discussed earlier.

What software do you use?

My brain.

What hardware do you use?

Pen, ink, watercolor, paper.

What advice would you offer to people entering the field of new media and technology?

Immerse yourself in the technology you are planning to learn. Set aside undisturbed time as if you were taking a vacation, perhaps a week or so. Go to classes. I prefer weekend or week-

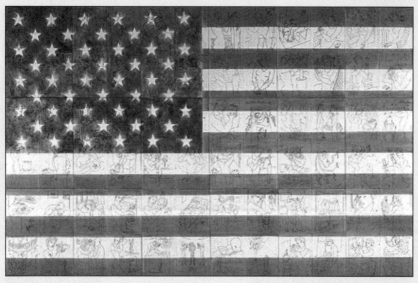

© Barbara Nessim 2000.

long classes to the ones that happen once a week over the course of a few months. Hook up with a friend who wants to learn it, too. *Enjoy* what you are doing. Learn because you want to learn it not because you have to learn it.

What advice can you give to students studying to be illustrators?

Learn about type and design as well as drawing, painting, and *creative* thinking. A good conceptual artist who also knows how to design and draw is valuable to any employer.

You will then be able to get an interesting job working with all the new media companies sprouting up everywhere. Learn how to work on a team. *Teamwork* will be the operative word for the future. You can also promote your illustration work as an extra activity.

Where they should focus their attention?

On being open to all the new things that are happening. Go to a conference. Read magazines with a broad focus, such as *Wired*.

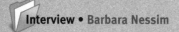

Idea/concept
↓
Research/sketching
↓
Script
↓
Storyboard/flow chart
↓
Animatic/working prototype
↓
Production
↓
Postproduction

Chapter Four

DIGITAL | Creativity

The Production Pipeline

n the professional design world, projects have a very specific

work flow. This is done to maximize quality, maintain cre-

ative control, and keep production costs within a budget. A pro-

ject's work flow is said to pass through the production pipeline,

and this chapter will explain the production pipeline in detail.

It is very important to understand the sequence of events that

takes place in the commercial creative process. This process has

evolved over the years, and it is an important element in any

creative project.

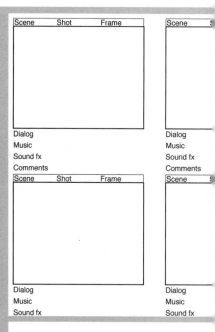

Preproduction
↓
Production
↓
Postproduction

[4.1] The three divisions of the production process.

Production is normally broken down into three stages: preproduction, production, and postproduction (see Figure 4.1). Preproduction is often the most creative phase of any project. During this period the creative and visual development is the focus. For animation, a storyboard is drawn and then put into a sequential form, known as an animatic. In design, many different creative approaches are tried before several sample designs are presented to the client. For Web sites, a series of flow charts are designed to give an idea of the navigation and content of the site. The production phase is when the actual artwork, audio, video, and programming is done. During postproduction, the project is edited and assembled into its final form. In addition to explaining the production process, this chapter will give detailed descriptions of the various members of the production team and what their roles are in this process.

The production process is followed very strictly by professional studios. It is a method that has evolved over time and, due to the high costs of production, it is generally done the same way by most companies. Although there are minor variations within each studio, the basic divisions of preproduction, production, and postproduction are universal (see Figure 4.2).

Preproduction

This is the early stage of the formation of a project. In feature films, it is called the development stage. For many people, this is the most creative part of the process. Since nothing is written in stone, ideas flow freely, and the goal is to come up with the best, most creative idea and design for the project.

In feature film companies, the development process starts with an intensive research phase. For high-budget films, this includes a trip to locations that are going to be used in the film. While on location, drawings, photographs, reference video, and all types of data are collected. Researchers at the studio go to libraries to gather designs, historical photographs, and reference, and they collect various creative and artistic treatments of the location and local culture. Illustrators are then commissioned to come up with a series of illustrations that might possibly define the style and look of the film. These illustrations are then set to the music proposed for the film and shown to the people who decide whether to fund projects and how it should look.

The following process has been generalized so that it can apply to almost any new media project, whether it is a Web site, CD-ROM, digital video, or animation. The purpose of using this process is to maximize the work effort and to give the best final product. The version here has been developed from my production experience over the years and conversations with producers, directors, designers, and other individuals from both large and small studios.

Idea/Concept

The first stage of a project is the development of the idea or concept. Sometimes this is called developing the theme. The challenge here is to limit the description of the whole project to a sentence or two. Doing so clarifies the original intention, and defines a solid basic idea that anyone can understand. Ideas that are too convoluted often do not succeed, since they are difficult to understand. Good examples of simple themes are "a young girl's search for identity" (Disney's *Mulan*) and "a love story between a poor boy and a rich girl set during a critical historical event" (James Cameron's *Titanic*). Bad examples of a theme are "this is a 3D animation that shows off particle systems," and "this Web site will be about video games." These last two are too general, too vague, and don't really define the content or idea. Other than a brief mention of the final form of the project, it is not necessary to include software or other creative techniques as part of the theme. The theme should describe what the piece is about.

This short description is also a very easy way to describe the project to potential creative partners or clients.

Once you have narrowed down your idea to a sentence or two, the next step is to expand this description. One recommendation is to look at this next step as a press release, that is, a one-page description that has the who, what, where, why, and how of the project in it (see Figure 4.3). Of particular importance in this next stage is to define who the target audience is. The level of sophistication of the content will depend on the audience. For example, a Web site geared for scientists will have radically different language and graphics than one for a musical group popular with teens.

The net result of this process is a brief, written description of the project. This description now has the advantage that it presents the project in a concise, one-page format that can be faxed easily. It is also easy to change. In the beginning stages of any project, you

---

THE PRODUCTION PROCESS

Idea/concept
↓
Research/sketching
↓
Script
↓
Storyboard/flow chart
↓
Animatic/working prototype
↓
Production
↓
Postproduction

[4.2] An overview of the production process.

Who, What, When, Why, Where, How

1 page in length

250 words, double spaced

[4.3] A press release is a good idea. It will give you a clear idea of what the project is all about.

should keep the approach simple and easily changeable. This keeps the mood creative and tempers calm when changes are made.

For feature films and other high-budget projects, the next step is often what is called a treatment. Treatments are often several pages in length and do a further breakdown of the who, what, where, why, and how. They often include a simple budget breakdown as well. Design documents may be longer and more extensive. What is important is the concept of stating the project in a few sentences first, and then going to a one-page description. Be careful not to do too much extra work at this stage. Time is money, and clients have been known to change their minds, although some clients do pay a concept development fee.

Research/Sketching

Once the idea, budget, production schedule, and other details have been defined, it is time to explore the project more completely. This is called the research/sketching stage. Since the idea has been clearly defined, research can now begin to expand the visual treatment of the project.

The research done at this stage is much more directed and focused than during the initial development stage. More specific designs and sketches are made, including rough outlines of the navigational flow, and so on. The Internet, library, magazines, and studio image files and reference collections are thoroughly researched. It is important to get as much background information regarding the project as possible.

It is also important that this stage be nonlinear, that is, not too much of a focus on the details of the work, but rather on defining the visual style and content. The specifics of the story will be finalized in the script stage.

It is a good idea to sketch out the most important visual treatments during this stage. It is also a good idea to do several different visual treatments of the most important elements to give a wider range of creative concept.

One handy method here is to have large bulletin boards in the studio. As sketches, downloads, photocopies, and so on are made, they should be pinned up on the board. Eventually, the visual approach and design of the project will evolve from this stage. In my studio, I use large a 4-by-8 foot panel attached to the wall.

Script

For any narrative or time-based work, the script is the stage where the sequence of the piece is defined. Scripts are generally written in two formats. In the two-column format, the video is on the left and the audio is on the right. The second format, which is used more commonly for feature films, is the stacked format, where one paragraph is the visual description and the following paragraph is the audio for the film. Both formats are typed double-spaced, and one page will take approximately one minute of screen time. So if you want to have a ten-minute videotape, you know that you need to have a ten-page script.

And now a word about revisions. The idea/concept and research/sketching stages are fairly nonlinear in their approach. The overall idea is to be as creative as possible and to define the look and, in interactive works, the feel of the project. The standard rule for revisions is three rounds. You make a first pass at the script and have a meeting with all those directly involved. Out of that meeting comes suggestions and changes. There is a second, and then a third meeting. If there continue to be major revisions after the third revision, a red flag should be sent up by you to your clients. Remember, time is money, and if a lot of revisions are still being made, something was wrong in the initial part of the production process. The treatment should have clarified the content, and it should not be changing dramatically at this stage. Countless revisions are fine if the client is paying for them, but that is a sign that your client really doesn't know what he or she wants. If the project has been clearly defined in the theme and the treatment, then major changes should not happen unless there is a really good reason.

Normally, after a third revision, the script will be approved. It is important that the approval be signed off by the client and mention made that additional changes and revisions will be charged extra. This is not to say that there may not be any future changes, but it guarantees that the production is on the right track.

Storyboard

A storyboard is a visual depiction of the script. Storyboards are small thumbnail sketches that usually take ten minutes or so to draw. They are normally done in black-and-white and follow the visual description in the script. For example, if the script says a close-up of a hand playing guitar, the visual will show that exactly.

| Scene | Shot | Frame | | Scene | Shot | Frame |

Dialog
Music
Sound fx
Comments

| Scene | Shot | Frame | | Scene | Shot | Frame |

Dialog
Music
Sound fx
Comments

| Scene | Shot | Frame | | Scene | Shot | Frame |

Dialog
Music
Sound fx
Comments

[4.4] This is a sample storyboard form. You can copy this and enlarge it to fit an 8 1/2 by 11 piece of paper or make your own. You can also buy storyboard pads in most art supply stores.

Usually one storyboard is done for every two to three seconds of screen time. Therefore, a minute of video would have about 20 to 30 storyboards. Storyboards are meant to show the key action in a visual sequence. These should be done before any of the visuals in between are done (see Figure 4.4).

Storyboards follow the same rule as the script. There are normally three rounds of revision. Again, if there are more than that, it is an indication that the script was not written properly. If the script has been approved, it should take no more than three storyboard meetings.

Storyboards are most often done for commercials, feature films, and animation. Very rough storyboards are done for live action.

Navigation or Flow Chart

A navigation or flow chart is a visual depiction of how the user will move and navigate through a Web site, CD-ROM, or other interactive application. It differs from a storyboard in that it is nonlinear. Instead, it is a series of boxes connected by lines that show the paths of information flow. There is generally a main screen or menu, which is usually where the user starts. There are keywords or graphic symbols on the main page that take the user to other areas of the Web site. For example, on my personal Web site, there are words and symbols for music, writing, and images.

There are many different types of branching structures, and the one you choose depends on the type of information to be presented. Two examples of branching structures are a wagon wheel configuration and a hierarchical organization. One easy way to work on a flow chart is to use a bulletin board, 3-by-5 cards, and push pins. It is easy to move the cards around and try different approaches to organizing the information. There are several software programs that allow this type of design work, too.

The next stage is the animatic/working prototype stage. Animatics are used for time-based media, and the working prototype is for a Web site or interactive application.

Animatic

An animatic is generally referred to as a motion storyboard. The storyboards are photographed either onto videotape or converted into a digital format and synchronized with either a scratch sound track or the final soundtrack, if it has been produced. By marrying these two elements, the proposed work can be seen in a linear form in real time. Animatics follow the same revision structure as the script and storyboard: The magic number is three. The function of the animatic is to see if the flow and pacing of the shots works. Although a storyboard is a good way to visualize a script, when the animatic is done, it is much easier to see if a scene is too long or too short and if the proposed sequence of shots works. Often additional storyboards are cut in, or camera angles are changed so that they support the story and plot line better.

For high-budget projects, more elaborate animatics are produced. The term *previsualization,* or pre-viz, is used to describe this work. Some even contain live action sequences that may have been shot with a camcorder or in some other inexpensive way. The purpose of this stage is to finalize the visual sequence before the real production work begins. It is much easier to shoot a scene informally with a camcorder than it is to change things when the actors and a whole crew are on the set.

Working Prototype

A working prototype is similar to an animatic, in that it is a rough working sketch of the final product. The individual sketches—3-by-5 cards are handy for this—are scanned into the computer and a rough navigational design is completed. Even though the final artwork has not been produced, the look and feel of the project can be defined at this point. This is generally done with a flow chart. The navigational design can be tested and modified at relatively low cost.

Everything discussed so far is part of the preproduction phase of a project. As you can see, most of it is done with word processors, computers, and sketches. Some technology is employed, but it is minimal. There are two major reasons for this. The first is that production time is expensive. For any studio to make a profit, the production machines must be working as much of the time as possible.

This usually means that several projects are in development and several projects are in production at the same time. The time on the production machines is billed at a much higher rate, whereas in pre-production, there are a lot of changes and some projects may not get approved. It is therefore best to keep the preproduction phase as creative as possible, while spending as little money as possible.

Final Preproduction Materials

Once the preproduction process has been completed, there are generally three major items that are produced. The first is a production book, which contains the developmental work, the script, storyboard, navigation design, and any other relevant material for production. These books are often copied and given to the key people involved in the production, so that everyone can have a clear idea of what the final product is supposed to be like.

The second item is a complete budget. Now that all of the parameters of the production have been defined and the overall production value determined, a compete estimate of the cost and time to produce the project can be made. It is important that this budget be as complete and accurate as possible. Once it has been approved, it is important that the client be informed that any changes above and beyond this budget are billed additionally.

The final item that is put together is a production schedule. Since the budget contains all of the estimated hours for the work to be completed, it is relatively simple to put together a schedule.

Production

The production process is generally overseen by two people: the producer, who is responsible for all aspects of the production, and the creative director, or art director, who is responsible for all the creative aspects of the project. They supervise the artists, video people, sound people, photographers, and the rest of the crew.

We will cover all the aspects of digital media production in detail in later chapters. For now, it is enough to say that the production book or design document defines all the creative work that has to be done. The budget and production schedule outline who will do the work and how long it will take. For a project to make money, all of these things must be kept under strict control. For example, if a Web site has 100 screens in its initial design, a budget of $20,000, and has to be done in six weeks, all of the artists, programmers, information architects, photographers, and so on need to be hired and scheduled to do the production in that time period for that amount of money.

Postproduction

Postproduction begins when all of the artwork, photos, video, animation, programming, and so on have been completed. The postproduction process involves the final assembly of the finished elements into their final form. For example, in a film or video project, production is the shooting of the live action, and postproduction is the editing process. In computer animation, it is the editing of the final rendered sequences and the adding of the soundtrack and front and end titles. For a Web site, postproduction is the editing, testing, and configuration of the site before it goes live. For interactive CD-ROMs, postproduction is the final assembly of the alpha version and the testing that brings it to the final release version.

Manufacturing and Distribution

Once the postproduction phase has been complete and the client approves the final version, the work is sent for manufacturing, printing, or duping. It is extremely important to have a final approval signed off by your client at this point, since the cost of remanufacturing is very high. Labels and packaging are generally produced during this phase. Once the final product has been delivered to the client, you are ready to move on to the next project—and to receive your final payment from your client.

Production Environments

Basically, there are two types of studios: large studios and small studios. Large studios generally have several hundred employees on permanent payroll. There is a very tight administrative structure in place, and all the different people who fit into the production process work at the studio. Large studios generally have high revenue accounts that allow them to keep such a big staff. Industrial Light and Magic (ILM), Disney, Warner Brothers, Dreamworks, Rhythm and Hues, Digital Domain, PDI/ Dreamworks, Organic Online, Rare Medium, Razorfish, and Agency.com are all big studios. The advantages of a large studio for a client are that they are a one-stop shop. Large studios generally provide all the services a client needs. Since they have such a large staff, turnaround is generally fast. Large studios also bring in freelance help when they are working on really big projects with tight deadlines.

Small studios generally have less than fifty employees. There are thousands of small studios that have fewer than five people. Most freelancers are in essence, their own studios. That is how I worked for most of my career as an independent producer, and it is still how I approach my commercial and personal creative work. I did as much of the creative work I could do and then hired freelancers or small studios to do the parts of the projects I could not do. This keeps overhead low and allows one to make more money on a per-project basis. A large studio with extensive studio space and a lot of employees needs to have a huge cash flow. Someone with a small studio and minimal overhead who farms out a portion of the work has a much lower overhead.

The falling cost and increasing capability of computers has allowed a lot of small studios to begin operation. Los Angeles is home to the major studios, but there are also hundreds of small studios that have a particular specialty and are generally fewer than five individuals sharing a loft space with a wide range of digital production equipment. The cost of configuring a computer to do professional digital media production is a fraction of what setting up a studio ten years ago was. One small piece of advice for those just beginning their careers who want to have their own studio some day: It is usually a good idea to get two to five years experience with a big studio before going out on your own. This will give you a good idea of how a large business is run and how the production process works. It also is a good way to make connections, meet people, and work on projects that will form the basis of your portfolio. Most large, well-known companies use large studios to do their production work. If you have worked for Disney and ILM, you will find it much easier to get work for your new studio than if you just graduated from college.

Scheduling

We also need to talk about setting up a production schedule. Simply put, the deadline is when the client needs it. A word to the wise: Clients often give artificial early deadlines to make sure the job will really be ready on time and to take some of the extra time to change and modify the job after the original deadline. By having the client sign off on everything, you are in a position to charge your client for these changes.

The simplest way to do a production schedule is to divide the time into three sections; preproduction, production, and postproduction. The numbers I am giving here are approximate, but they will help get you started. Preproduction usually takes 30% of the time of a project, production usually takes 50% of the time, and postproduction takes 20%. So, if you have one month to do a project, you would spend roughly one week on preproduction, two weeks on production, and one week on postproduction. If you have 6 months (24 weeks), you will spend about 5 weeks on preproduction, 16 weeks on production, and 3 weeks on postproduction. If you are a student and have one academic year (9 months), you should spend September and early October in preproduction; late October, November, December, January, February, and early March in production; and the rest of March and April in postproduction. You should finish the project at the end of April or early May. The downfall of most students is that they plan to complete the project at the final deadline, rather than to finish it a week or two (ideally, a month) early, so that they can go back and fix mistakes, refine the editing, and so on. If you are a student, always try to finish a project at least a week before the deadline, so you can spend that final week polishing it and taking care of any unexpected problems.

As you can see, the figures I have given are approximate. The point I am making here is that there should be some flexibility in this process. Preproduction usually does not vary that much, and often, in a rush situation, the preproduction process is considerably shortened. Also, if the client has an extremely clear idea of what they want, they may have already done most of the preproduction. The same goes for postproduction. The wrapping up of a job usually takes a limited amount of time.

The production process will vary the most. Always take this into consideration when planning a job. Every job is different, and unexpected problems—especially with computers—always come up.

The right way to make a production schedule is to break down the three phases into smaller phases, look at each task, estimate how many hours each task will take, and put all of this into a calendar, with a week-by-week breakdown. Schedule production meetings and reviews for every Monday so that you can track the production. By making adjustments along the way, both you and your client will have a very clear idea of how the project is progressing and whether it is on track. Production scheduling and budgeting take years of experience to learn well. Good producers are worth their weight in gold to clients with tight deadlines and big budgets.

Budgets

There is a very simple way to deal with budgets. When your client asks you how much it will cost, reply by asking "How much do you have?" That said, I could also write a whole book on budgeting. Most professionals give their client a range of options. All clients will have a budget in mind when they contact you. It is in their best interests for you to do the job for less, and it is in yours to get a higher budget for the project. The old expression "time equals money" should always be kept in mind when discussing budgets with clients. Although it is difficult for many people to discuss money, it should always be done up front and in writing or e-mail. A great source for costs and hourly rates is the *Graphic Artists Guild Ethical Pricing Guide.* I use it for reference. The price range will vary and depend on the client, and sometimes the prices seem a bit high, but they always form a start for my dealings with clients.

The Production Team

The production team can be a single individual or several hundred, depending on the budget and studio environment. Freelance artists are very often one-person production teams and take on all the roles. Large Web design firms and feature film companies often have several hundred employees. These people tend to be very specialized and are involved in only a small part of the entire production process. When this occurs, the roles of the producer and director become extremely important, since they are the people responsible for maintaining the creative consistency of the project. The following descriptions cover the wide range of new media production, including video, animation, Web production, CD-ROM, and photography. Obviously, all of the different categories cannot be included, but the most common ones are.

Producer

The producer is responsible for the overall management of the project. Producers are generally involved with the budget, scheduling, and hiring of the creative individuals involved. Producers are very often the money people, or they report to the money person. Producers generally follow projects from beginning to end and are intimately involved with projects from the beginning. It is the role of the producer to make sure that the original creative intention, budget, and schedule are all on track. In larger studios, several assistant producers may work on different sections of a project.

Director

The director is generally responsible for the creative execution of the project. Unlike producers, directors are not overly involved in the business aspects. Directors supervise and work with the creative team to execute the project as originally planed. This includes involvement on the original design and planning of the project. Directors have an intimate understanding of budget and scheduling issues, and seek to provide the highest quality result within the parameters defined by the client or producer. Directors very often rise up through the ranks of the artists, since they must totally understand the creative process involved. In design, the more common term for this type of individual is art director.

Artists

This is a very general term, but *artist* refers to the people who do the actual creative work (i.e., the sketching, digital scanning, image making, etc.). Artists are generally involved in the preproduction stage, where they do sketches and illustrations to develop the project. They are also very important in the production process, where they complete the final artwork under the supervision of the director. Large studios employ both traditional and digital artists and integrate their skills in the production process. Digital media artists should know the software they are using inside and out. They also need to have creative talent and the ability to produce high-quality work.

Designers

The term *designer* generally refers to an individual who works with type in some way. For example, a designer would be the person doing the layout and design of a Web site. They generally work with material provided by production artists and put it together into the final form. Designers need to have an intimate understanding of typography (e.g., familiarity with a large number of typefaces and the mechanics of typography). They also need to understand color, layout, and composition.

Video

Video people have a broad range of specialization. They can be camera operators who do the actual shooting. There are also people who specialize in the lighting of scenes. Audio people are a very common subspecialty on video shoots. Other than the single person

who does it all, the most common minimal video crew is the camera operator, audio person, and lighting person. In video studios, there is also a video engineer, who is responsible for keeping all of the equipment operating.

Audio

Audio people handle all the aspects of sound, from recording to editing and mixing. Recording studios do not generally have large staffs. The main divisions in audio are the producer and engineer. The producer oversees recording and mixing. The audio engineer sets up the microphones and works the mixing board and other recording equipment.

Computer Animation

Computer animation has become increasingly subdivided in the past few years due to the growing sophistication of the software and the development of large studios producing computer animated features. There are three major roles in computer animation. The first is modeling. Modelers are responsible for building the mathematical models that become the characters and environments. The second specialty is animation. Animators do exactly that: They animate. They bring the characters to life and allow them to act. Animators need to have acting ability, since they act through their characters. They need to have a deep understanding of motion, particularly the expression of personality through body motion. Finally, technical directors have a wide range of specializations. They are responsible for assembling all the final elements into the finished product, including compositing of the elements, lighting, and sometimes animating effects.

Web Production

There are a wide variety of roles in Web design firms. Web design is generally a team effort. A typical small team for Web design includes a producer, designer, production artist, information architect, and programmer. We have already discussed the responsibilities of the producer, designer, and production artist. Information architecture is a new job description that has evolved over the past few years. The role of the information architect is to work with the data structure of the Web site. These people are responsible for determining how the Web site will work, what data formats are needed, what type of programming and software are appropriate, and so on. Information architects work with designers and programmers to make sure that the design, interactive elements, and content all work together efficiently.

Programmers

Programmers write code and deal with computers on a fundamental level. There are generally two types of programmers, ones that are application specific and ones that write code from scratch. For example, an application-specific programmer might be a someone who works for a Web design firm and who works specifically with HTML. A programmer who writes code might be someone who works for a special effects house that needs a highly specialized piece of code written for a particular special effect.

Systems Administrators

Systems administrators keep the technology working. In very small studios, one staff member usually handles this role. In a large feature film animation studio of, say, 300 people, there would probably be about 50 technical staff. Duties of the systems administrators generally include installing and maintaining software, keeping the network operational, managing files and backing up data, as well as fixing any technical problems that crop up. There is a tremendous need for systems administrators.

While a great many specialized jobs have been left out, the preceding descriptions are the most common roles in new media production. In a one-person studio, you will wear all of the hats. In small studios people generally have broader responsibilities. Large studios tend to hire specialists. Your personality and the kind of studio environment you prefer will determine the type of career you will choose.

Summary

This chapter outlined the production process in a general manner. This process has been used by studios over the years to give a practical, cost-effective structure to the creative process. By dividing it into the three stages of preproduction, production, and postproduction, a studio is able to control the process and maximize both the quality of the final product and the profit made on the project. The essence of the production process is the original idea/concept, fol-

lowed by a research/sketching stage, which produces a script, flow chart, storyboard, animatic, or working prototype. Along with a production schedule and detailed budget, these are the basic elements of the preproduction or development process. Once this has been finished, the actual production or the artwork, Web site, animation, or other digital media is done. Once the production phase is finished, the postproduction phase begins. Postproduction is characterized by the assembly of all the elements into a final, finished form. This includes editing, testing, duplication, packaging, uploading the Web site to a server, outputting the animation to videotape, and so on.

We also talked about the production environment and the different people who compose the production team. At the top of the pyramid is the producer, who is responsible for the entire production. The director is responsible for the creative execution of the project. Designers, artists, video experts, audio engineers, editors, programmers, and systems administrators all contribute to the production of the final work. Production teams can vary from a single individual to several hundred individuals depending on the size of the project and the budget.

Graphic Artists Guild, *Graphic Artists Guild Handbook of Pricing and Ethical Guidelines,* North Light Books, Cincinnati, OH, 2001. www.artistsnetwork.com/nlbooks; www.gag.org

A must-have for all freelance artists and digital media studios. This book gives pricing on a very wide range of design projects and sample agreements, contracts, and other documents for all aspects of design. This book will easily pay for itself and should be on your book shelf.

Gerald Millerson, *Video Production Handbook,* Focal Press, Woburn, MA, 1992. www.focalpress.com

An excellent book on video production. In addition to a good review of the video production process, the book contains a lot of excellent practical information.

Frank Thomas and Ollie Johnston, *Disney Animation, The Illusion of Life,* Abbeville Press, New York, NY, 1984. www.abbeville.com

Although focused on traditional, Disney-style animation, the book looks at the complete production process and much of the information can be applied to other media. An excellent reference book and a must-have for anyone interested in animation.

Ralph Singleton, *Film Scheduling/Film Budgeting,* Lone Eagle Publishing, Beverly Hills, CA, 1984.

A good source of forms and procedures for film scheduling and budgeting.

1. Go through the production process with a project you are thinking of doing. Write down the theme, do a one-page press release, sketches, and either a storyboard or flow chart. Put together a production schedule for the project.

2. Do some research on job roles. Pick an area of digital media production in which you are interested. Go to on-line job sites and locate open positions for this type of work. Research the studios offering the jobs. Make a list of the experience you would need if you wanted to apply for the position you are interested in.

Steven Heller

INTERVIEW

Art Director, *The New York Times Book Review*
Co-Chair MFA/Design, School of Visual Arts

Steven Heller is the art director of the *New York Times Book Review* and the co-chair of the MFA/Design program at the School of Visual Arts. He is the author of more than 70 books on graphic design, popular art, and satiric art. His most recent books include a biography of Paul Rand and *The Swastika: Symbol Beyond Redemption? Design Literacy, Design Literacy Continued, Graphic Style: From Victorian to Digital, The Graphic Design Timeline, Design Dialogues,* and *Typology.* He is the recipient of the Art Director's Hall of Fame Special Educators Award, Pratt Institute's Hershel Levit Award, and the 1999 AIGA Medal for Lifetime Achievement.

What are the most important qualities of a contemporary designer?

Intelligence, taste, and the ability to communicate ideas in an accessible, if not memorable, manner.

How do you define good design?

Well, there are two answers. One is how I define design itself, which is the marriage of

form and content. The other is how I determine good design. This is more complex because it is rooted in subjective criteria—that is, taste. I feel that good design attracts the eye and imparts a message as it leaves a sense of satisfaction. Good design is that which achieves the primary task and makes the receiver hungry for more.

How has the use of the computer and new media changed the design process?

Speed is the first benefit. But speed has its drawbacks, too. Designers are now capable of doing many "finished" things in the time it once took to explore only one. Speed has placed more expectations on the designer, which is fine, but it has made the designer lazy. With speed comes haste. With haste comes considerable waste.

What does the computer bring to the creative process?

Speed, again. It enables the creative person to explore many more options. This is a double-edged sword. It also enables to creative person to borrow more freely from the big closet of ideas.

What advice can you offer to new designers or other people entering the new media field?

Learn history. Be aware of past accomplishments. Repeating them is fine, as long as one adds something new to the stew.

What type of background is required to enter the new media design field?

I suspect that a willingness to learn all the programs is useful. But you have to define what aspects of the field you are talking about. I think storytellers will find new media quite a wonderful realm. But they just have to have stories to tell. Techno-folk need an instinct for gadgetry and more.

What courses would you recommend for future designers?

The traditional courses should be stressed at the outset. Drawing, composition, type design and typography, design history, and so on. Then let the e-courses come.

What is most lacking in the education of design and new media students?

Sorry to be a broken record, but history. Also, the basics of type and typography seem to be atrophying every year.

How has traditional print media been affected by digital media?

I think that we anticipate greater, faster, and more frequent change in print. This is a bad precedent to maintain. Print is print, and motion and Internet are something other. Related but not kissing cousins.

Where do you see Web design heading?

This is a hard one. I am a print maven, and so I still see the Web through a print lens. It *must*

extend beyond these confines. It is a new medium and so it must develop its own vocabulary and syntax. What this will be I'm not sure. Already, it has developed its own cliches.

With respect to typography, what do you see as the advantages and drawbacks of digital media (kerning, manipulation, etc.)?

This is not print. But the evolution of type has been a bumpy road. I believe that the Web will redefine the nature of typography. Which should not mean that we fail to teach the traditional methods of type as a baseline for future discovery.

How has the Internet changed recently, and where do you see it heading?

Everyone is on it. Designers are using it more and more, and they are designing for it in ways that could not have been predicted. I see it as an authoring platform. I see designers becoming more authorial in limited ways. The Web is just another vehicle for presenting ideas—telling stories—and designers will take a more direct role in this, I'm sure.

What is the future of design?

Oy. I have no idea. Design—ordering and aestheticizing data—will always be part of our experience. The Web is a lure for students who want to be creative. The future of design will build on the past.

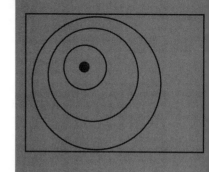

Chapter Five

DIGITAL Creativity

Design and Typography

An understanding of design and typography is essential
for any new media designer. Words and concepts are
transmitted through design and type. The proper use of type, in
terms of layout and design, can have an enormous impact on the
comprehension and reception of your message. This section will
provide a basic understanding of design and typography and will
explain how to use this knowledge in designing for new media
and the Internet.

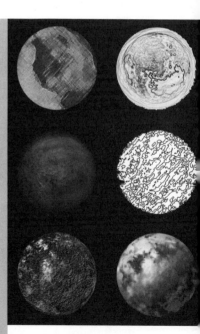

Height = 3

Width = 4

[5.1] This is the aspect ratio of video screen space and computer screen space. There are slight variations, but this is the norm. For example 640 by 460 and 800 by 600 resolution fit this exactly. It is a good idea to have several sizes of this frame handy. For example, turn an 8 ½ by 11 piece of paper in the landscape format and draw an 8" by 6" box in the center. You can use this for designing.

Design

We will start with a theoretical discussion of design. Ask any designer what the rules are and most will say that there are no rules. What they mean is that each design challenge is unique and poses its own design problems that need a solution that is new, fresh, and creative. We will review the basic principles of design so that we can place a frame of reference around this approach. Knowing your design principles will help you break the rules and come up with creative, fresh designs. One of the most important elements to remember about design is that it is an active, changing field. Design is fashion. What worked and was popular a year ago will not work this year. The general public and consumers of design need constant fresh, exciting images and concepts to grab their attention and to motivate their involvement with it.

To understand design, we need to start with a very simple approach: 2D and black-and-white. The first issue to look at when talking about design is space division. Whether you are working with a computer screen, magazine, or movie screen, there is the concept of space. This is the area that must be filled with the content of the design. For the purposes of this discussion, we will look at the computer screen space, which is roughly the same as a video screen. It is wider than it is tall and has a ratio of 4:3 (see Figure 5.1).

It is best not to divide this space down the middle. This creates vibration, and the eye keeps switching from one half of the screen to the other (see Figure 5.2). It is generally better to make the division closer to one edge, top or bottom, right or left (see Figure 5.3).

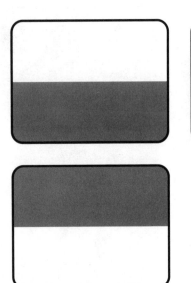
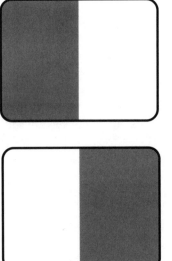

[5.2] These examples show the even division of screen space. As you can see, your eye vibrates from side to side. Try to avoid this when planning your design. There are rare occasions when this effect might be desired, however.

One rule that has endured over time is called the rule of thirds. This means that you divide the screen into three divisions, both top to bottom and right to left. The recommendation is that you try to keep the areas of interest at the intersection of the lines. Although

[5.3] These examples show an uneven division of screen space. You can see that they are more pleasing to the eye than exact division. Look at various Web sites and see how they use this method.

there are times when you will put something in the middle of the screen, it is generally better to follow the rule of thirds (see Figure 5.4).

Another approach to design is to use what is called the focal point, that is, the area of the design that the eye focuses on. Looking at the sample screens, we can see that no matter where the focal point is placed, the eye always goes to that point (see Figure 5.5). The most important part of any design should be where the focal point is. The basic function of design is communication, and if your audience looks at the most important part of your design, you have succeeded.

A variation of the focal point approach is to use a bull's-eye. The bull's-eye approach evolved out of traditional painting theory and the

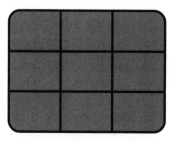

[5.4] The rule of thirds is used in both design and photography. The idea is to put the center of interest at the intersection of the lines. This gives a more pleasing composition.

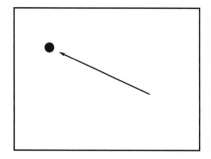
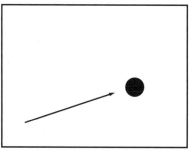

[5.5] A focal point draws your eye's attention to it. For advertising, the focal point should be the most important part of the message. Look at a variety of designs, put a piece of tracing paper over them and locate the focal point and trace how your eye travels over the design.

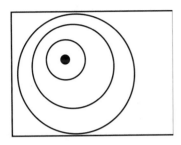

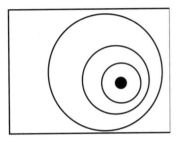

[5.6] The bull's-eye uses a circular composition to direct your attention. This can be further accentuated by using perspective and depth. Repeat the previous exercise by locating compositions that use the bull's-eye and defining them with a tracing paper overlay. By doing this, you will begin to see how designers compose their images.

use of dimension in constructing the space on a canvas. Just as each object in traditional painting needs a highlight, middle tone, and shadow, the bull's-eye deals with foreground, middleground, and background. Each of these elements helps the composition to draw your eye to the most important part of the image (see Figure 5.6).

Another more modern approach to design is the grid system. This system divides the space into a grid and the design follows the choice of the grid (see Figure 5.7). The design of the grid needs to reinforce the movement of the eye to create boundaries and shapes that direct its attention to the area on the screen that is the most important. The grid system is very helpful when designing documents with multiple pages, such as books, magazines, and Web pages.

Form Follows Function

One of the cardinal rules of design is that form follows function. Although most obvious with industrial design, it is also a very important principle for Web design and interactive applications. No matter how brilliant the design, if the user cannot navigate easily and intuitively through a Web site, the design is a failure. This is one of the reason for the emergence of the information architect on the Web design team. Designers are experts in typography, space, color, composition and form. Information architects are experts when it comes to the look and feel of a Web site and the factors that influence navigation through it.

Principles of Design

Above and beyond the division of space and the development of proper functionality, other areas need to be addressed when talking about design, such as color and the use of other media. Readability and legibility will be discussed in the section on typography.

Color

Color is another very important element of design. We can direct the attention of the eye through composition and design techniques, and we can direct the attention of the eye through the use of color. Color also carries with it many other associations.

We mentioned the technical issues of color. Colors formed by light are additive from red, green, and blue. Red and green give yellow, blue and green give cyan, and blue and red give magenta. When they are all added together, they give us white. Pigments

DIGITAL | Creativity

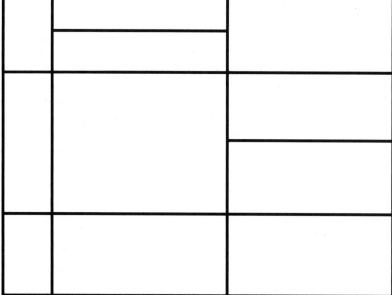

[5.7] The grid system is widely used. It greatly simplifies the design process and gives conformity to any series of designs. Analyze different grid systems and begin a collection of ones that you like.

behave in a different way. Their colors are subtractive, and for printing purposes, the primary colors are looked at as cyan, magenta, yellow, and black. When pigmented colors are added together, they give us black (see Color Plates 2 and 3).

In addition to these properties, colors have three basic attributes: hue, saturation, and value. Hue refers to the actual color itself. Saturation is the amount of color that is present. A high degree of saturation is rich with color and intense. Value refers to the shade, or brightness of the color. Value is measured on the gray scale.

Colors also have subjective attributes that are based on their psychological associations. For example, blue and green are generally referred to as cool colors, while red and yellow are warm. Simple associations of blue are ice, water, and sky. Associations with green are foliage, nature, and growth. Red and yellow can be associated with the sun and fire. Since these associations are emotional and sometimes not totally rational, color science from this point of view is not an exact science. However, the use of color is critical in the design process. As colors change with fashion, so they do with design. A full treatment of color is beyond the scope of this book, but careful observation of the use of color in design will give the designer more insight into the proper choice of colors for a particular design objective.

New Design Considerations

Earlier we talked about dividing space, composition, directing viewers' attention, and color. These are all visual concerns. With the increased use of audio and video on the Web, these factors must also be taken into consideration as part of the overall design approach. Audio is a very powerful medium, and it is not limited by screen space. Audio fills the entire space occupied by the viewer. Video can be live action, 2D or 3D animation, or a combination of these elements. This forms a time-based, narrative design element. It requires the constant involvement of the viewer and can be informative and entertaining, and it can be a way to focus the attention of the audience. As the Web and new media develop, it is the responsibility of the designer to gain literacy with these media and to be able to incorporate them effectively in their overall design. The production of audio, video, and 2D and 3D animation will be discussed in later chapters, but it is important to mention that they are vital elements in the design process with new media.

Introduction to Typography

Typography has a long history, from a communicative, design, and cultural perspective. Verbal communication has the advantage of the proximity, body language, and intonation of the person speaking it, as well as the interactive advantages of a conversational format. Written communication is formalized by the rules of grammar and the definitions given to particular words and concepts. Environmental and cultural influences play strongly into written communication. One common example is the many words the Eskimo culture has for snow. Another example is the rapid influx of computer terminology into everyday English. The English language has 26 characters that fit easily onto a computer keyboard. The traditional Chinese language is pictorially based and has several thousand characters. The relationship of these issues to typography will be addressed using English, since this is the language most commonly used on the Internet. It is important to note that the international nature of the Internet be kept in mind when using words that may have different meanings to various cultures.

Fundamentals of Typography

The fundamental element of type is the letterform. The letterform has several parameters that define it, including the height of the letter, the ascender (e.g., *B,f,d*) and the descender (e.g., *y,g*). Letters are also divided into upper and lower case. A typeface is a specific design of a character set. There are thousands of typefaces. A font is a specific sized set of a typeface (e.g., 10-point Times Roman). Type is generally divided into serif and nonserif typefaces. Serifs are small decorative elements on the corners and edges of type, whereas nonserif typefaces are often referred to as block letters. Other groups include script (connecting/nonconnecting) and novelty typefaces.

Typefaces

Typefaces vary widely from simple block lettering to fancy script fonts. The choice of a typeface depends on any number of things. One of the major considerations is the medium for which the type is going to be used (see Figure 5.8). Print is a high-resolution, static medium that can reproduce very fine detail. Viewers who are experiencing print media often have the book or magazine within several inches of their eyes. Video, on the other hand, is a low-resolution

Helvetica

ABCDEFGHIJKLMNOPQRSTUVWXYZ
1234567890-=\~!@#$%^&*()_+
abcdefghijklmnopqrstuvwxyz

Arial

ABCDEFGHIJKLMNOPQRSTUVWXYZ
1234567890-=\~!@#$%^&*()_+
abcdefghijklmnopqrstuvwxyz

Times New Roman

ABCDEFGHIJKLMNOPQRSTUVWXYZ
1234567890-=\~!@#$%^&*()_+
abcdefghijklmnopqrstuvwxyz

Verdana

ABCDEFGHIJKLMNOPQRSTUVWXYZ
1234567890-=\~!@#$%^&*()_+
abcdefghijklmnopqrstuvwxyz

[5.8] These four fonts are the ones most commonly used on the Web. Most computers, both Macintosh and PC, have them.

[5.9] This example gives you an idea of how point size affects the relative importance of type.

12 Point Type
14 Point Type
20 Point Type
24 Point Type
36 Point Type
48 Point Type
60 Point Type

format. Type needs to be bigger to be readable and the television viewer is often several feet away. Fine lines and detail are lost on video. The Internet places even further restrictions on typefaces. Not all computers have the same typefaces, and they do not appear the same on all screens. Monitor sizes also vary. Therefore, it is important to know what a typeface is going to be used for before choosing it. The best way to do this is to view a sample of the typeface on the final medium.

Type Size

Type is generally referred to by the size of the letters. Type has been traditionally referred to in point sizes (see Figure 5.9). This standard comes from print, but it is used almost everywhere. For a rough approximation, 72-point type is about 1 inch high. Thus, 36-point type is a half inch tall, 18-point a quarter inch, and so on. For print text, point sizes in the 9 to 14 range are good. The Internet uses size for type. Sizes for HTML range from 1 to 7.

Type Style

Typefaces have different styles. The most common are bold, italic, underline, condensed, and extended. These keep the same basic design of the typeface but modify it slightly. The use of styles is one way to let certain phrases or words stand out from the rest of the text. A type family is a collection of all the typefaces of a specific design (e.g., Helvetica, Helvetica Bold, Helvetica Bold Condensed, etc.).

Spacing

Type forms words, words form sentences, sentences form paragraphs, paragraphs form documents, and so on. As we move through this list, we encounter letter spacing, kerning, word spacing, and line spacing, or leading. When a font is created, the person designing it specifies what letter spacing will normally be used between the letters. This spacing can be increased or decreased and is used both for design work and to fit the copy into a specific area. *Kerning* is a term used mostly for working with the spacing between individual letters. Kerning is most often used for important words, especially when they are large on a screen or page. Proper kerning will make a significant difference in how a word looks. *Word spacing* refers to the space made between the words, not the individual letters. This can also be increased or decreased depending on the look the designer wants or to fit copy.

Once the letters and words have been spaced, we can also increase or decrease the space between the lines. This is called *line spacing,* or *leading.* For print the normal increments are single-spaced, space and a half, or double-spaced. Leading is normally referred to as the point size of the letters, followed by the leading (e.g., 12/14 or 20/24).

Align type right
Align type right

Align type center
Align type center

Align type left
Align type left

Tab type
Tab type
Tab type

[5.10] It is generally a good idea to use the alignment tools and tabs, rather than the space bar to align type. It is cleaner and more predictable.

Alignment

Alignment is another way that we can format and layout type. Alignment has four common formats. In align center each line is centered over the previous one. Align left means that all the lines are set against the left margin. Align right sets each edge along the right (see Figure 5.10). Justified type aligns to both edges of the column. Another way to describe type is to call it flush left or flush

right, or ragged left or ragged right. Asymmetric alignment is done by manually editing spacing, and it is used for design and layout purposes.

The Creative Use of Type

When using type, the first and foremost principle is that it should communicate the idea and content of the message, whether it be a Web page, advertisement, book, poem, or CD cover. Too often, not enough care is taken in choosing the words to be used. This phase of the project is called the copywriting phase. Too much copy, and the screen is filled with text; not enough copy, and the image overrides the text and blurs the intended meaning. This can be used for a positive or negative effect, again depending on the purpose of the message. In magazines and Web sites, visuals attract attention first and lead the viewer to read the text. Type can also be a design element in and of itself. We have all seen type-only ads. Whichever route is taken, the first step is to define the copy that will be in the Web site, ad, or project.

Layouts

Layouts show the visual organization of all elements on a page. Whether the computer is used or not, it is the first attempt to define the spatial elements of both image and type onto a screen or page. Layouts start in a very rough way to give the designer and client an idea of what they are looking at. As the graphic approach is narrowed, more detail is added to the layouts until the comp, or comprehensive drawing, stage is reached. For example, what first may have started out with rough shapes and blocks for text, now has recognizable sketches for the images and real type in the text blocks. This is the best design process for working with type. Use it as a graphic element first, and then add the words and copy. This way, the design is more predominant than the text. Ideally, text and image should fuse into an overall design, where the composition draws the attention of the viewer and encourages them to read the type, while the overall style and appeal of the screen is enhanced by the design elements. Design and content should not compete; they should reinforce and complement each other.

Choosing a Typeface

Choosing a typeface can be simple, or it can be a long, drawn-out corporate process. Most large corporations have a corporate identity document, which defines their logos, colors, typefaces, and other items that identify their corporate image. This is based on extensive research of their corporate goals, target market, what their competitors are using, and so on. As more corporations focus on their global image, and as media like television and the Internet place increasing restrictions on how logos look in different media, many companies have redesigned their logos and corporate images to fit into the new media mold. Logos are becoming simpler with less detail, and many companies are using their initials or less complicated typefaces. Many companies also use typefaces that are common to most computers.

Aesthetics and style have a lot to do with the choice of a typeface for a company or project. Typefaces have long been associated with popular culture, as evidenced by their evolution. Typefaces of the Art Nouveau period were fluid and emphasized curves. Art Deco typefaces became angular and precise. "Computer-looking" typefaces became a style unto their own, based both on their trendy graphical approach and the early limitations of computer typography. One of the current graphic trends is toward the use of a more organic look. Another is to look back an era of high style (e.g., the trends of cigars and martinis). Popular culture and trends will continue to define and be defined by design, particularly graphic design. So, to answer the question, the typeface should conform to the style, image, and look that your project needs. If it is highly technical and corporate, the look should be clean, tight, simple, and sans serif. If you are doing a Web site for a restaurant that is organic, cultured, eclectic, and ethnically themed, you should choose the colors common to the ethnic background and graphics and typefaces that support this earthier image.

Working with Type

When choosing a typeface, there are many things to consider. First and foremost—and easiest—are the issues of legibility and readability. Although they sound familiar, they are two different concerns. Legibility means simply that you can read the type. Generally, speaking, this means that it is not too small. Remember again that the final medium determines the minimum point size. Someone looking at a high-resolution computer screen two feet away can read much smaller type than someone watching a television ten feet away. Readability means the ease with which one can read the text. For example, extended runs of text in capital letters are hard to

read. Certain typefaces lend themselves better to graphic use, such as headlines or titles, than they do to body text.

A good general way to work with type is to isolate the most important concepts and ideas and place them in the heading or subheading. When using body copy, make sure that the text is clear and concise. The level at which the copy is written must reflect the audience it is directed toward as well. Scientists and children require radically different writing styles.

Working with Type and Image

Screens and pages that are all text are boring. Sometimes they are necessary, but the addition of graphics, whether they are photographs or graphic elements add much to a design. One common mistake made by all beginning designers is to simply place text over an image without giving any thought to the content of the image. When we were looking at layouts before, we talked about the concept of type and image being represented as shapes first, defining the proportions, and then the design evolved from that. Taking this one step further, if we are working with a photograph, we need to analyze the photo in terms of its composition and form and design the type so that it fits with the image and they complement one another. One way to do this is to make a photocopy of the photograph and sketch the predominant lines in the photograph. This will give you an idea of the composition and the directions the viewers gaze will take when looking at the photograph. When this is combined with the proper type placement, the viewers' eyes can be guided across the photograph and to the type, thus achieving the objective of involving the person in the design.

Letting Images or Graphics Tell the Story

Although we have focused on using type in this section, it is also important to remember that type may not always be the best solution. Graphics can also take the place of type on certain occasions, especially when they are universally understood graphics and the project will have an international audience. We are all familiar with the universal symbols used in airports. In some ways, these symbols are a fusion of design and typography.

CASE STUDY

SVA Subway Poster Design

The School of Visual Arts is well known for its series of subway posters. Many different designs have been produced over the years by well-known designers and artists. In recent years, we have been doing a series of "Art is . . ." posters. A design by Milton Glaser used the phrase "Art is Whatever," in which the *hat* in *whatever* used a graphic of a hat. I was on a plane going to a conference and began thinking of ideas for a poster. I started with thinking about words that incorporated the word *art,* similar to what Milton has done with *whatever.* I did a search on my computer for *art* and came up with the word *earth.* I immediately began to think of a computer graphic globe as the main theme for a poster using the phrase "eARTh is." I sketched a rough layout, and when I returned to New York, I ran the idea by Silas Rhodes. He liked the idea and we set up a meeting to discuss it. In preparation for the meeting, I created a series of 2D globes based on some maps and clip art I had located. I tried layouts with a realistic globe as well. I liked the computer treatment (see Figure 5.11). I also tried layouts with various globes in a symmetrical layout: 4, 9, and 16. The idea here was to show variations on the numerous globes for more visual interest. During my meeting with Silas, we both agreed that a single globe had more impact than many, and that we should go with a computer graphic, rather than a realistic image (see Figures 5.12 and 5.13). With this in mind, I began my creative exploration in earnest. I worked with a variety of 2D images, but no matter what I did, there was still that hint of a Photoshop manipulation. The technique was being dominated by the software.

[5.11] (above) This was the first globe test that I really liked. It had an artistic look to it, and the colors were pleasing.

[5.12] (right) This was the rough layout with a single globe in it.

[5.13] (below) I tried a few layouts with a variety of globes. This one had 9. I tried another with 16.

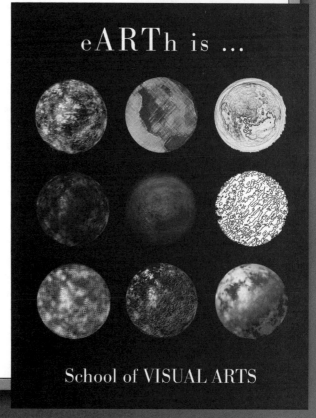

eARTh is...

School of VISUAL ARTS

[5.14] (above) This was the final 3d globe render. We decided to go with a 3D look, rather than a 2D painterly style.

[5.15] (right) I tried a few frames and background colors. This frame was too dominant and the background color did not complement the globe.

It wasn't working. I then went to Alias/Wavefront Maya™ and began to experiment with 3D globes (see Color Plates 26–30). This began to bear more fruit. The image had more dimension to it, and I had a great deal of control over its surface properties. I finally decided on a copper/green/brown globe (see Figure 5.14 and Color Plate 31) and rendered it at high resolution. I created a few variations for Silas to choose from. When I placed the globe and text on the poster, it did not have enough impact. The globe looked lost and not terribly interesting. I then began to think more about the "eARTh is . . ." copy. There were two elements to the verbal pun. One played on *earth* and one played on *art*. I got an idea. Why not frame the globe to give it more of an "art" feel? I scanned in several frames and then met

again with Silas. I provided him with several layouts using different frames, globes, and background colors (see Figure 5.15 and Color Plates 32 and 33). We decided on the final image (see Figure 5.16 and Color Plate 34). I then worked with art director James McKibben to produce the final design. This discussion should give you a glimpse into how the creative process for graphic design works. It is always important to explore a range of alternatives before deciding on your final design.

eARTh is...

UNDERGRADUATE PROGRAMS

Advertising
Animation
Art Education
Art History
Cartooning
Computer Art
Film & Video

Fine Arts
Graphic Design
Humanities & Sciences
Illustration
Interior Design
Photography

GRADUATE PROGRAMS

Art Therapy
Computer Art
Design
Fine Arts
Illustration
Photography

CONTINUING EDUCATION
DIVISION

School of VISUAL ARTS

209 East 23 Street, New York, NY 10010-3994   Tel 800.366.7820   Fax 212.725.3587   www.schoolofvisualarts.edu

[5.16]
The final poster.
© 2000 Visual Arts
Press. Creative
Director: Silas H.
Rhodes, Artist:
Bruce Wands,
Art Director:
James McKibben.

Summary

In this chapter, we talked about the basics of design and typography. Design takes years to master, and it is best learned by understanding the division of space, composition, and the effective use of color and typography.

Typography also takes years to master. An intimate understanding of type, knowledge of many typefaces, and a strong sense of balance and proportion are the fundamental tools of the typographer and the designer. The creative use of type as a design element is also an integral part of this tool set. It is important to be familiar with all aspects of typography, including fonts, sizes, styles, layout, and design. The correct use of type with images is one of the things that separates a designer from a novice. The best way to look at this is to make sure that the type and image complement one another. Focus on the composition of the design, the readability of the type and copy, and the interplay between the type and the graphical elements.

Marcelle Lapow Toor, *Graphic Design on the Desktop,* John Wiley & Sons, Inc., New York, NY, 1998. www.wiley.com

A good overall approach to design, including typography, logo design, the design process, color, and designing for the Web.

Rob Carter, Ben Day, and Philip Meggs, *Typographic Design: Form and Communication,* John Wiley & Sons, Inc., New York, NY, 1993. www.wiley.com

A comprehensive look at typography and its use in design.

Francis Ching, *Design Drawing,* John Wiley & Sons, Inc., New York, NY, 1998. www.wiley.com

A solid approach to design drawing.

Wucius Wong, *Principles of Color Design,* John Wiley & Sons, Inc., New York, NY, 1997. www.wiley.com

A good theoretical book with sections on design principles, color principles, color design, and color expression.

James Craig, *Basic Typography: A Design Manual,* Watson-Guptill Publications, New York, NY, 1990.

A solid practical book on typography with a traditional approach.

Linda Holtzschue and Edward Noriega, *Design Fundamentals for the Digital Age,* John Wiley & Sons, Inc., New York, NY, 1997. www.wiley.com

A good theoretical and practical book. Approached from an intellectual viewpoint, with chapters on art and design, digital design, point, line and plane, and color.

BIBLIOGRAPHY

1. Take a look around the Internet and collect five samples of typography and design you like. Look through several magazines and pick five examples of typography you like. Look at some films and videotapes and choose five samples of typography you like. Compare the 15 samples you have chosen and make a list of how the samples differ. Your goal is to understand what makes choosing for the Internet, print, and film and video different.

2. Choose a Web site and redesign it. Use the Netscape or Internet Explorer browser window as the basis for your designs. Make five to ten variations of the Web site you have chosen. Look at them in a group critique and discuss what works and does not work with both your and the original design.

EXERCISES

Bonnie L. Hammer

INTERVIEW

Design Production Manager, Zagat.com
Personal Web Site: www.hammerized.com

Bonnie Hammer represents the new generation of digital creative professional. She is currently the Design Production Manager for Zagat.com and previously was the Production Manager for iVillage.com. Before relocating to New York, she spent 5 1/2 years in Los Angeles as a freelance artist doing special effects for film and video games. She has worked at Boss Studios, Metro-Light Studios, R/Greenberg Associates, Anderson Video/Universal Studios, RFX Inc, SimEx Digital Studios, Atomix Studios, Knowledge Adventure, and Adrenalin Interactive. Her feature film credits include *Cliffhanger, Last Action Hero, Mortal Kombat, Under Siege 2, Three Wishes,* and *Virtuosity.* TV projects include Fox TV, and Sony Entertainment Television. Multimedia Titles include *Undersea Adventure* and *3D Dinosaur Adventure.* Computer Games include *Ten Pin Alley* and *Vampire the Masquerade.* She received an MFA in Computer Art from SVA and a BFA in Graphic Design from the Rochester Institute of Technology.

What do you see as the important milestones in the development of new media?

Bringing the Internet to the personal desktop realm. The growth of AOL, MSN, Prodigy, and CompuServe, and the Netscape and Internet Explorer graphical interfaces.

How do you begin a new media project?

I begin with a spec of the project and then a mock up of the page in either Photoshop or Illustrator. We always have a kick-off meeting with the producer, designer, art director, and project manager. It is usually held during this process as well.

How has the use of new media and the computer affected this process?

In very similar ways, except everything is digital from the conception.

What software do you use?

Photoshop™, Illustrator™, Image Ready™, Fetch™, BBedit™, StuffIT™, Flash™, MS Word™, MS Excel™, MS Outlook™, In Control™, Netscape™, Internet Explorer™, HTML, Palm Desktop™, Quark Xpress™.

What hardware do you use?

Power Macintosh, G3/G4, PC, iMac.

What advice would you offer to people entering the field of new media and technology?

Learn both the PC and the Mac. Have a good understanding of Photoshop, Illustrator, Image

Ready, Fetch, and HTML. Design your own Web site and upload it. Surf constantly and get familiar with the Internet. You can never ask too many questions. Take classes to stay in the loop. With all of the rapid developments in the technology, it is virtually impossible to know all of the software packages, programming, video, and audio skills.

How important is it for a new media artist to know everything?

A new media artist should concentrate on design typography and layout skills, rather than go for specific software and hardware. Anybody can learn software and be trained on hardware, but not everybody has design talent. I would tell them to work on their personal portfolios and Web sites.

Where they should focus their attention?

The best advice I ever got was to get out a pencil and paper and make two columns. In the first column, list all the things that you are good at and in the second, if money weren't an issue, what would you rather be doing for eight or ten hours a day? Then connect the dots and whatever matches up is the answer on where you should focus your attention. It worked for me.

What is most lacking in the education of design and new media students?

Design skills are most lacking and making realistic projects for the real world to showcase in their portfolios.

What are the important elements of a new media portfolio?

Design, layout, typography, use of fonts, and color and object placement.

Where do you see Web design heading?

I see Web design becoming more animated with flashed graphics as Internet speed becomes less of a design issue. In five to ten years, I see the convergence of television and Web design.

How do you see the Web affecting other media, such as print/news, traditional art, TV, movies, animation, and galleries?

I see all these media converging. However, it will happen slowly. For example, the television and the computer will eventually become one box.

How important is sound in new media?

This percentage breakdown can be argued, but I feel that it should be sound 60% and visual elements 40%. Right now, audio is growing quickly on the Internet, and it is becoming more important in Web site design.

Where do you see multimedia heading?

The ability to randomly access any portion of an animation, or work, is unique to multimedia, and it allows interactivity.

How important are traditional animation skills?

Animation skills are extremely important.

How important is programming in the work you do?

Knowing HTML is fairly important, but Java scripting and Unix are even more important.

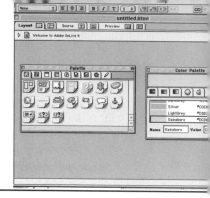

Chapter Six

DIGITAL Creativity

Web Design and Production

We are in the middle of a revolution. Technology is

racing ahead much faster than we can adapt to it.

No more evident is this than with the Internet. The development

of the graphical browser interface and widespread adoption of

Netscape and Internet Explorer have led to a whole new form

of digital global communication within the past five years.

It is important to keep reminding ourselves that the World Wide Web is still in its developmental stages. The half-life of software and data structures on the Internet is three months. Even with this continuous rate of change, the Internet has evolved into a tremendous economic and cultural networked environment. The Internet was designed to be able to adapt rapidly to change. Much of this was laid down when the original structure of the Internet was designed. The use of multiple platforms and operating systems was built into the Internet. This is one of the reasons it has succeeded in such a big way. We have all seen the fortunes of computer companies and software companies rise and fall, but the Internet has maintained steady growth and will continue to do so for many years to come. The purpose of this chapter is to give you an understanding of how to create and design Web sites for the Internet. Web sites are the fundamental content unit of the Internet, composed of information (textual, graphical, audio, and video) and links to other sites and resources. The subset of a Web site is a Web page—that is, to keep it simple, a single HTML document. Web sites are composed of many pages linked together. To design Web sites effectively, it is important to understand the constraints that one is working with, the nature of the networked environment of the Internet, and how to convey your message in a manner that takes advantage of these limitations, rather than be hindered by them. Before we get started in the process of design, we should take the time to understand some of the major design terms used and the underlying structure of the Internet.

The Team

Web design is generally a team process. Although many designers do create Web sites on their own, large Web design firms consist of hundreds of people, each doing a very specific job. Small design firms have people who do a great many different things. Before a Web site is started, the team must be assembled. There are many factors governing this, including budget, production schedule, scope of the site, and ongoing updates. Web teams can number in the hundreds on down. A typical small team is three individuals (see Figure 6.1). For simplicity, this chapter will deal with Web site production from a single designer's point of view.

[6.1] A typical small Web design team. Teams can range from two people to several hundred depending on the site.

Concept/Idea

The first thing you need to create a Web site is an idea. What will the Web site be about? There are thousands upon thousands of Web sites. What is going to make your Web site unique and different? What will your Web site contain? Who is the target audience? All of these questions must be answered before you even sit down to the computer. One of the best ways to get ideas for a Web site is to look at other Web sites. Go to some of the search engines and type in some of the keywords that you will use for your Web site. Look at the design, navigation, and use of text and graphics. This will start to give you an idea of what you want your Web site to be. Then follow the Web design production process (see Figure 6.2).

After your initial stage of research is done, make a list of all the elements that your Web site will contain. This will start to give you an idea of how much work you have ahead of you and exactly how you want to structure the site. If you are doing a corporate site, this is much easier. Most companies already have a logo, letterhead, business cards, brochures, a location, services, and merchandise. A lot of content is already created for you. If you are doing a student site, check out what other students have done. One of the best ways to look at student sites is to log onto art school sites and look at the different approaches. Web sites are as different as people. As with most projects, it is important to narrow down your concept and idea to a single page and to include the who, what, when, where, why, and how of the Web site. Also define the visual and graphic style of the site and define the information that it will contain. This gives you a basic approach to the site and forces you to narrow down what your ideas and concepts are, rather than trying to include everything into your site.

Define Content and Gather Information/Resources

Web sites are essentially data. Because of bandwidth restrictions, you need to make sure this data is in a form that is suitable for the Web. Also, you must make sure that the content is clearly defined and streamlined for delivery over the Web. Some sites are huge

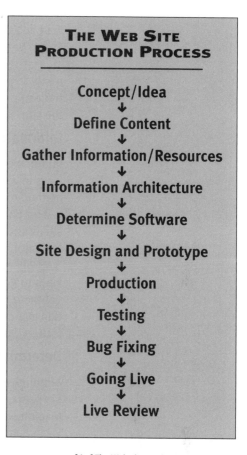

THE WEB SITE PRODUCTION PROCESS

Concept/Idea
↓
Define Content
↓
Gather Information/Resources
↓
Information Architecture
↓
Determine Software
↓
Site Design and Prototype
↓
Production
↓
Testing
↓
Bug Fixing
↓
Going Live
↓
Live Review

[6.2] The Web site production process. Memorize it and always use it. It will cut down on time spent and give you the best results.

warehouses of data (e.g., Amazon.com and Barnesandnoble.com). Other Web sites have a finite content (e.g., a music site). Simple music sites typically have the CD cover graphics, music files, lyrics, a way to purchase the CD, and photos of the band. Whatever the project, precise definition of content is critical to the success of the site.

Information Architecture

Information architecture is a relatively new term that refers to the ways in which information is arranged on a Web site. A simple method of information architecture is to draw a site map. A site map is a graphic view of the Web site, how the information in the Web site is structured, and how you get to it. Information architecture is intimately involved with the design of the site. Each box on the site map will eventually become a page in the site. If there are multiple ways to get to a box, there need to be multiple navigational tools to get there. The information architect also looks at how the information is grouped, what the expectations of the users will be, and other factors that involve the actual use and navigation of the site.

Determining Software for the Web Site

Although HTML is the most commonly used tool for making Web sites, there are dozens of software packages that create Web sites. Macromedia Dreamweaver™, Adobe® GoLive™, and Macromedia Flash™ are three of the most popular (see Figures 6.3–6.5). If your site is going to use audio or video, certain decisions have to be

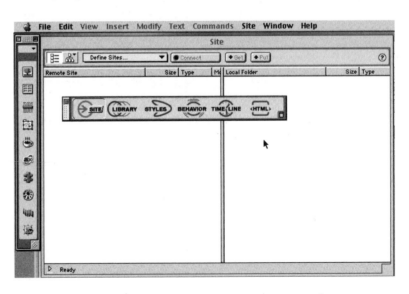

[6.3] A look at the Macromedia Dreamweaver interface. It is one of the leading Web design software packages.

DIGITAL|Creativity

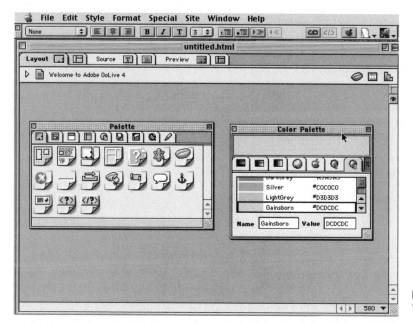

[6.4] Adobe GoLive is another leading Web design software package.

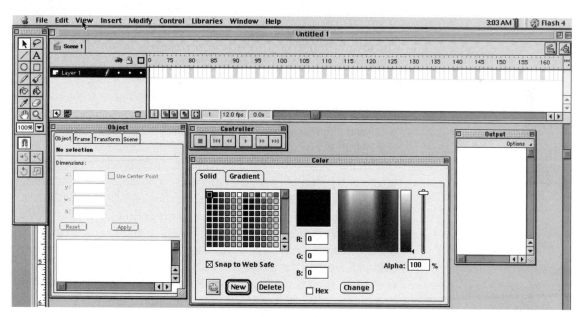

[6.5] Flash uses vector technology to allow for animation and quick download times.

made about file formats and what technologies will be used for your viewers to hear and see the audio. Will it be primarily a PC user site or a Mac user site? Will I stream the media, or should I use downloading?

Determining what your content is and how the site will be structured needs to be done before you choose what software you will use. Again, you can break it down to three basic packages. You will need a text editor for the text, most likely Microsoft Word. You will need an image editor for the graphics, most likely Photoshop®, and an HTML editor, such as Dreamweaver, GoLive, or Flash.

Site Design and Prototype

The next step in creating a Web site is to do the design work and develop a simple working prototype. This will tell you that your concept works and that the look and feel works in practice. The prototype is generally done with placeholders, and the final images, graphics, and text are added afterward. If the site is not too complicated, the placeholder stage might be skipped and the final artwork and text prepared as the site is put together.

Web site design always needs to be thought of from two perspectives. The first and most important is the visual and content issues. The primary purpose of a Web site is to deliver information. Second, it has to deliver that information in a way that will engage the viewer. This demands style, interest, attractive graphics, informative text, audio, and/or video. Web site design also needs to be considered from the back end, or technological, viewpoint. If the best-designed site in the world takes ten minutes to download, no one will visit it. It will be a total failure. Designers must work within the constraints of an ever-changing medium. For this reason, the new-media designer must be a designer and technician rolled into one— or work at a firm where there is a technician who can patiently and eloquently explain why certain design ideas won't work or who can devise an elegant solution so that they can work. In either case, once the content has been defined and the information architecture planned, most of the major barriers for the designer have been overcome. The content will give a designer a good feel for what the site will look like, and the information architecture gives the basic structure on which the design will be based.

Metaphor and Visual Style

It is difficult to come up with any standard approach to design. The strength of any design is its individuality. This section will address techniques for defining the design approach to a project.

When coming up with a design for a Web site, it is always good to go back to one of the fundamental rules of design: form follows function. When thinking about a design approach, take a careful look at the site from the perspective of a potential user. What do users expect to see and how do they expect to use the site? What are they looking to get out of the site? How long is a typical visit to the site?

Next, take a close, hard look at the company and the content provided. As mentioned earlier, corporate sites already have a lot of design research behind them in their corporate logo, typeface, and printed matter.

The next step is to enter a very creative work phase. Your client's competitors' and similar sites are an important resource, as are extended keyword searches and visual research. Collect as many graphic and design ideas that revolve around your project as you can. Put them up on the wall and look at them together. Start sketching and designing.

One good technique is to make copies of the Netscape and Internet Explorer browsers and use them as design templates, much as you would use a storyboard for a video or commercial. Experiment with different Web typefaces, and try approaches using different software programs. Load the sample graphics on a server and see how the design downloads and works.

The use of metaphor for Web sites has gained popularity as a design style. There are only so many ways that you can incorporate text, logos, and graphics to make an interesting site. One way to make your site stand out is to use metaphor. What do we mean by metaphor? Well, Webster defines it as an implied comparison, or the transferring of a word or phrase to the meaning of another. For example, comparing stock trading to racing, or sleeping to lying on the beach. In a visual sense, you create a graphic and visual environment that supports and enhances the intention of your Web site through association.

Since Web design is generally a team effort, while the design process is proceeding, the information architects and programmers are busy building the prototype with placeholder or other graphics.

The navigation and look and feel of the site is intimately related to the design of the site, and there is generally a lot of back and forth between the designers and the information architects. For example, the interface may be an image map with several hot spots on it. This image may change several times during the design process. Or the client may want to see how an image map works versus a set of navigation buttons.

It is very important to remain very free during this phase. Early on, the overall budget has been approved, and the amount of back and forth with the client is generally a function of the budget of the project. Low-budget Web sites have less of this type of interaction.

When we have reached the final stage of the design process, several screens of the site have been completely designed, and the working prototype is a very clear model of what the final site will look like and how it will operate. It is very important to get the client to sign off on the design at this stage. After this, the real bulk of the work begins and it will be very expensive to initiate major changes from now on.

One word of caution: Your client hired you to design the site based on your design style, reputation, and creativity. When meeting with clients, it is generally a good idea to give them a few choices but not too many. If you have come up with 25 different approaches, narrow it down to 3 or 4 to present to your client. It is also not a good idea to present only a single idea. You want your client to feel involved in the design process but not in control of it or in a situation where they feel controlled by you. This is a delicate balance, but remember that you are the design professional and your take on the design style is going to be better informed than that of your client. Client-dictated Web sites always tend to have too much text, too much information, and not enough design. Learning how to work with and handle clients is a major part of being a successful designer.

Creating and Preparing Content for the Web

Once the design phase has been completed and approved by your client, the bulk of the work begins. This is the preparing of all the elements for inclusion into the site. Based on the approved design and the information architecture, the production department has a good idea of how many pages, graphics, amount of text, typeface, audio, video, and links will be needed. Production artists are generally grouped according to their specialty. Designers with a strong background in typography work with the art director to make sure that all the correct copy is included and designed to the specifications of the design document.

A Web site can be broadly defined as an interactive collection of text, images, sounds, video, and links. This set of data is located on a server and is accessed by a Web address, or URL (Uniform Resource Locator). A really simple way to define a Web site is to look at it as a collection of folders on a computer. Proper Web site design mandates that you keep your Web site data in orderly folders.

HTML

HTML stands for the Hypertext Markup Language. Although some people argue that it is not a true programming language, most people describe it as a simple programming language that formats the source material you have created so that it can be displayed on the Internet. There are many versions of HTML, as well as spin offs, like Dynamic HTML (dHTML) and XML, the extensible mark up language. There is also other software, like Flash, which uses different methods for formatting the data and needs plug-ins to allow the browser to interpret its pages. HTML is by far the most widely used format on the Web. Also, by using HTML, you are guaranteeing that the largest audience possible can view your site. Many sites give the user the option to use either HTML or Flash to view the site.

HTML Text and Tags

HTML is used to format text, images, sounds, video, and so on. You can use a word processor like Microsoft Word or a simple text editor to create an HTML document. One great way to learn about HTML is to use the View Source option in your Web browser. This allows you to look at the HTML source code for a Web page. HTML places tags before and after the text to define what it is. To define an HTML document, or Web page, you need to have <HTML> at the beginning of the document and </HTML> at the end of the document. The <head> tag contains information about the Web page, such as the title. The <TITLE> tag defines the title of the Web page. The <BODY> tags are used to define the main text contents of the web page. <P> defines a new paragraph. The height of text ranges from 1 to 6, and it is defined by <H1>, <H2>, <H3>, and so on. Although HTML does not have the sophisticated type-handling capabilities of a program like Quark XPress, it can do the standard functions of choosing a font, making it bold or italic, using alignments, spacing, line breaks, and so on.

Fonts

One of the weaker areas of the Internet is its ability to use fonts. There are several reasons for this, the primary one being that HTML must be able to be viewed on a variety of computers. Not all computers have the same fonts. Macintosh system fonts differ from Window system fonts. Therefore, HTML is written in such a way that if a particular font is not available, a substitute font will be used. This is a nightmare for designers and typographers. Several work-arounds and compromises have been made. The first is that a limited number of fonts are used for Web pages. The four major fonts used in Web design are Helvetica, Ariel, Times New Roman, and Verdana (see Figure 6.6). If you limit your font choice to these, you are relatively secure in knowing that your Web page will look the same on most systems. Other work-arounds more specifically define fonts. Another widely used method is to include type in your Web site as an image. That way, exactly what you want will be downloaded, but images take longer to download than text, so this method must be used carefully. It is hoped that in the future, typographic conventions on the Web will evolve. It is already happening to some extent, but it must always be kept in mind that the Internet is a lowest-common-denominator type of environment. To reach the most people, you must conform to the most widely used standards and conventions.

Helvetica
Arial
Times New Roman
Verdana

[6.6] These are the four basic fonts used for Web design. Get to know them well.

Color and Images

Images are very important for Web design, both for informational and design purposes. They can be scanned images, photographs, drawings, art, illustrations, and graphics. They can serve to inform or entertain, and they can also be used to navigate through a site. For example, buttons or graphics can be used as navigational devices. An image map can be set up, where, for example, you click on different parts of a map or photograph to go to more specific information about an image or area.

Before we discuss preparing images for the Web, we should talk about color. Color is handled in a very specific way on the Internet. To make it simple, you need to understand what is referred to as the Web-safe color palette. Many of the computers connected to the Internet can display only 256 colors. Originally, this was due to limitations in the hardware, but bandwidth issues also come into play. Images with 256 colors are smaller than photographic color images. The smaller the image (in terms of data), the faster it downloads. Download speed is critical to the success of a Web site. If viewers have to wait too long, they will more than likely respond to the site in a negative way. As a result, unless it is the choice of the viewer to wait for a download, you must use the 216 Web-safe color palette for all other elements. The Web-safe color palette is shown in Color Plates 11–13, and the values are hexadecimal, which is how they are used in HTML. The Web-safe color palette can be used for background colors, type colors, and images conversions, so that they will look the same on all computers.

Now that we have agreed that the vast majority of our images need to be converted to 216 colors, let's talk about using and preparing images for the Web. The critical issue with images is quality and download time. For all Web designers, this is a compromise. Most designers approach this compromise from both sides. There are times when the image is very important and download times must be longer, and then there is the instance where the image must be made smaller (both in physical size and file size) so that it can be downloaded quickly. Typical file sizes for the initial hit on the Web site range from 40k to 60k. This includes all of the text and data on the initial screen. Some people use a "splash page" of minimal size to get people into their site and allow for additional data to be sent when the once they're there. If the image is going to be much larger, most designers will make a small reference image and then give the user the option to download a larger, better-quality image. Two software packages widely used for this purpose are Adobe Image Ready™ and Macromedia Fireworks™. This software is specifically designed to allow designers to interactively choose between image quality and file size.

Image File Formats

The Web will recognize several different types of image formats, but the two most widely used formats are GIF and JPEG. Another up-and-coming format is PNG. There are also vector graphic formats, like those used in Macromedia Flash and Adobe Acrobat®. GIF stands for Graphical Interchange Format. It compresses files so that they are relatively small. It also reduces the number of colors to 256. GIF files are used for graphics, small images, and wherever solid color areas are used. GIF files can also be easily animated, and

GIF animations are a real standard on the Web. They play quickly and are universally usable, with minimal download time. JPEG stands for Joint Photographic Experts Group. JPEG files are generally used for higher-quality photographs. JPEG files can store up to 16 million colors and have a better compression algorithm than GIF files. It is a variable compression rate that can vary depending on what the designer needs for a particular image. One tip: Always keep your original JPEG file. Each time it is saved, it is recompressed. This is called lossy compression. So if you open and close a file multiple times, it will begin to lose its original quality. PNG is the Portable Network Graphic format. It is newer than GIF or JPEG, and has advantages over each one. It has lossless compression and can display up to 16 million colors. It also has 256 levels of transparency, giving it added creative flexibility. It is still a new kid on the block as far as the Internet goes, but we should see it being used and supported more as the technology advances.

Gamma, or the brightness of images, also needs to be mentioned. There is a significant difference in the way Macintosh and PC computers display images. Images that look good on the Macintosh are generally darker on the PC. Always be sure to check the gamma of your images on both platforms before putting them on your site. The other major important factor regarding images is size. As mentioned earlier, the total size of graphics for a page should be in the 40k to 60k range. This can be accomplished two ways. The first is to limit the number of colors. The fewer colors, the smaller the file size. Also, images tend to be smaller on the Web. A full-screen image is generally not a good idea, unless the user is willing to wait for it. Designers generally try to keep the size of images as small as possible.

Vector Formats, Macromedia Flash, and Adobe LiveMotion™

Vector files take much less space than bit maps. Therefore, they download quicker and to some extent are more desirable for the Internet. Vector files define a graphic mathematically, rather than pixel by pixel. The first company to take advantage of this for the Web was Macromedia, with their software Flash. Flash is very popular on the Internet, with an expected 30–40% penetration as of 2000. In response to Flash, Adobe developed LiveMotion, which works in a similar manner. Adobe also has a software package called Acrobat, which uses PDF files. This stands for Portable

Document Format. This is used extensively for putting downloadable software manuals on-line and on CD-ROM. Several 3D companies are also exploring a modified version of this approach, including Brilliant 3D.

Links

Links are used to connect one Web page to another or to different areas of the Web. In addition to creating links to pages, you can create links to images, files, and e-mail. When using links, be sure to you let your user know what the link is going to. Use design elements, such as color, text, and images to define links. This will make it easier for users to understand your navigational process.

Sound and Video

Separate chapters are devoted to sound and video, where how to create them will be covered in detail. A few tips regarding using sound and video in your Web sites will be discussed here. Both are very data intensive. Sound has less data than video. Both are very powerful communication media. Now that methods for using sound on the Internet have been widely accepted, it is important to consider sound when designing a site. Sound can be included in a site in two ways. One is through the downloading of sound files. These should be small and related to the impact of the site. Longer sounds, such as speech and music can be downloaded or streamed. MP3 audio is a very popular format for music. The most popular format for streaming audio is from RealNetworks. For video, Quicktime and RealNetworks are the two most popular formats.

It is not the purpose of this chapter to teach HTML and Web design software. There are many good books for this, and a few are listed in the bibliography. The point here is that HTML is not rocket science, and Web design is an art that combines a deep understanding of design and the technical limitations of the Internet. Web design can be done by using a Web page layout program like Macromedia Dreamweaver or Adobe GoLive or by coding pages in HTML. A seasoned Web designer recently told me that most good Web designers usually put the Web site together using a text editor and then check their HTML using a program like Dreamweaver. How you work depends on your personal preference.

CASE STUDY

www.brucewands.com

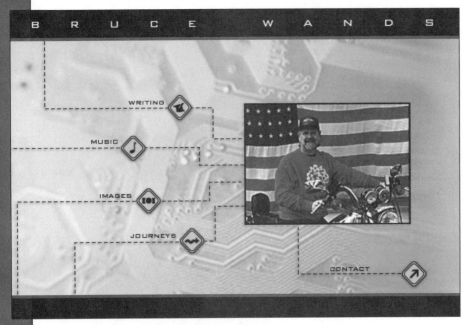

[6.7] The latest version of www.brucewands.com. I use the metaphor of motorcycles and travel to give my site a unique look. Anne Rothschild is the designer I work with.

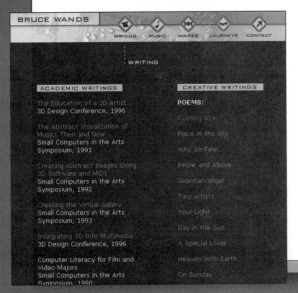

My Web site is a personal site. It is designed to give me a venue for my academic and creative writing, music, images, photography, and computer art. It also provides a venue for my travels and the creative work that results from it. I plan to sell merchandise on my site, including music CDs, art and photographic prints, and my books and poetry. The site was de-signed in cooperation with Anne Rothschild. We first started by defining the content and style I was looking for. I wanted a contemporary design that reflected travel, motorcycles, and my creative persona. We chose to use the motorcycle metaphor and have road sign graphics, with a printed circuit background motif to emphasize the high-tech elements. What we finally came up is shown in Figure 6.7 and Color Plate 35. The writing page gives viewers a choice of the academic and creative writing. I change the

[6.8] This section of my site is where I keep academic, creative writing, and poetry. I am in the process of writing music and poetry books and using new media, CD-ROMs, and DVDs to publish my creative work.

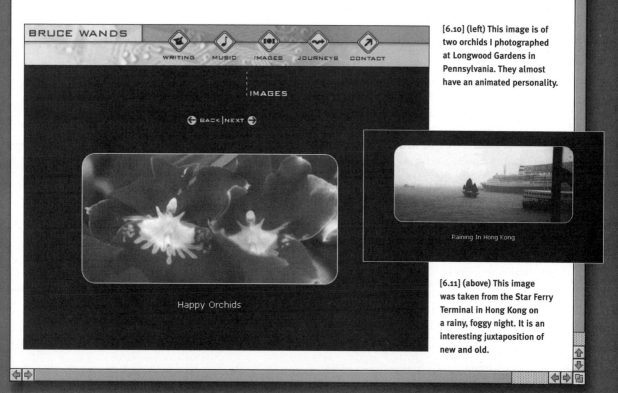

papers and poems from time to time to keep the site fresh (see Figure 6.8 and Color Plate 36). Figure 6.9 and Color Plate 37 show the images section. We opted for a graphic approach that will allow me to change the number and type of images I use. I have a combination of photography and fine art images in this section and update it periodically. Samples of two of the images taken on my travels are shown in Figures 6.10 and 6.11 and in Color Plates 38 and 39.

[6.9] This is a look at the images section of my site. The matrix was designed with flexibility in mind. It can be easily reshaped depending on the images and content I decide to include.

[6.10] (left) This image is of two orchids I photographed at Longwood Gardens in Pennsylvania. They almost have an animated personality.

[6.11] (above) This image was taken from the Star Ferry Terminal in Hong Kong on a rainy, foggy night. It is an interesting juxtaposition of new and old.

CASE STUDY

**Voyage of Discovery, The National Trust
Creative Director, Jeremy Gardiner**

The Voyage of Discovery is a Web site for
the British National Trust. It revolves around
the journey of the Grand Turk, a British
frigate replica. It was produced by Jeremy
Gardiner and several other individuals
through his company Panopticon. What follows is a complete view of the project, from
the original proposal and sketches, to the
final finished artwork.

PANOPTICON PROJECT PROPOSAL
CLIENT: National Trust
PROJECT TITLE: Voyage of Discovery
SPECIFICATIONS: Design of Web site
for Coastshow

Introduction

The star of this site is the Grand Turk. She
will be a constant presence during the
Voyage of Discovery. Each of the site's section header pages will feature a large background graphic showing a detail of the
ship in painterly detail accompanied by a
large swash capital echoing the page's subject matter. These elements will be contrasted by the site's typography, which will
feature generously spaced uppercase fonts
appropriate for a maritime subject. The
site will offer information on virtually
every aspect of the frigate's Voyage of
Discovery, including:

- Virtual tour of ship
- Audio tour of ship
- Map and itinerary for voyage
- Captain's log

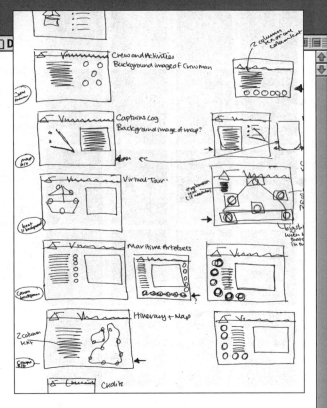

[6.12] This is the original sketch Jeremy Gardiner made for the
Voyage of Discovery Web site. This is the best way to start thinking
graphically. It is best done before you sit down at the computer.
Courtesy of Jeremy Gardiner.

- Information on the Neptune appeal
- Listing of crew and their dockside
  activities
- Links to other sites
- Maritime history
- Navigation then and now

The site's architecture will be kept very
simple, so access to the many informational subsections of the site will be virtually
instantaneous. The design of the site will
strike a perfect balance between visual ele-
gance and information access, providing a
meaningful experience to both casual visitors and prospective patrons to her ports
of call.

Site Structure

The overall shape and size of a site hierarchy can depend on a number of factors but should always reflect an appropriate division of information based on the needs of its users. While users often want to get to the information as quickly as possible, they do not want to get lost in the process. The Grand Turk site will offer users six different paths off the main page. There will be virtually no cross-links between the sections, so for the user, this broad, flat hierarchy provides an efficient and perfectly clear navigational space.

Page Structure

To create the visual richness of the site, the pages will be formatted in a seamless mixture of bit-mapped and HTML-set text. Simple tables will establish page grids, which will juxtapose page titles in an asymmetrical relationship with the running text. Intelligent use of alignment settings within these table cells will allow for the relatively easy creation of architectonic relationships of type and image. The striking page backgrounds will be saved as large JPEG files. Spanning 750 pixels across and as much as 900 pixels up and down these background images will not tile, even on the largest computer monitors.

Searching

One of the best measures of success for a Web site is the simplicity with which users can locate the particular information they are seeking. The voyage itinerary will offer the user the ability to search the schedule for the nearest port to them. The design of the page will also include a map of the coastline where each port of call will be highlighted. There will be background information and a photo-

Introduction

from here the user can access all screens. The user returns to this screen each time they click on 'sail home'.

Map & Itinerary

the background map details various ports of call. When the user clicks on one of the names, such as 'Liverpool' text will be displayed on the left detailing when the Grand Turk will arrive and perhaps details on how to reach the port via walking, car or public transport.

Virtual Tour (a)

Maritime Artefacts (a)

Crew & Activities

At the moment this screen contains no information or interactivity. It may be that this page features several 'crew members' with a brief outline of the activities that the visitor to the Grand Turk may expect to find and perhaps take part in.

Captain's Log

This page will probably be the most text heavy with updates on where the Grand Turk it and its crew have been up to. This may be partly fun (as in cannon firing) or totally practical - schedule updates etc., This has yet to be finalised. It may be that data from previous days is also accessible in which case some form of 'backwards/forwards' navigation control will be need to be included

Credits

The 'Coast Show' logo concludes the website visit. This page simple gives details of those people who have worked on this site, i.e. picture taking/gathering, design, sound, programming etc.,

Virtual Tour (b)

when the user clicks on one of the 'bubbles' as detailed on the ship image in 'virtual tour (a) the screen will go to 'virtual tour (b) which has houses the 'virtual tour'. To make another choice/to view another 'bubble' the user clicks on the small boat to return to the first 'virtual tour' screen - or the user can click on the 'sail home' icon to return to the introduction (choice) screen).

Maritime Artefacts (b)

maritime artefacts (a) has information on how to access the object movies for each of the 'artefacts'. When the user chooses an item to look at, maritime artefacts screen (b) appears. This screen allows the user to view the chosen image/object in 360 degrees. Information relating to the 'artefact' appears on the left hand side and changes for as appropriate to the object being viewed.

[6.13] This is the final flow chart for the Voyage of Discovery Web site. Courtesy of Jeremy Gardiner.

bubble of each port. In case of bad weather and a change in schedule the itinerary will be updated on a regular basis. User's interested in naval history can locate background on Grand Turk in a Then and Now section and can find images and information on important artifacts. One aspect could include object movies of navigation instruments from the past and present. There will also be a captain's log, which will updated on a weekly basis. Links to other sites of interest will include the National Maritime Museum and other National Trust sites.

The Tours

While the Voyage of Discovery site will offer a wealth of useful information for both prospective visitors and members of the National Trust, perhaps its most unique offering are its two interactive tours. Users from around the world, many of whom will never have the opportunity to see the Turk in person, can partake in a virtual visit,

[6.14] The front page of the site. It is clean, simple, and to the point. Courtesy of Jeremy Gardiner.

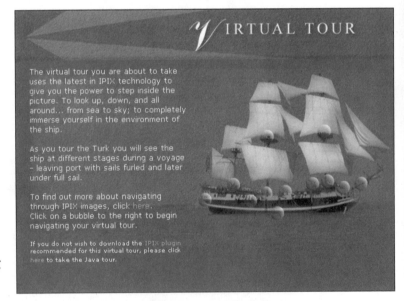

[6.15] This site uses IPIX technology to give a VR experience on the Web. You can go to different parts of the ship and get the feeling of presence by being able to look in almost all directions. Courtesy of Jeremy Gardiner.

gaining an almost firsthand feel for the frigate's wonderful design. The most dynamic of these tours will include the interactive photobubble. Using cutting-edge technology, the exterior and interior of the frigate will be captured in a 360-degree fish-eye image. With a player program downloadable at the site, users will be transported to the deck of the ship, the crow's nest, or the Captain's cabin, where they can look around at will. Interaction with the viewer is remarkably simple and the sense of immersion is very convincing.

After the proposal had been accepted, the next step was to put together the team. The team for this project included: Creative Director, Jeremy Gardiner; Interface Designer, Susan Overton; Web Integration, Luc Pestille; Product Testing, Ashley Richards; IPIX and QTVR Photography, Veronica Falcao; National Trust, Head of Education and Interpretation, Gareth Binns; and Researcher, Emily Lutyens. At this stage, a sketch of the basic navigation was completed (see Figure 6.12). A

[6.16] (left) This is a view from the ship's wheel and where the captain stands. Courtesy of Jeremy Gardiner.

[6.17] (right) This is a view from the bow looking toward the stern of the ship. Courtesy of Jeremy Gardiner.

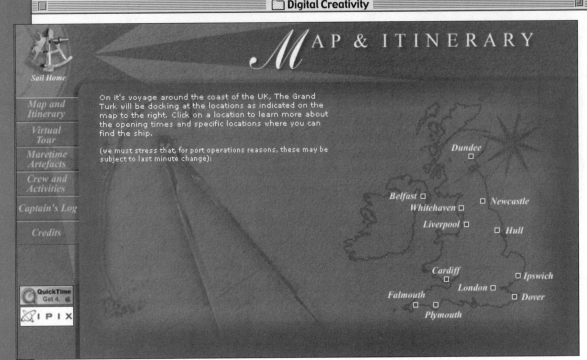

MAP & ITINERARY

Sail Home

Map and Itinerary

Virtual Tour

Maretime Artefacts

Crew and Activities

Captain's Log

Credits

QuickTime Get 4.

IPIX

On it's voyage around the coast of the UK, The Grand Turk will be docking at the locations as indicated on the map to the right. Click on a location to learn more about the opening times and specific locations where you can find the ship.

(we must stress that, for port operations reasons, these may be subject to last minute change):

Dundee

Belfast
Whitehaven
Newcastle
Liverpool
Hull

Cardiff
Ipswich
London
Dover
Falmouth
Plymouth

[6.18] (above) This page gives you a look at the itinerary of the Grand Turk. Courtesy of Jeremy Gardiner.

more complete and final flow chart is seen in Figure 6.13 and Color Plate 40. The main page for the site is shown in figure 6.14.

One interesting part of this Web site is the use of IPIX technology for a virtual tour of the ship. By downloading the plug in, you can look up, down, right, and left to get the feeling that you are actually on the boat. This is accompanied by sounds that were recorded from the viewpoint to give added realism. The menu for the virtual tour can be seen in Figure 6.15 and Color Plate 41.

CAPTAIN'S LOG

To find out what's been happening onboard The Grand Turk, have a look at the Captain's Log.

May 12th - London - Ipswich
Left Greenwich 07:00 and arrived Ipswich 10.00 (following day). Average speed - 5 knots. Travelled 110 nautical miles. Progress very slow due to North-Easterly winds of 6 - 7 on the bow. Very rough trip (bow under water, waves crashing over deck).

Wonderful welcome in Ipswich by the Royal Hospital School armed guard and band. Sailing day very good weather, cannon exchange with Royal Hospital School. Despite a rough trip, crew morale very good, excited about starting the trip and arriving at the first port.

May 18th - Ipswich - Hull
23 hour trip, left Ipswich 17.00. 151 nautical miles, average speed 8.5 knots. Very heavy rain for part of the trip, zero visibility. Leak in the cabin which blew the radar. Day sail very rough. Crew morale still high.

May 23rd - Hull - Newcastle
148 nautical miles. Average trip, managed to get the sails up. 8 cannons fired as we passed Souter Lighthouse - hundreds of kids waving as ship went by. Enjoyed being part of the

[6.19] What more intimate view of life aboard the ship than to peruse the captain's log? Courtesy of Jeremy Gardiner.

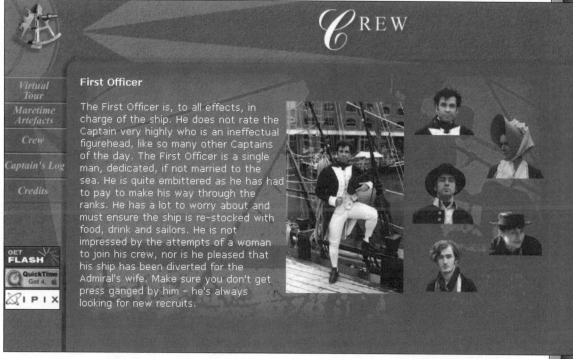

CREW

First Officer

The First Officer is, to all effects, in charge of the ship. He does not rate the Captain very highly who is an ineffectual figurehead, like so many other Captains of the day. The First Officer is a single man, dedicated, if not married to the sea. He is quite embittered as he has had to pay to make his way through the ranks. He has a lot to worry about and must ensure the ship is re-stocked with food, drink and sailors. He is not impressed by the attempts of a woman to join his crew, nor is he pleased that his ship has been diverted for the Admiral's wife. Make sure you don't get press ganged by him - he's always looking for new recruits.

Virtual Tour

Maretime Artefacts

Crew

Captain's Log

Credits

GET FLASH

QuickTime Get 4.

IPIX

[6.20] This section gives the viewer information about the crew. Courtesy of Jeremy Gardiner.

Figures 6.16 and 6.17 and Color Plate 42 show what you actually see when you use the virtual tour software.

The various parts of the site include a map and itinerary (see Figure 6.18), a Captain's log (see Figure 6.19), a description of the crew (see Figure 6.20 and Color Plate 43), as well as descriptions of various artifacts that would have been carried aboard (see Figure 6.21 and Color Plate 44).

[6.21] Artifacts are presented so that you can look at them in three dimensions. Courtesy of Jeremy Gardiner.

ALL IMAGES © 2000 RICHARD BORGE.

CASE STUDY

**Rich Borge, Illustrator,
www.richborge.com**

[6.22] This is the opening page of Rich Borge's site. You immediately get a sense of his creative style. Navigation is simple and clean. © 2000 Richard Borge.

This Web site and the one that follows it define a new breed of illustrator, digital illustrators who are using the Web to their advantage. The field of professional illustration has changed dramatically in the past few years. Traditional illustration was used mostly for print, editorial illustrations in magazines and newspapers, and so on. Digital technology and the Internet changed all that, in some ways for the better and in some for the worse. The rampant proliferation of clip art and the reuse of digital illustra-

ILLUSTRATION · EXECUTIVE SERIES · PHOTOGRAPHY · CD COVERS/GRAPHICS · STOCK · AGENT · HOME
ALL IMAGES © 2000 RICHARD BORGE. UNAUTHORIZED DUPLICATION IS PROHIBITED.

[6.23] Rich has a very unique and recognizable style. He combines various media in his digital work. © 2000 Richard Borge.

[6.24] The use of 3D sculptures gives Rich's work a whimsical and humorous approach to image making. © 2000 Richard Borge.

tions has made the bottom drop out for many artists. On the positive side, those who have embraced and used new technology have benefited greatly from the changes. Rich Borge and Pamela Hobbs are two such people. Rich Borge has a unique style. I first met Rich through his faculty position at SVA. I loved his approach to illustration. With a background in painting, sculpture, and illustration, Rich would create objects, textures, and other illustration elements traditionally, then scan them into the computer, and compose them in Photoshop. When you first go to Rich's Web site (see Figure 6.22

[6.25] This illustration makes use of 2D and 3D elements. © 2000 Richard Borge.

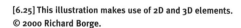

[6.26] This illustration was black-and-white on the Web site. Most make rich use of color. © 2000 Richard Borge.

and Color Plate 45), you are immediately informed of his unique style. In addition, the interface is intuitive and clean. When you click on illustration, (see Figures 6.23–6.27 and Color Plates 46–48), you can look through a variety of his work. When you look at stock, you now have access to his stock illustration collection (see Figure 6.28). He also has Executive Series and CD Covers/Graphics sections. In addition to a clear and concise marketing scheme, Rich has partnered with Gravity Workshop to sell greeting cards, posters, prints, and other items on-line (see Figure 6.29). This approach to e-commerce is a perfect example of how an artist can take advantage of the Web. Rich also includes links, a client list/bio, and contact information on his site.

[6.27] Another good use of 3D elements. © 2000 Richard Borge.

DIGITAL | Creativity

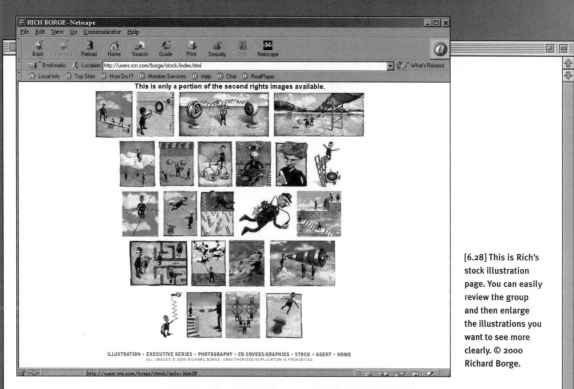

This is only a portion of the second rights images available.

ILLUSTRATION • EXECUTIVE SERIES • PHOTOGRAPHY • CD COVERS/GRAPHICS • STOCK • AGENT • HOME
ALL IMAGES © 2000 RICHARD BORGE. UNAUTHORIZED DUPLICATION IS PROHIBITED.

[6.28] This is Rich's stock illustration page. You can easily review the group and then enlarge the illustrations you want to see more clearly. © 2000 Richard Borge.

[6.29] (left) A good example of how digital illustrators are marketing their work on the Web. © 2000 Richard Borge.

[6.30] The opening of Pamela Hobbs' Web site. It uses Macromedia Flash and is animated and includes sound. © Pamela Hobbs pam@pamorama.com

CASE STUDY

Pamela Hobbs, Illustrator, www.pamorama.com

Pamela also represents the new breed of illustrator. Although her style differs radically from that of Rich Borge, both share a similar approach to marketing and advertising their work. Pam's site relies on Macromedia Flash and incorporates animation. When you enter, you are immediately drawn into Pam's playful style (see Figure 6.30 and Color Plate 49). Her interface is animated and easy. As you glide the mouse left and right, you can see the various parts of the site, including animation, fine art, merchandise, and stock art (see Figures 6.31–6.34). Pam's selection of stock art is divided into editorial, icons, and kids (see Figure 6.35 and Color Plate 50).

animation

fine art

merchandise

stock art

[6.31–6.34] Roll-over images compose the animated interface to move around Pam's site. © Pamela Hobbs pam@pamorama.com

© Pamela Hobbs pam@pamorama.com

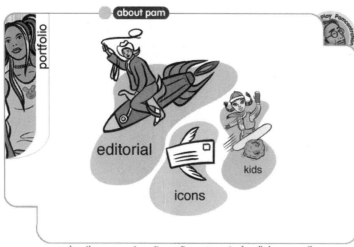

[6.35] Pam's stock work is arranged in three major categories: editorial, icons, and kids' illustrations. © Pamela Hobbs pam@pamorama.com

When designing a Web site, it is always important to test the site on both the Macintosh and PC computers. Figures 6.36 and 6.37 demonstrate the difference between the PC and Macintosh versions, respectively. There is a noticeable difference in the text on the left side.

[6.36–6.37] These two screens demonstrate the difference between type on the Macintosh and type on the PC. © Pamela Hobbs pam@pamorama.com

Pam's artwork translates well to the Web. It is bold, stylized, and colorful. Figure 6.38 demonstrates some of her icons. Icons come in handy in international situations. Pamela is well-known in London, the United States, and Japan. She had the foresight to include her bio in both English and Japanese (see Figures 6.39 and 6.40).

In keeping with her fun approach to life, Pam has included a game called Pamcentration with her site. You must choose the correct matches to finish the game (see Figure 6.41). I didn't do so

[6.38] Examples of Pamela's icons.
© Pamela Hobbs pam@pamorama.com

portfolio

about pam

about Pamela Hobbs

パメラ・ホブス

イラストレーター。 英国ロンドン出身。 ハワイとニューヨークで活躍後、

サンフランシスコに移住。現役として仕事に励み、かつ美大の教鞭もとる。

他に個展や、イラストの講演会など、積極的な

主なクライアントは、SONY、SWATCH、CBS、FOX

ホーム・ページ www.pamorama.com で、どうぞ作

作品へのご意見、ご要望がございましたら、電

日本でのイラストご注文は、独占代理人アマナ

(03) 3470 · 4325 にご連絡ください。よろしくお

About Pamela Hobbs (English)

animation · merchandise · fine art

[6.39–6.40] Pamela includes her biography in both English and Japanese. © Pamela Hobbs pam@pamorama.com

portfolio

about pam

about Pamela Hobbs

Imagine a world of scooter-driving, go-go boot-wearing, martini-drinking, Tiki torch-owning hipsters. Welcome to Planet Pam: the groovy, "retro-modern" domain of award-winning British illustrator Pamela Hobbs who spends here working time between London, Tokyo, SanFrancisco, and New York.

Pamela has taught at the California College of Arts and Crafts, as well as the School of Visual Arts and the Parsons School of Design. A popular guest speaker, Hobbs has charmed audiences from Ohio to Oslo.

Hobbs' client list includes some very cool products Absolut, Swatch, and Sony and a slew of media heavyweights Paramount Films, CBS Fox TV, Business Week, Time, Conde Nast Publications, and The New York Times and more.

Her illustrations reflect the attitude of the times as well: a cheerful and uncritical view of the future, and a welcome alternative to Y2K doom and gloom.

Text by Grace Lou

About Pamela Hobbs (Japanese)

animation · merchandise · fine art · stock · links · email pam

well. It took me 55 seconds (see Figure 6.42). Oh, well—better luck next time!

Another way to get people involved in your site is to have links—and cool links (see Figure 6.43). Change them from time to time, so that people will not get bored.

[6.41–6.42] Fun is a big part of Pamela's philosophy. "Pamcentration" is a game you can play again and again. I didn't do so well. 55 seconds! © Pamela Hobbs pam@pamorama.com

links

links
see more of Pam's work

Adobe web site

Mac World web site

Bill Graham Presents

Graphic Artists Guild

the ispot

Pam's
kool picks

SHIFT

Supernatural Design

Rampt.com

Danger Media

animation • merchandise • fine art • stock • links • email pam

[6.43] Having a list of links is always a good way to get people to enjoy the information they can get on your site. © Pamela Hobbs pam@pamorama.com

Finally, Pam has included a merchandise page. She has a wide range of products that feature her artwork, such as T-shirts (see Figure 6.44). She even has an on-line order form (see Figure 6.45).

merchandise

Book | 1 | 2 | 3 | 4 | 5 | 6 | 7 | 8 | 9 | 10 | 11

animation • merchandise • fine art • stock •

[6.44] Pamela has a wide variety of merchandise for sale. Another way the new breed of illustrator maximizes their income from their creative work. © Pamela Hobbs pam@pamorama.com

[6.45] Making it easy for people to order merchandise increases sales. © Pamela Hobbs pam@pamorama.com

stock

order now!

All work is available in digital format and can be sent via email or FedEx.

Name: Bruce Wands

Email: brucewands@aol.co

Company: Wands Studio

FedEx number:

Item number:

animals
business
food
health
holiday &
vacation
people
sports
technology

Usage

Digital Creativity book

Turnaround time:
○ Urgent (additional charges apply)
○ Standard

Send

animation • merchandise • stock • links • email pam

DIGITAL | Creativity

Summary

Web design is the hottest new field in design. It will continue to be so for many years to come. It is important to understand that it is a new field and still defining itself and still evolving. In five years the World Wide Web will be nothing like it is today. There will be full-frame video, high-quality audio, and much easier interaction and navigation. New technologies like 3D environments and voice recognition will be further developed. With this in mind, we still need to develop and create Web sites with our current tools. The process of Web design was reviewed, along with the team of people needed. It is important to understand that Web site design is mostly a team effort. It is difficult for one person to master all of the skills needed to create complicated Web sites. The step-by-step process of approaching Web design was reviewed, including concept development, metaphor usage, content creation, programming, HTML and other design issues.

Hopefully, the case studies in this chapter have given you some ideas regarding your own site and commercial sites you may be asked to produce. It is important to make sure that sites you create have a definitive style that makes them stand out from run-of-the-mill sites. Use your imagination and refer to the chapter on creativity whenever you reach a stalemate. Always use the same production process when designing sites. There is a lot of detail involved in Web site production. By following this process, you will keep the time spent down and the dollars earned up. Remember, Web design is a dynamic field. Creativity remains a constant, but the techniques and capabilities of the Web will continue to change rapidly for some time to come.

BIBLIOGRAPHY

Michael Baumgardt, Adobe *Photoshop 5.5 Web Design,* Peachpit Press, Berkeley, CA, 2000. www.peachpit.com

This is one of the best practical books I have seen on Web design and production. It approaches the topic very clearly and with good detailed information on all of the issues regarding producing a Web site.

Darcy DiNucci, Maria Giudice, and Lynne Stiles, *Elements of Web Design,* second edition, Peachpit Press, Berkeley, CA, 1998. www.peachpit.com

This is a good overview of Web design, and a good introduction to the use of HTML.

Ruth Maran, *Teach Yourself HTML Visually,* IDG Books Worldwide, Inc, New York, NY, 1999. www.maran.com

This book is designed in a very visual way. It goes through the basics of HTML in an easy-to-see and understand manner.

David Siegel, *Creating Killer Web Sites,* second edition, Hayden Books, Indianapolis, IN, 1997. www.mcp.com/hayden

This was one of the earliest and most popular books on Web design. The second edition is more comprehensive and covers the field more from a theoretical and design approach.

Jennifer Niederst, *Web Design in a Nutshell,* O'Reilly & Associates, Cambridge, MA, 1999. www.oreilly.com

This is an excellent reference book on HTML. It is very comprehensive and has all the nuts and bolts of HTML coding.

Lynda Weinman, *Designing Web Graphics,* third edition, New Riders Publishing, Indianapolis, IN, 1999. www.lynda.com

Lynda has written several good books on Web design. This one is her most recent.

EXERCISES

1. **Design a personal Web site. Start with a site map and then use either HTML or an application like Dreamweaver or GoLive. Keep your first site simple, with a biography, contact information, and a small portfolio of your creative work. Later chapters will focus on photography, sound, and animation. As the semester progresses, expand your site to include these additional elements.**

2. **Pick one area of Web design (e.g., typography, music, images, video) and do a research project on it. Locate several sites that focus on a particular area (e.g., a music site or a video site). Look at how the sites were designed. What methods were used to make the site work for that particular content? What software and file formats were used? Bring this research to class and discuss it with your classmates and teacher.**

DIGITAL | Creativity

" Pamela Hobbs

Illustrator, www.pamorama.com

As much as she talks about acid jazz, sushi, and tequila, and about how hard she likes to play, this 33-year-old British commercial illustrator doesn't want to let on to the fact that she works even harder. This wrought-iron work ethic, combined with her dedication to cool, have made Hobbs wildly successful internationally. When she isn't off to Tokyo serving her Japanese clients, as she was last month, Hobbs is churning out work in her studio in San Francisco's Mission District or back at her old location Black Hat Studios in London. She's worked for everyone from sexy accounts like Swatch Watch and Pop-Up cards to the "really nice guys" of the Berkeley Mac Users Group (BMUG), and she promises that all English people are not like the characters in an Austin Powers film. Ms. Hobbs has served on the faculty of computer graphics departments at the School of Visual Arts, Parsons School of Design, and the California College of Arts and Crafts.

How do you define your illustration style?

I am known for my distinct sedate modern style. My illustrations are a combination of texture, pattern, and sophisticated inked drawings, all united using various software applications.

Where can we see your work?

My artwork has been widely exhibited and has been featured in *Print, How, Step by Step Graphics, American Illustration, Mac Life Tokyo,* and *Time.* Clients include Swatch, *Time* Magazine, CBS Fox TV, Sony, *PC World London,* Absolut Vodka, Adobe Systems, *Business Week,* SEIBU Japan, *Wired,* and others (see Color Plates 51–54).

You combine traditional and digital imagery in your work. How did that style evolve?

I try to combine my traditional work with the computer so it has more of a human touch to it. I used to think I would do everything on the computer, but why do something with technology if you can do it more efficiently by hand? I can't completely copy my ink and brush line on the computer, so I keep sketch books to stay aware of what I'm trying to create. Once I have my main drawing, I scan it in and the rest evolves as I create on the computer. I do things like texture and color on the computer because that's what it does well.

What advice would you give to aspiring illustrators?

As a computer artist, I think it's really important to try to be personable, accessible—to get your own style, to do your own thing rather than to try and re-create a look on the computer. Try to make it as individual as possible. I stress that the individuality should come through, not just an effect.

How has the Web influenced your career?

My site (www.pamorama.com) connects to people nationally and internationally. I am often asked to do lectures, sometimes at the very last minute, and it's nice to know if I forget to bring something with me or my Zip disk fails, that I can be at MacWorld Japan and dial up the site during the lecture and say, "Hey here's the site, be sure to log on check it out, and drop me a note and tell me what you think." People love that. In Japan, everyone's so shy, so they won't always ask questions after a lecture for fear of being rude, and you think, "Oh no, I bored them to death, they hate me." But when I returned from Tokyo last month there were hundreds of e-mails from people all asking tons of questions! It took us days to answer all those, but I think it's important to do so if you're giving people your contact information. Web sites are a way to cross international barriers; with visual language and communications we wouldn't normally have the pleasure of experiencing first hand. I mean, I always wanted a color fax machine so I could just fax the artwork right then and there, and now we've got it, but it's a lot better as you don't have to buy paper for it, so maybe you have to buy a big computer and a load of software, but really you can do it all for a lot less now—maybe the same price as a fax machine. Best of all, it's not like the telephone that's intruding upon some angry person telling me didn't I know its 5 AM and I woke them up. Or better yet, it's 7 AM and they woke me up!

What are your favorite Web sites?

This week? or next? This week they are:

http://www.shift.jp.org
http://www.supernaturaldesign.com
http://www.ntone.com
http://nosepilot.com—*just bear with it.*
http://www.threeoh.com
http://www.k10k.net
http://www.kiiroi.nu
http://www.australianinfront.com.au

How do you see illustration evolving in the future?

My artistic and technological visions change as I see the industry change. I tend to get excited by the new challenges this enterprise brings about. My work represents adaptation and unification within my self, and my surroundings. Staying on top of the latest thing in technology is important. However as a creator, I believe its vitally important to keep in mind that you are first and foremost an artist. Your creative vision is a graphical strength that must not be overwhelmed by the gadgets and gizmos of industry.

What software do you use?

It's an old-school thing—what you first are introduced to you tend to be married to—however over the years I have been using various software applications depending on the task at hand. I have done beta testing with Adobe and have used several products of theirs in conjunction with third-party applications. It's what works best for the individual and the client. If my client prefers one over the other, then I comply to their needs. After all, it's the end result that counts.

How do you see the balance between traditional and digital skills?

When cameras were first invented, people were afraid of the outcome. Computers originally had the same bad image. However, I have always felt the computer was an extension of what I do. With or without it, I am a creator first and foremost. As a tool, the computer has led a new generation of people into the millennium; it has now allowed so many voices to be seen and heard. I have always recognized the power of its capabilities upon my professional and personal work, but not let it pilot me.

What is your advice for students studying digital media?

If anyone is to grow they must try new things, I can't say that it's not happening right in front of us all. Everyone seems to be a Web designer; however, I think one needs to keep in mind that there is a lot more to this under the surface. You do have to just jump right in, and submerge yourself into this field; if you're just trying to get your toes wet, it's never going to be lucrative. Working until 5 AM on tight deadlines might be fun for me but hell on earth for someone else—it's all speculative.

Describe one of your favorite projects.

A lot of work in the United States is advertising and editorial work. Every day brief deadlines reach a new ultimate unrealistic pinnacle. However without the introduction of e-mail, myself and many others in this field of work wouldn't be able to produce high-quality work under such short deadlines. I take jobs that I love, and I work with clients who love and appreciate a new and sophisticated style of work that they feel represents them in the best possible manner. I don't just draw pictures and images, but I feel that it's important to relate the correct concepts and visions to the audience at hand. Every day, even every hour, my job takes me into a new realm and a new challenge with many twists and turns. I work more and more with teams of programmers, technicians, and art directors. I believe that this new remote virtual office is the wave of our future.

What are your thoughts on digital fine art?

Fine art is fine no matter what medium its created in. Technology, like the rest of my business is about inaugurating a body of work that speaks to the viewer, and not about the technology itself.

Who are some of your favorite illustrators/fine artists?

This week:

Fine: Gary Hume, Damien Hurst, Pierre et Gilles, Nick Knight (photographer).
Illustrators: Anja Kroencke, Hiroshi Tanabe, Martine Sitbon.

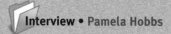

Chapter Seven

DIGITAL | Creativity

Digital Photography

We are all familiar with the old saying, a picture is worth a thousand words. In the digital world, images are invaluable for a number of reasons. One of the most important is that the international nature of the Web makes imagery much more universally accessible. Knowledge and meaning are often more easily communicated through a photograph than with text.

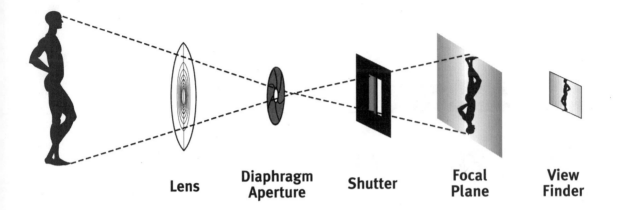

Lens   **Diaphragm Aperture**   **Shutter**   **Focal Plane**   **View Finder**

[7.1] A classic view of the photographic process. Light reflecting from the subject passes through the lens, is controlled by the aperture and shutter and focused on the focal plane. The viewfinder serves as a vehicle for the photographer to see the image.

Digital photography emerged several years ago, and lower costs and higher resolution have contributed to its rapid growth and widespread use. For professional photographers, digital photography has not eliminated the use of film but added another dimension to the craft. All of the traditional photographic principles apply to digital photography. The major area of change occurs after the photograph is taken. The use of digital storage is rapidly replacing film. Stock photo collections that were previously archived on film are now being converted to digital form. There are a number of reasons for this. Digital archiving allows copies to be equal to the original, and digital data is somewhat less fragile than film. Finally, accessing images through a database is much easier than manual methods. You can find many stock photographic companies on the Web. Another reason for using digital photographs is the ability to retouch, color balance, and manipulate these photos with image-editing software. It is now possible to create images that were not technically possible a few years ago. This new area has also spawned a new appreciation for photographic imagery and broadened its horizons. Digital photography starts with a subject in an environment, the lighting conditions, the lens being used, the speed of the action, and the camera (see Figure 7.1). However, before you go on location and take the picture, you must get the assignment. Digital photography is used for Web sites, advertisements, product shots, portraits, public relations and event photography, and fine art photography, to name a few.

Photography started in the 1800s with black-and-white tintypes and glass negatives. Later the process moved to paper. In the early

DIGITAL | Creativity

1900s color photography developed. Although the technology of color photography improved greatly, the use of film for photography lasted several decades. The widespread use of digital photography has happened in the last five years. The technical background of digital photography relies on using a charge coupled diode (CCD) to record the image, rather than film. Since the image that is captured is digital data, it can be easily brought into the computer, manipulated with an image-editing program to improve it, and then printed or published electronically on a Web site. Since digital media can be reused, it costs less to produce digital photographs and allows for the photographer to gain more control during the creative process. Since digital media is available immediately, you do not have to wait for the film to be processed. In the production environment, this time saving is very important.

Photographic Production Process

This chapter will start with a description of the digital photography production process (see Figure 7.2). It will be followed by a review of the technical issues of digital photography. The creative applications of digital photography and ways to make better pictures will be discussed in depth. Professional techniques for making digital photographs will be explained.

Meet Client

The first step in any commercial assignment is to have the initial meeting with the client. The contact with the client may have been initiated by a response to an advertisement, a referral, or viewing of your Web site. The purpose of the initial meeting is to get an idea of what the client wants, and what the budget and schedule is. The goal of this meeting is to get the assignment from the client. One helpful way to conduct this meeting is to use your portfolio as a point of reference. Since you know the process of producing the images in your portfolio very well, it will give the client a jumping-off place to describe what they want.

DIGITAL PHOTOGRAPHY PRODUCTION PROCESS

Meet client, show portfolio, discuss assignment
↓
Define objectives clearly
↓
Define project with brief description, sketch or composite image
↓
Preparation for the shoot
↓
Location or studio shoot
↓
Digital correction and editing
↓
Image archiving
↓
Prepare image in final format (print, web, CD-ROM)
↓
Deliver to client

[7.2] The photographic production process. It works for both digital and traditional photography. Following this process will enable more control over the final product.

[7.3] This image is in the process of being color corrected in Adobe Photoshop.

Define Objectives

It is very important to find out what it is exactly that your client wants and what the photographs are going to be used for. Photography for a magazine ad is much different than photography for the Web. It is also important to find out what context the photograph will be used in. Will it be shown on its own or combined with text or illustrations? The use of the photo will also determine the budget. If it is going to be a critical part of an ad campaign, the budget will most likely be higher than if it will be one of several hundred images in a Web site.

Define Assignment

Once the general use and objectives of the client have been defined, it is often helpful to both parties to define the assignment in a brief description. This forms a basic letter of agreement and gives both parties some assurance that they are both on the same

DIGITAL|Creativity

page. It is usually at this stage that a budget is determined and a production schedule drawn up.

Location or Studio Shoot

Now that the initial work has been done, it is time to take the photographs. This will vary widely depending on the assignment. It may be a location shoot or a studio shoot. Studio shoots tend to be easier because the environment in the studio is controlled. Next on the list is interior location shoots because you do not have to rely on the weather. The last is outdoor location shoots, since you do have to depend on the weather conditions and time of day. It is a good idea to have a longer deadline for outdoor shoots. You may also want to ask the client what time of year is best. The visual difference in most locations between summer, fall, winter, and spring is enormous. Also, the angle of the sun will drastically affect the outdoor lighting. One option to this is to travel to a location. This is normal for many high budget shoots, where an outdoor location is critical.

Digital Correction and Editing

Once the photographs have been taken, they are brought into the computer and color corrected and edited. Digital color correction can be done in a wide variety of software programs, but Adobe Photoshop® is the most common (see Figure 7.3). The first step in working with an image is the process by which the image is brought into the computer. If the photograph is made with a digital camera, this is generally a simple matter. It is important to make sure the image was shot at the right resolution. Other methods of bringing a photo into the digital realm are flat bed scanning, drum scanning, and photo CDs.

Image Archiving

It is important to make sure that images are archived properly. Digital media is somewhat less fragile than film, but it is still volatile. The standard archiving procedure is to make three copies of the files. One goes to your client, one is kept in your studio, and one is kept off site to guard against theft and natural disaster. CD-ROM is generally the most stable and cost-effective method of storage.

Preparation of Image in Final Format

Once the image is in digital format, it must be prepared in the final format that the client wants. This can be a print or images for a Web site or a CD. This can be done at the photographer's studio, or at a commercial output service.

The Digital Camera

The basic components of a digital camera are the body, lens, viewfinder, storage medium, and shutter. There are several types of digital cameras. Price is probably the simplest way to describe them.

Before you purchase a digital camera, do your research. The first thing you need to do is to make a list of what you will use the camera for, which features are absolutely necessary, which ones you would like to have, and what your budget is. An hour on the Internet will give you the best idea of which camera to purchase.

Point and Shoots

These are the least expensive digital cameras. They generally run from $100 to $500. They are very easy to use. They are completely automatic, and the the higher-priced cameras have more sophisticated controls. The least expensive ones have a fixed lens, usually a wide angle, and no exposure control. As the price goes up, features like a zoom lens, macro capability, and adjustable resolutions are added on. To get the best camera for your money, look on the Internet and read the reviews. Important features to look for in this price category are a good zoom lens, variable resolution (the higher the better), macro capability, and manual exposure controls.

Prosumer

Prosumer refers to equipment that is in the consumer price range but has professional features. Cameras in this range can cost from $500 to $2,000. These cameras are generally entry-level profession-

[7.4] An early Sony Mavica digital camera. It has a convenient built in floppy disk drive and takes pictures at 640 by 480 resolution.

al cameras, and long-term purchases for consumers. Most have a good zoom lens, macro focus, and more sophisticated exposure controls. Figure 7.4 shows a Sony Mavica digital camera, which sells for about $700. Many feature an LCD panel and a viewfinder, so you can see the image in a few different ways. The LCD also acts as an interface to the many options that these cameras offer. They generally also allow you to capture images at several resolutions. Most of the photography in this book was done with a Nikon CoolPix 990. I am very happy with this camera. It is easy to use in the automatic mode and has a wide range of manual controls for more serious professional photography. This is important for professionals. Images for the Web do not need to be high resolution, but if the image is going to be printed, it must be of good quality.

Professional

Professional-level cameras can cost as much as $50,000 and are generally found in large professional photographic studios. They produce images equal to or better than film and allow the photographer an infinite range of control over the image. Professional cameras also allow interchangeable lenses to be used. Another aspect of professional cameras is the addition of digital backs to existing cameras. For example, the Hasselblad camera has been a professional standard for years. High-resolution digital backs are now available for this camera, allowing for an easy transition from traditional to digital photography.

Technical Issues

The Charge Coupled Device

The heart of any digital camera is the charge coupled device (CCD), which converts the image coming through the lens into digital form. A CCD is a matrix of photosensitive elements that correspond to the pixels in the final image. They are covered with an array of red, green, and blue filters to allow them to create colors. When the device is turned on, and an image is focused on it, varying levels of light strike the surface. Depending on the intensity of the light, a varying amount of charge is sent to the device controller and memory. This data is collected and stored digitally.

The way the data is stored depends on the resolution of the image. Although some cameras may allow for different resolutions, the standard resolutions are 640 by 480, 800 by 600, 1024 by 768, 2048 by 1532. The larger the image, the more memory required to store the image.

Memory requirements for digital cameras vary. When taking a photo you should always consider the final resolution that will be required. Photos for video and the Internet can be lower resolution than those needed for print.

Digital cameras store images in a wide variety of formats. Like any new technology, most manufacturers are committed to their own systems and only a few general systems have evolved. The simplest format is that used by Sony Mavica. These cameras allow you to use a floppy disk for storage. Sony also uses memory sticks, which are easy and convenient to use. The Nikon camera uses CompactFlash memory (see Figure 7.5). Other cameras may have no removable media at all and require you to download the images from your camera.

[7.5] A PCMIA card adapter for CompactFlash memory. It will plug directly into an Apple Powerbook computer and give instant access to digital images. The memory cards come in a range of sizes. This memory card has 16 MB of data. For serious digital photography, buy as much memory as you can afford. For example, 64 or 128 MB cards.

Lenses

The lens takes the image from the outside world and focuses it on the CCD to make it a digital image. A camera lens is normally made of several pieces of plastic or glass, which focus the image onto the exposing medium, or CCD. Lenses combine convex and concave lenses in shape, since they have to take a larger world, the image, and fit it onto a smaller, flat world, the CCD. The focal length of the lens is the distance between the center of the lens and the focus

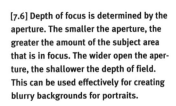

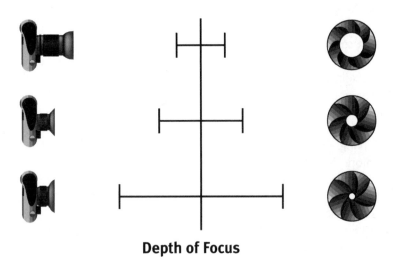

[7.6] Depth of focus is determined by the aperture. The smaller the aperture, the greater the amount of the subject area that is in focus. The wider open the aperture, the shallower the depth of field. This can be used effectively for creating blurry backgrounds for portraits.

Depth of Focus

plane of the camera. The depth of focus is determined by the size of the aperture, or opening, of the lens. The smaller the aperture, the large the depth of focus, and vice versa. Depth of field determines how much of the picture is in focus (see Figure 7.6). A narrow depth of field has only a small portion of the image in focus. The rest of the image is soft. A wide depth of field has a large part of the image in focus. This also corresponds to the aperture settings of the lens. The three main configurations of lenses for photography are normal, telephoto, and wide angle. (see Figure 7.7). They are the same for video and film.

The normal range approximates our vision. Objects photographed with this type of lens appear the same as they would if we were looking at the real scene. This is the most commonly used lens since it is basically what the normal eye sees.

By definition, the telephoto lens has a narrow field of view. It compresses and flattens the perspective of the image, for example, making a city street seem very crowded. Since it has such a narrow field of view, tele-photo lenses allow you to be farther away from the sub-ject and still fill the frame. This is valuable when you cannot get close to your subject, as at a sports event or concert. Telephoto lenses are also used for portraits. The ideal focal length for a portrait lens is 105 mm.

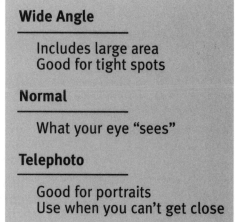

Wide Angle

Includes large area
Good for tight spots

Normal

What your eye "sees"

Telephoto

Good for portraits
Use when you can't get close

[7.7] These are the general rules for using the three main types of lenses.

A wide-angle lens allows the image to include a larger part of the subject. It allows the photographer to get closer to the subject. It is very useful in interiors, where you want to see a large portion of a small room, for example. Wide-angle lenses also give a larger depth of field. This is important in photos where a large area needs to be in focus. Since the subject seems to be further from the background, it is also helpful in emphasizing the main subject of interest. Wide-angle lenses can also distort the perspective. What is near the cen-ter of the field becomes distorted and seems closer to the viewer. What is in the background seems farther away. This increases the illusion of depth in photographs taken with wide-angle lenses.

Zoom lenses, also called variable focal length lenses, cover a range of focal lengths (e.g., 35–105 mm, 100–200 mm, 70–210 mm, 28–43 mm). The advantage of a zoom lens is that several different lens effects can be had with a single lens.

Digital cameras often have a single lens, while more professional models allow for interchangeable lenses. The quality of the image is very dependent on the quality of a lens. While some lenses are a fixed focal length, others have a zoom feature, either expressed as 3:1 or 35 mm–105 mm. When choosing a camera, focal length and the capabilities and sharpness of the lens are important factors. The wider the zoom range or focal length, the more versatile the camera.

Most single-lens cameras have a slightly wide-angle lens, and it is recommended that you get as close to your subjects as possible when using this type of camera. The combination of having the subject large in the frame and the separation of the foreground from the background will also emphasize the subject.

Some cameras also feature a digital zoom, which works electronically, rather than optically. Although this is helpful in some situations, the image of the digital zoom is not always of the best quality.

The ability of a lens to do macro photography is really important, especially for professional photographers (see Color Plate 55). Products, logos, and all sorts of other items need to be photographed at a close distance.

Exposure and Shutter Speed

Exposure refers to the amount of light that is allowed to pass through the lens and onto the film or CCD. Shutter speed is the length of time the shutter stays open to record the image. Shutter speeds can vary from several minutes to 1/2000 of a second. The most-often-used shutter speeds range from $1/125$ to $1/1000$ of a second. In traditional cameras, the shutter is a physical mechanism that opens and closes. In digital cameras the process is controlled electronically.

Exposure

Finding the proper exposure is one of the greatest challenges in traditional photography. This same challenge exists in digital photography but there many more options. In traditional photography, exposure means the amount of light that gets recorded. Underexposure means that not enough light was recorded, and overexposure means that too much light was recorded. Most cameras determine the proper exposure automatically. Often there are several settings, depending on the lighting and time of day. Professional cameras also have a manual setting.

Camera Equipment

While the camera is the basic piece of equipment needed to take photographs, every professional photographer travels with a camera bag or a vest where they keep a wide variety of items. Bags come is a variety of styles and sizes, and the choice is a matter of personal preference and related to how much you want to carry and what is needed for an assignment. One good tip is to include a list of equipment with your bag, so that when you do travel, you can make sure you have everything you need.

A typical camera bag list would include:
- Lens tissue and brush for cleaning the lens
- Assorted filters for various light conditions and color conversion
- Cable release
- Small tripod
- Large tripod
- Gray/white color cards
- Tape, staples, pins, putty
- Small screwdriver
- Extra batteries (lots of them!)
- Extra film or memory cards
- Dust-proof plastic bags with silica gel for damp locations
- Clamps to support the camera

Tripod

Keeping the camera stable is very important, especially in low-light situations, where slow shutter speeds are required. It is often difficult to hand-hold any exposure of more than $1/30^{th}$ of a second without the image blurring. Tripods must be as stable as possible, and allow for a wide range of adjustment. The head of the tripod should be adjustable so that it tilts, twists, and swivels. There are several different types of tripods for a wide variety of uses. A monopod is a single expandable pole that helps keep the camera stable. It is lightweight and easy to carry, but it offers only minimal support. Lightweight tripods have three legs but fewer options than standard tripods. Standard tripods have adjustable legs, supports for the legs, and an adjustable head with swivel and tilt controls. Large-format tripods and studio tripods are not portable, but they are essential in a photographic studio, where heavy cameras and precise positioning are essential.

[7.8] The type of lens also determines how close you can get to the subject. This will have an effect on both perspective and the intimacy between photographer and subject.

Creative Photography

Creative photography comes with experience and study. Although sometimes great pictures just happen, they can happen more often if you apply creative theory to your photographic process. Many of the same principles that guide painting and drawing apply to photography, including viewpoint, composition, contrast, shape, form, color, texture, pattern, and lighting.

Viewpoint

The viewpoint of the camera is critical in determining the impact of the photograph. Most amateur photographers take all their photos at eye level and stand in front of their subjects. By creatively positioning the camera and examining the subject for interesting angles, the quality of your work will improve. See Figure 7.8 for an example of how the distance of the camera from the subject is also related to the lens type. In this case, a wide-angle lens puts the camera close to the subject and a telephoto lens, far away.

Composition

Composition is critical in photography. In drawing and painting, the artist can compose an image from imagination. Photographers must compose an image within the viewfinder. They must adapt their instrument to the image, rather than applying the image to the medium as a painter would. One of the important words in composition is *balance*. The elements in the image must have an innate balance for the viewer to remain focused on the image for any length of time. The orchids in Figure 7.9 and Color Plate 56 balance each other, and the eye moves between them.

Contrast

Contrast is the difference between the black and the white. A high-contrast image has a narrow range from black to white. Extreme high-contrast images have only two shades, black and white. In computers, the full range of black and white is usually 256 levels. A low-contrast image is one that does not have strong highlights or strong shadows, for example, when the sun is obscured by clouds (see Color Plates 57 and 58).

DIGITAL|Creativity

[7.9] This photograph demonstrates how a limited area of focus can create an interesting composition.

Shape

Shape refers to the graphic elements of a photograph. One of the most important graphic elements is the silhouette. Much of what we see is identified by pattern recognition, and silhouettes are one of the best ways to allow viewers to get the meaning as quickly as possibly. When composing your images, try to define the characteristic lines that define the subject, and then shoot from an angle that defines these lines in an aesthetic way. Your photographs will be more successful. The image in Color Plate 59 is designed by a vertical curved shade. The photo in Figure 7.10 and Color Plate 60 plays off the falling quality of the fern fronds. It also relies on the pattern created by the fronds. Figure 7.11 and Color Plate 61 use repetition to emphasize the subject matter.

Form

Form refers to the three-dimensional aspects of an image. Lighting is critical in defining form. Always refer to the classical painting approach of highlight, middle tone, and shadow. These three elements will add dimension and form to your subject. The use of different focal lengths will also allow you to add or lessen dimension.

[7.10] This image takes advantage of the pattern and shape of the ferns.

For example, being very close to your subject and using a wide-angle lens will greatly exaggerate the three-dimensional nature of your subject. Figure 7.12 and Color Plates 62 and 63 use the lighting conditions to emphasize the three dimensional nature of the lilies.

Color

Color has enormous impact on the viewer. Color carries emotional information, along with aesthetic information. Musicians play the blues, while a person who is not feeling well feels a little green. Colors are generally grouped into two categories, warm and cool. Warm colors include red, orange, and yellow. Some associations made with these colors are warmth, fire, passion, and excitement. Cool colors include blue, green, and violet. Associations with cool colors include night, solitude, sadness, and contemplation. When

DIGITAL | Creativity

composing an image, take a moment to analyze the color values in the scene. It is generally a good idea to have a single color scheme for an image. This can be a dominant color and interplay between complementary colors, or a choice between highly saturated or desaturated colors (see Color Plate 64).

Texture

Texture refers to the character of the surfaces you are photographing. For example, the shape could be an automobile, the form is the body of the automobile, and the texture is the surface of the fender or the leather interior. Texture adds interest and detail to an image. Lighting from the side or top increases the detail in the texture, while lighting from the front diminishes it. Texture can be positive

[7.11] Repetition makes this photo have interest. The eye is led from left to right as it moves over the photograph.

[7.12] The asymmetric composition of this image emphasizes the calm surface of the water and the texture of the leaves.

or negative. The texture of an old man's face gives him character and interest, while revealing it on a young woman makes her look older.

Pattern

Patterns generate strength through repetition of something within the image. It emphasizes a particular graphic element. Two important elements of defining pattern in a photograph are viewpoint and lighting. The viewpoint of the camera has to be such that the pattern emerges from the image. Lighting, such as highlights or shadows, also reinforce the development of pattern in an image.

Lighting

Lighting for photography is critical, since there is no exposure without light. To understand light, we must look at its components. The main ingredients of light include intensity, size, color, direction, time of day, color temperature, the use of filters, and flash. Color temperature varies with the light source, as seen in Color Plate 5.

The Sun and Light

Our main source of light is the sun. At sunrise, the atmosphere affects the color of the light and dramatic colors often occur. Clouds have a major impact on the nature and character of sunlight. As it rises in the morning, the shadows are long. As the sun moves toward the midheaven at noon, the shadows diminish in size and the character of the light becomes harsher. Light from overhead highlights the tops of objects and gives them downcasting shadows. As the sun starts to fall, the shadows again begin to lengthen, and the color of the light begins to change, due to the increased effects of the atmosphere (see Color Plate 65).

Artificial Light

Artificial light is created with a variety of electrical lights. The most common are incandescent lamps or ordinary light bulbs. Fluorescent lights are also used. Professional photographic lights include photofloods and quartz halogen lights.

Flash

Another method for adding light to a photograph is flash. Flash photography adds light for only a very brief period. There are several ways to use a flash. Most professionals use commercial-grade flash units in their studios, rather than constant lights. Professional flash units do not generate as much heat as lamps do, are extremely reliable, and produce very consistent light, both in terms of brightness and color. Depending on the shutter speed, flash can either stop an action or create the effect of motion blur when using a slow shutter speed. Many cameras have a built-in flash. Although this is helpful, it tends to have a rather predictable look. That is the subject nearest the flash is the brightest, and since the flash is coming directly from the camera, shadows are eliminated and the subject looks flat. The flash from a camera is generally a weak source of light, and there is usually a very quick fall off of the light. This tends to make the background look dark. For example, when shooting a group of people with flash, it is best to have them all at the same distance from the camera to take maximum advantage of the flash.

Fill In

One of the best uses of flash is not when the lighting conditions are poor but rather to fill in shaded areas. Fill-in flash adds detail to shadows and can make your subject stand out a bit better when used in daylight. This is particularly true when a strong light source, like direct sun, is creating harsh shadows. Fill-in flash will soften the shadows and give a more pleasing image.

Bounce Flash

A technique for making flash look better is to use a bounce flash. That is, flash reflected off a wall or ceiling. This has the effect of adding softer and more natural light to a photograph. To do this, you must have a flash with a movable head or one that can be used off the camera. If the flash is reflected off the ceiling, you will get a diffuse top lighting. If it is reflected off a side wall, you will get diffused side lighting. Another method is to tape a piece of white poster board to the flash unit to diffuse and scatter the flash, rather than have it face directly at your subject. Finally, you can cover the flash with a diffuser. If you don't have a diffuser, you can improvise with tracing paper or a thin white handkerchief.

Using a sync cord lets you hold the flash at a variety of angles, giving you more control over the direction of the light and more control over the final image. The most common use of a hand-held flash is to extend your arm and raise it slightly, holding the flash at approximately 45 degrees toward your subject.

Red Eye

We've all been victims of red eye, either as a photographer or as a subject. Red eye is caused by light reflecting off the retina, which is the back of the eye. In a dark setting (where flash is often used) the

  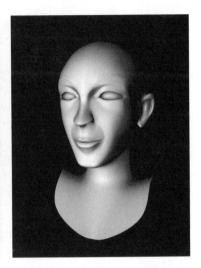

[7.13–7.18] These figures show the different effects of the direction of the light source.

pupil dilates to let more light in. When a flash hits the eye, it does not have time to constrict the pupil and red eye results. Red eye can be eliminated in several ways. Many newer cameras have a red eye feature, which sets off one or more brief flashes just before the final exposure, so that the pupil has time to constrict. You can also raise the lights in the room before taking the photo or ask your subject to look at the light and then look at the camera. Another method is to use an off-camera flash, so that the angle of the flash is not directly into the pupil. Finally, the digital photographer can open the photo in an image-editing program and simply paint the red eye out.

Studio Lighting

Photography in a studio has many advantages. One of the most important is that you can have total control over the lighting. Figures 7.13–7.18 show the effects of artificial light. Figure 7.13 shows a balanced light setup, and Figures 7.14-7.18 show light from the bottom, front, left, right and top, respectively. Some studios have skylights and windows to supplement the artificial light, but natural light is very fickle and although it is very valuable in capturing a particular moment, it is very seldom reliable enough to repeat that moment. Studio lighting setups vary with the subject matter. We will discuss a few typical lighting setups that can be easily done in a small studio.

DIGITAL | Creativity

Table-Top Photography

Table-top photography is very common and most often used to photograph small objects for Web sites, print ads, and so on. The basic elements needed are a subject in the proper environment, camera, tripod, lights, and a table (see Figure 7.19). The table must be large enough to place the objects on, and it should be very sturdy, so that there will be no vibration. It is recommended that a studio tripod be

[7.19] An example of a typical table–top lighting set-up. The umbrellas diffuse the light, so that there are no harsh shadows.

used for its stability and flexibility. You will need a variety of backdrops. This will include poster board, seamless paper, and drapes. It is always helpful to have a variety of props close at hand. Your subject may be a wine bottle, but adding a half-filled glass and some grapes can add character to the photo. Miscellaneous supplies, like tools, clamps, wire, tape, and an electric glue gun make setting up the photos much easier and will save you from having to make a lot of trips to the hardware store.

Lighting for studio photography is generally handled by flash. If your budget is limited, you can use photofloods or halogen lamps. The basic lighting principle for table-top photography is to use diffuse light. Direct light is harsh and does not allow detail to be highlighted. Diffuse light does. There are many ways to achieve diffuse light. A diffusion screen can be placed in front of the light, or the light can also be bounced off a reflection card, such as white foam core board. The placement of lights follows the classic lighting scenario of using the key light to establish the center of attention, direction, and mood of the lighting. Fill lights can soften the shadows and add detail to the object.

Portrait Photography

There is an art to taking a good portrait. The goal is to reveal the character of the person being photographed. This can be accomplished with a simple headshot or by placing the person in an environment that reflects his or her personality. It is very important to put the person at ease and to give them some freedom of movement. By maintaining a conversation with the person, you can maintain eye contact. Moving from side to side on the camera will get different eye positions and maintain more intimacy. Shooting portraits in direct sunlight should be avoided. It creates harsh shadows and makes the person squint, which is unflattering. If portraits are taken outside, they should be taken in the shade or an area where there is no direct sunlight on the person's face.

Portraits are more easily taken in a studio. You have more control over the lighting. A flash is best, since it avoids continuous glare and hot lights. Use the key/fill/background lighting setup and a large aperture, so that the background is slightly out of focus. This will draw more attention to the face. The focal length of the lens should be about 100 mm. This will make the face look the best. A longer lens also moves the photographer away from the person and allows them to feel more at ease. A wide-angle lens will distort the

[7.20] A self-portrait taken with supplemental lighting from high beams on a van. The face is illuminated better than if there were no additional light. Otherwise, the visor on the hat would make the face dark.

perspective and make the subject's nose look distorted and large. It is a good idea to have the person wear clothes that they are comfortable in and to choose an appropriate background. Informal portraits can also be very revealing. These are best taken in the environment the person feels most comfortable in—for example, an artist in a studio or a mechanic in a garage. The self-portrait in Figure 7.20 and Color Plate 66 was taken outside with additional light furnished by the high beams of my van.

Location Photography

Location photography depends on three major items: location, weather, and time of day (see Color Plates 67 and 68). The location is generally determined by the photographer or client (see Color Plates 69 and 70). Whenever possible, it is very important to scout the location first. Take several rolls of film or as many digital images as practical. You are looking for good camera angles to use and good places to photograph from, and you are determining which types of lenses you need, analyzing the local practical lighting conditions, and deciding whether you need to augment the light in some way. A real luxury is to be able to visit a location at different times of day so you can see how the sun affects the quality of the light and how the shadows fall. A thorough scouting trip will make a huge difference in the success of your final shoot. Showing up at a location with a model, assistant, and other people relevant to the shoot without a scouting trip will only make for a longer day and add an element of risk to the shoot.

[7.21] Adobe Photoshop allows the brightness and contrast of this photo to be adjusted interactively.

The Digital Image

Once the images have been shot, the next stage is to use digital techniques to improve, enhance, and bring the images to the level you want them to be. Digital image processing has revolutionized photography. Digital cameras have made significant advances in imaging, but image processing applies to both film and digital photography.

Scanning and Digitizing

Negatives, slides, and prints can be converted into digital form in a variety of ways. The least expensive but somewhat time-consuming method is to use a scanner. In fact, scanners actually qualify as cameras, although they have a very shallow depth of field and are generally used for graphics. However, many objects can be digitized on a scanner. For example, anything that is flat, such as leaves or specialty art papers, qualifies itself as a subject for "flat photography" or scanning. Some unique results have also been achieved with squashing something down onto a scanner and digitizing it.

DIGITAL | Creativity

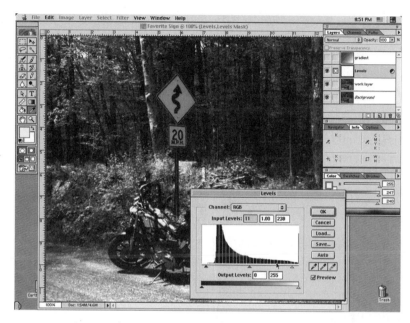

[7.22] Adobe Photoshop now allows the color balance of this photo to be adjusted interactively.

Scanners vary in price and their quality has improved considerably in recent years. Inexpensive scanners can be bought for a few hundred dollars. Many flat-bed scanners have transparency adapters that allow you to scan a slide or negative. The results are decent, but if the image is going to be printed large, there are better scanning methods. The next step up from a flat-bed scanner is a slide scanner. Nikon and Polaroid, among others, make these scanners and they are designed specifically for slides and negatives. These generally give better results than a flat-bed scanner for this type of media, but they are much more expensive. The next level is the drum scanner. These scanners are used for professional-quality scans and give excellent results. They are very expensive and are generally found in professional photo labs and output service bureaus. If you want to take the easy way out, the Photo CD is a good route. Your images are delivered on a CD in a variety of resolutions. Whichever route you take, and this will depend on the final use of your image, you end up with a digital file.

Digital Image Processing

Once you have a digital file, you can work with it to make it what you want. Before the days of digital image processing, all of the magic had to occur either during the exposure of the film or in the

dark room. Since the film and the paper were light sensitive, this type of creative work was often referred to as a "dark art." Digital processing has brought this type of work into the studio and made it accessible to all. Like any new widely distributed powerful technology, the results vary with the creative abilities of the user. However, the arrival of Adobe Photoshop has been a boon to image makers. Photoshop is commonly used for photo retouching and image manipulation. For example, brightness and contrast adjustments can be made easily (see Figure 7.21). Photoshop is also used for color correction (see Figure 7.22) and to crop and recompose photographs.

On top of the normal photographic operations, new software also allows for advanced image-processing operations. Compositing and layering are now much easier and not hampered by physical limitations. In addition, filtering and image processing allow an infinite variety of special effects to be applied to an image. The barrier between photography and illustration is being broken down.

Output

New advances in digital printing have made photorealistic printers a common part of many professional and personal computer systems. For a few hundred dollars, photographers can get ink jet printers with resolutions of 1,440 dpi, and they can e-mail and deliver digital files to their clients. By using page layout software, photographers with a knowledge of design and photography can expand their business to include full-service design and photography.

Summary

In this chapter we have looked at the field of photography. Unlike some media that have been significantly changed by digital tools, the vast majority of traditional photographic principles apply to digital photography. We talked about the production process for photography and the technical aspects of digital imaging. The concepts behind taking good photographs were reviewed, including lighting, exposure, aperture, shape, and contrast. Finally, we looked at the digital process as it applies to a photographic image once it has been digitized.

John Hedgecoe, *The Photographer's Handbook,* third edition, Alfred Knopf, New York, NY, 1998.

Although this is a traditional photography book, it is by far the best book I have found on photography. I highly recommend it to anyone who owns a camera, traditional or digital.

John Odam, *Starting with a Digital Camera,* Peachpit Press, Berkeley, CA, 1999.

This is a good overview of digital photography. It describes both theory and techniques. There are a lot of helpful examples and illustrations.

Tom Ang, *The Art of Digital Photography,* Amphoto Books, New York, NY, 1999.

This is a good, visually oriented book that covers digital photography from the basics to professional practices, including advice for exhibiting your own work.

John Hedgecoe, *John Hedgcoe's New Book of Photography,* DK Publishing, New York, NY, 1994. www.dk.com

This book is a more visual approach to photography than *The Photographer's Handbook*. It is full of color samples of John's work and explains the techniques he used to achieve the results. It's a traditional photography book that is very useful to the digital photographer.

Michael J. Sullivan, *Make Your Scanner a Great Design and Production Tool,* North Light Books, Cincinnati, OH, 1998.

This is a great look at how to maximize the use of your scanner. It is included here since it related directly to bringing images into your computer.

Norman Kerr, *Lighting Techniques for Photographers,* Amherst Media, Buffalo, NY, 1998.

This is an excellent guide to lighting for the still photographer. The approach is both theoretical, and practical.

1. **Pick a subject and take a series of photographs related to it. Be creative. Use different lenses, exposures, and apertures. Take photographs that emphasize shape, contrast, color, pattern, and other compositional techniques. Pick the best 15 to 20 images and make a small exhibition.**

2. **Use photography to illustrate a narrative process such as a story, poem, journey, or other sequence. Then combine this series of photographs with text that you write. Combine the text and images into a Web page.**

"" Matthew Schlanger

INTERVIEW

President and CEO, Black Hammer Productions, Inc. www.blackhammer.com

Matthew Schlanger has been an interactive media developer since the 1970s. As president of Black Hammer for the past five years, he is responsible for the direction of the company's business development, marketing, and account management programs. Prior to founding Black Hammer in 1995, Matthew was creative director and senior programmer for the award-winning CD-ROM *Ocean Voyager,* developed for the Smithsonian Institutue and the interactive game *Gahan Wilson's The Ultimate Haunted House.* His video art and creative work have been exhibited at the Whitney Museum of American Art, IBM Gallery of Science and Art, American Film Institute, The Kitchen, and New Museum. He is on the faculty of the MFA Computer Art department at the School of Visual Arts in New York. See color examples of his work in Color Plates 71 and 72.

When did you enter the digital realm?

As a video artist in the 1970s, most of the processes and hardware I used focused on an analog paradigm (analog processing and analog control derivative of voltage control audio synthesis), yet I also used early computers to control the analog as well as for image processing. I built several Jones frame buffers, which looked like the analog gear, but were digital devices, yet with no CPU. To control the buffers we used analog inputs and a Z80 with a custom-built I/O interface. The Z80 was quickly replaced by the Amiga 1000. At the Electronic Television Center, in the late 1970s we had an S100-based computer running a Cat frame buffer, which was used for image processing. It was crude and programmers were writing in C to move the pixels around.

What was your background prior to your entry into the field of new media?

I was a video artist but was also building my own video processors and dabbling with engineering and a good deal of electronic hardware construction. I also taught video production, mostly at SVA. I worked in television and independent production. I designed video and image processing systems for varied clients, often bridging the gap between broadcast hardware and the early commercial image processing devices (NU-VISTA, etc.). Independent production included shooting about 200 interviews with Holocaust survivors for the Museum of Jewish Heritage.

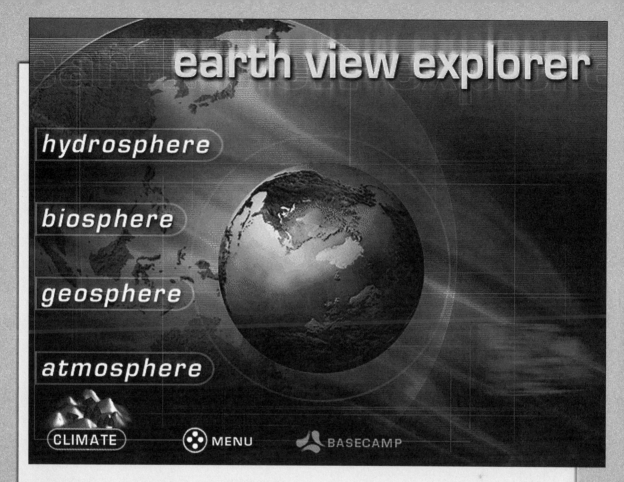

earth view explorer

hydrosphere

biosphere

geosphere

atmosphere

CLIMATE   ● MENU   BASECAMP

What made you decide to work with new media?

I was always working with the notion of interactivity. A component of my video work included the creation of interactive installations. I discovered Hypercard and became aware of interactive work being created in C for the Museum of Jewish Heritage. At the same time, there was an Amiga revolution going on, and people were talking about the coming of CD-ROM drives. What I was seeing inspired me, especially early work that used video disk, speaking to the prospect of adding interactivity to my work. I was becoming disenchanted with the art world, and I wanted to move to a medium where I could have more of

Earth View Explorer. Screen capture from a CD-ROM created for Lamont-Doherty Earth Observatory of Columbia University by Black Hammer Productions, Inc. Design Direction by Pauliina Raitosola. Earth View Explorer is an educational product intended to aid in the instruction of earth science and was funded by the National Science Foundation.

an impact. This is why I began with educational software design and later games.

What aspect of your background have you found most helpful in your transition to new media?

Almost everything. Video production and art provided many jumping off points: having developed a strong sense of design and composition, understanding animation and movement, having worked for years in a time based medium, programming, music and sound composition, electronic circuit construction and engineering, system design. Teaching translated to management and communication. Even building hardware for artists at the Experimental Television Center was an entry into interface design, albeit a hardware interface. I felt early on that coming from a time-based medium, I had already studied composition in time with sound. I had to add the notion of interface and interactivity, game design, taxonomy, and information architecture.

Who has influenced you most within the field of new media art?

Early on I took a graduate course at NYU with Donald Payne called Interactive Educational Software Design. Prior to that I had discovered the book *Human Computer Interface Design*. With Payne, I was exposed to cognitive science and many issues that laid the groundwork for my early work in new media. My first trip to the Computer Game Developer Conference was inspiring.

What do you see as the important milestones in the development of new media?

The modem and the establishment of the World Wide Web. Early ABC and IBM laser disc and hybrid laser and computer work. Several CD-ROMs developed in the first wave of new media. The establishment of the Computer Game Developer's Conference. HTML, Netscape 1.0, 2.0, 3.0, Java, XML, Macromedia Director, Shockwave, and Flash.

Describe your creative process.

My personal creative process varies based on the medium. In video, I was attracted to real-time image processing. There video composi-

tion and animation was a process of composite layering of periodic waveforms manifested as sound and visual form in real time. The process was not dissimilar to how a sculptor would manipulate clay. At Black Hammer, my creative role is concept development and management. The process is a collaborative one. I am a strong believer in preproduction.

How do you begin a new media project?

At Black Hammer we begin to develop software for clients with a requirements assessment. This includes a rigorous examination of the goals and requirements from many perspectives. The end product of the process is a functional specification, which includes a detailed description of every aspect of a project and its functionality.

How have the use of new media and the use of the computer affected this process?

The basic process of preproduction and production is nothing new. Both film and commercial video production have employed rigorous preproduction and production paths. Computers have helped organize preproduction and production in many ways. Microsoft™ Project allows for extensive planning and tracking, and you can create, modify, and update gantt charts in a flash. Excel, Filemaker, and a slew of others can be tailored to suit many needs. We track all beta testing in a Filemaker database served outside the firewall. No more piles of index cards.

What are the major constraints you have encountered in working with new technology?

Bandwidth. I went from video, at 60 fields full resolution each second to early CD-ROM, where I was able to animate maybe 7 sprites a second. If broadband were to achieve ubiquitous distribution, then the Web would finally achieve the bandwidth of single- and double-speed CD-ROMs, CD technology from 8 to 10 years ago. As a computer-based artist you are limited by the tools that are available on the market. There is always the tendency that works created with the same tools look alike. The trick is to transcend the limitations of the tools you use.

Technology is a rapidly changing and complex medium. Because of the diverse skill sets required to work in the field it is often necessary to collaborate. What effect does this have on the creative process?

I began as an artist who did everything myself: image, sound, technology, design, and program-

ming. I have learned to create teams of people with compatible talents. I have also learned to leave space for other people. The way to get the best work from someone is to allow them to own what they do. Specialization is the natural outgrowth of the multiplication of creative tools and systems. Collaboration allows for the accomplishment of tasks which no one individual can achieve alone.

What are you working on now?

We just completed a Bill Nye (the Science Guy) Web site for Noggin. We are building a Web-

Experimental Television Center. Screen capture from a website created for the Experimental Television Center by Black Hammer Productions, Inc. Design Direction by Pauliina Raitosola. The Experimental Television Center was created in 1970 by Ralph Hocking to support electronic media art.

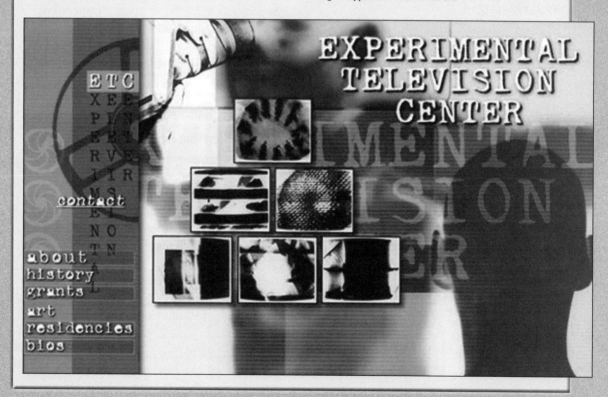

based flight booking system for business jet owners and working on our eighth CD-ROM project for Scholastic. There are several new and ongoing Web projects in-house.

What software do you use?

Mostly Word, Netscape, and Excel. But at Black Hammer the popular software includes BBEdit, Flash, Director, Illustrator®, Photoshop®, Dreamweaver, Fireworks, Homesite, and AfterEffects.

What hardware do you use?

We use everything. I still prefer Macs.

Where should students focus their attention?

Focus on what you are most talented in.

How do you think the Web has changed traditional design?

For new media in general, design must answer to function, interactivity, and information architecture.

Where do you see Web design heading?

More animation using vector-based software.

How do you see the Web affecting other media, for example, print/news, traditional art, TV, movies, animation, galleries?

We have already seen design elements established on the Web cross over to print and television. The constraints of the Web combined with a massive number of designers studying each other's experiments have seen a fast evolution of look and feels. Each medium will continue a dialog with the others.

How easy or difficult is it to incorporate company identity/branding into new media projects?

This is fundamental to what we do at Black Hammer.

How important is sound in new media?

Very important. The Web is finally seeing a more liberal use of sound. Good use of sound dramatically extends the impact of animation. Ideally, every animation should have a component sound and every sound should have a component visual.

What are the important considerations for audio in new media?

The image is confined by the dimensions of the screen. Sound fills the space in and around the screen, a much larger space. Furthermore, most people tend to take more information through the ears than the eyes. Given this disproportionate relationship, the designer must be very careful about balancing image/sound constructions. The overuse of filling space with music is lazy and a pitfall to be avoided.

How is analog video different from digital?

As video processing and production use the same tools for both analog and digital output; the difference is the resolution. Analog delivers a constant 60 fields/second at full resolution and never drops a frame or stutters. It depends on your compression and codec, but digital video is typically small with some kind of codec artifact and the frame rate is generally 15 frames per second or less (MPEG can be full motion but is still limited by size).

With the current bandwidth constraints, what types of modifications have you had to incorporate into the work you create?

For CD work we like to use full-screen, full-resolution with a QuickTime codec (Smacker also has yielded nice results). This requires reducing the amount of area changing on the screen at any given time, and other tricks to reduce bandwidth. This affects both the motion and graphic design. Video for the Web must be small and designed appropriately. When we have used MPEG for CD we did not really need to change the designs much.

Where do you see video moving in the future?

Newer high-definition formats will eventually penetrate the broadcast and professional markets. In the immediate future, high-quality equipment in very small packages, plus computer-based editing software will continue to put video production in the hands of many more people. In the past, broadcast quality hardware could only be afforded by industry.

What do you think about webcasting?

Webcasting is great for niche work. Those trying to extend cable-like programming to webcasting are missing the point. At this time I am more interested in individual efforts. The hard part is consideration of the global reach.

What is your take on the development of interactivity?

When film was invented, cameras were set before stage performances yielding long one-shot proscenium-perspective works. The grammar for film remained to be written, and it took years for that grammar to develop. The Web and CD-ROM also borrowed from earlier media, yielding the new media shuffleware. As fast as the grammar for new media is developing, we are still at the beginning of a long process.

Where do you see multimedia heading?

Surprisingly CD-ROMs have not disappeared, and DVD-ROM has not caught on—yet. As the best prospects for broadband peak at 2X CD-drive bandwidth, I don't see CD-ROM (or DVD-ROM) entirely disappearing in the near future. The ability to randomly access any portion of an animation or work is unique to multimedia and allows interactivity.

How important are traditional animation skills?

Very. The principles still apply, but sometimes the tools are different.

How important is programming in the work you do?

Very. I started in new media designing, managing, and programming CDs and Web games. Programming is an area of creative expression. Most good new media programmers are the better interface architects.

How do you see the collaboration between engineers and artists affecting the use of the media?

This is nothing new. At the Experimental Television Center we used to work with the engineer to build and design hardware that reflected our vision. There must be dialog, and the engineers must be brought into the design process early. Don't just design and then tell the engineer to build it.

What is the outlook for the future of digital media?

In 100 years film has changed very little, the two major advances being the addition of sound and color. Video technology has essentially not changed much either, although there is greater access to higher-quality tools and a paradigm shift from network to cable TV. The new digital media are based on the computer and software. Computers double in processing power and storage space at alarming rates. Software advances do not need time for manufacturing to catch up with engineering advances. Hold onto your seats.

What careers will be important?

Programmers. Idea and content generation. There will always be a place for good managers and designers.

What emerging technologies will become important?

Wireless. Digital book technology.

DIGITAL Creativity

Video Production

In this chapter, we will explore the video production process in detail as it relates to producing digital video for new media and the Internet. You will learn the process of creating video from concept to finished product. Video theory will be explained to provide a basis for the understanding of digitizing video. Traditional and digital video production will be compared and contrasted. Production techniques will be reviewed for those wanting to create digital video for the Internet. The basic principles of editing will be explained.

The Video Production Process

Video production has its roots in film production. As media evolves, many of the technical factors change dramatically, but the principles behind the use of the time-based camera as a narrative tool do not. It is therefore important to have a sound knowledge of film theory as it relates to video production. The difference between analog and digital video production from the camera point of view is not significant. Where the dramatic changes have occurred is in editing. Analog video editing was tape based and time consuming. Digital video allows nonlinear editing, which gives users much more creative freedom in completing a video production. We will start with a review of video theory as it relates to new media and the Web. It must also be remembered that there is a huge consumer base of VHS and so an understanding of analog video is important.

The Analog Video Signal

A sweeping beam of electrons creates video across the screen at a very rapid rate (see Figure 8.1). Like film, video is in essence a series of still images. Persistence of vision gives us the illusion that the images are moving and are continuous. If you look closely at a video screen, you can see that it is really a series of lines. The most common video standard is NTSC. This stands for National Television Standards Committee, but it is humorously referred to as Never The Same Color. Due to the analog nature of the video signal, it is rare to find consistently good color. The NTSC signal is combined into a single wire, which is why the signal is so poor. Both the color and black-and-white information are combined.

The reason RGB computer monitors have more consistent color is that they have four wires going into them: red, green, blue, and sync (see Figure 8.2). The NTSC video signal is composed of 525 lines. These are looked at electronically as two sets of lines, the odd lines and the even lines. One set of odd or even lines is called a field. Both sets together are called a frame. Video plays back at 60 fields or 30 frames per second. By tracing the odd lines first and then the even lines, the image on the screen remains bright and

INTERLACED VIDEO

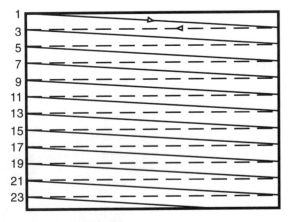

[8.1] This shows how the electron beam travels across the television screen. The first field pass does the odd lines, and the second field pass does the even lines, making sure that the image looks stable on the screen. This is called interlaced video.

does not flicker. Conveniently, AC voltage is 120 volts and 60 cycles per second in the United States, making synchronization easier. If we look at this more closely, there are technically 29.97 frames per second. The reason being that by offsetting the frame rate slightly from 30 frames per second, artifacts from the AC voltage can be minimized. We'll talk more specifically about frames rates later when SMPTE time code is discussed.

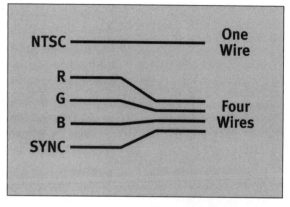

[8.2] RGB video is composed of four elements: red, green, blue, and sync. It is very high quality. NTSC video is combined into a single wire and is not as good as RGB.

The analog video signal has four main elements. If you look at them on a monitor, they are picture, brightness, color, and tint or hue. From a technical standpoint, they are looked at as the black level, video level, chroma, and phase (see Figure 8.3). Picture and black level determine where the threshold of the black is in the signal. Brightness and video level determine how bright the picture is and also what the contrast of the picture is. The less distance between the black level and brightness, the less contrast. Color and chroma determine how much color is the video signal. With no chroma, the picture is black-and-white. When the chroma is too high, the picture is too colorful and fuzzy. Hue and tint determine what the colors look like. When a face appears green, the color is out of phase.

These levels are measured in a video studio by two instruments, the waveform monitor and the vectorscope. The waveform monitor looks at the picture or basic video level and the brightness or contrast. The vectorscope looks at the amount of color or chroma and the phase. Passing the video signal through a processing amplifier or more commonly a time-based corrector can control all of these levels. Most time-based correctors have a video processing amplifier built in. The standard method for measuring these colors and adjusting a video monitor is to use color bars, which are standardized and used as a reference. That is why you see color bars at the beginning of most videotapes. Standard practice is to leave about one minute of bars before you begin recording. On a demo tape, you normally have about fifteen seconds. This gives you a chance to adjust the monitor, so that your videotape will look its best when you show it.

Black Level = Picture
Video Level = Brightness
Chroma Level = Color
Phase = Hue/Tint

[8.3] These are the four elements of the video signal. Knowing how to make a monitor look good is a very valuable and easily learned skill.

Adjusting a Video Monitor and Signal

All video monitors have controls on them so that they can be adjusted. There is a standard procedure for adjusting a monitor, and it is highly recommended that you follow it. Your video will always look better. This procedure can also be followed when you are digitizing video into the computer. Some software programs have waveform monitor and vectorscope software, but the ones that do not usually have the same four controls of black level, white level, chroma, and hue.

1. Turn the color control all the way off, so that the signal is black-and-white.
2. Set the black level so that it is dark but the picture is also fairly visible.
3. Set the brightness level so that there is a good range of contrast between the darkest elements of the picture and the brightest. You may need to go back and forth between the picture level and the brightness level a few times.
4. Now that you have gotten the best possible black-and-white picture, slowly bring up the color until it looks good: not too weak and not too saturated.
5. Set the hue control so that the colors look correct. One easy way to do this is to use a fleshtone as a sample. Another way is to look at the color bars and make the yellow color bar a golden yellow and the cyan bar a strong cyan. Adjusting these two colors will generally bring the other colors into adjustment. Remember, using color bars is the best way to standardize analog video.

Analog Formats

There are several analog video formats, as well as digital video formats (see Figure 8.4). The simplest way to look at them is to divide them into consumer, prosumer, and professional formats. The most common consumer format is VHS. This stands for Video Home System and is actually of a fairly low quality. A better-quality NTSC format is 3/4 inch videotape. This used to be a major standard, but it is slowly being replaced by VHS and digital video formats. Above this is SVHS and Hi-8. These formats require special connectors, and they separate the black-and-white information from the color information. The most widely used professional analog standard is Beta SP. There are many other video formats, but these are the most widely used, and the ones you will most likely encounter.

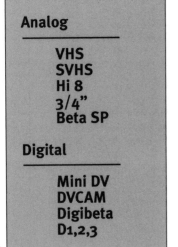

Analog

VHS
SVHS
Hi 8
3/4"
Beta SP

Digital

Mini DV
DVCAM
Digibeta
D1,2,3

[8.4] These are the most common video formats. As technology evolves, they are bound to change.

Digital Formats

Digital video has also gone through a lot of format changes, but it is starting to settle in. The consumer level of digital video is DV. There is the mini-DV and DV cam. The professional standard is D1. There are a lot of standards, like D2, D3, Panasonic 1/2 inch, etc. The advantages of digital video over analog video are huge. One of the biggest problems with analog video was generation loss. Every time you made a copy of a videotape, the quality was degraded. The previous standard procedure with video was to put your original footage onto an edit master (one generation lost) and make copies from it (two generations lost). This was usually a best-case scenario, since edit masters were valuable and often several dubbing masters were made from the edit master and another generation was lost. An important thing to remember when you are producing a program that will end up on videotape is to be sure to test it on the medium on which it will be delivered. There are considerable differences among a computer RGB monitor, Beta SP, and VHS tape. It may look great on the computer, but after it has been edited on Beta SP and then dubbed to VHS, there will be significant color changes. A broad generalization is that the picture will get fuzzier, the reds will increase in intensity and the blues and greens will decrease in intensity. You also have to be careful of patterns and thin lines. Because of the interlaced signal, these patterns may vibrate. If you carefully test on VHS during the production process, costly mistakes can be avoided.

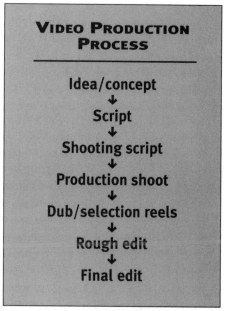

Video Production Process

Idea/concept
↓
Script
↓
Shooting script
↓
Production shoot
↓
Dub/selection reels
↓
Rough edit
↓
Final edit

[8.5] The basic video production process. Try to follow it for every project you do and you will get the best results.

Video Production Techniques

Producing video starts with a concept and idea, just as in photography (see Figure 8.5). After the early stages of preproduction have been completed, it is important to write a detailed and complete script. Although video is less expensive to shoot than film, a script is absolutely necessary. Without a path to follow, a tremendous amount of time will be wasted throughout the entire process.

Script

When writing a script for video, two things must be considered: the video (what the viewer sees) and the audio (what the viewer hears).

In narrative video projects, the audio is very straightforward. What the actors or narrator say is what the audience will hear. For music videos, the audio is also easy, since it is usually prerecorded. Abstract and fine art videos have a more experimental approach toward image and sound.

Once the script has been written and approved, a shooting script is developed. Video is almost never shot in sequence. The script is looked at in terms of how to make the shooting process as simple and cost effective as possible. This usually means that all the exteriors are shot at the same time, and all the interiors are shot at the same time. The script is also analyzed in terms of when particular actors are needed and for which scenes. It makes sense to use the actors for as few days as possible, since they are generally paid a daily rate. Locations also affect the shooting script and schedule. It is best to do all location shots at the same time, rather than bring the crew back and forth. A production book evolves out of this process. You now have a picture of the process through which the shooting will be done. Planning is critical for video production. The better the planning, the better the final product. Planning also includes determining what equipment will be needed, how many crew members, and so on.

Camera Techniques

Following is a list of common camera shots and moves and how they are used.

Long shot (establishing shot)
> This sets the tone for a scene (or film) and gives general information about what is about to happen. They generally are used in the beginning of a sequence or production to give the overall feel of the picture and again at the end to give a sense of resolution and completion.

Medium shot
> Medium shots are the most common and are used mostly for action. They give a sense of perspective in the scene and allow the viewer to have a more general picture of what is going on.

Close-up
> A close-up shot is a vehicle to get the viewer more involved in a scene. They are used most often for dialog. One becomes more involved with a character and begins to take on their viewpoint during a close-up. They are also used for moments of emotional intensity and intimacy.

Zoom

A zoom (or truck) indicates the camera moving in or out of a scene. They work in a narrative sense, just as they work in a mechanical sense. A zoom in tends to direct the attention of the viewer to where the director is moving the camera. It also indicates more involvement. A zoom out removes the viewer from a situation and nurtures less involvement.

Every shot and camera move must have a reason. The camera is the viewer's window into the world of the director. The way that this world is presented determines how the viewer reacts to this world.

Lighting

Lighting for video is an extremely important area to study. Lighting can be broken down into two basic elements: studio lighting and location lighting. We will first discuss the fundamentals of lighting, and then the basic techniques used in studio lighting and then talk about location lighting.

Lighting Fundamentals

Several basic parameters of lighting must be understood before we talk about the practical aspects of lighting a scene. The basic characteristics of lighting include intensity, contrast, color temperature, direction, and the quality or nature of the light.

Intensity refers to the amount of light, how much light exists and how bright it is. This is very important for video because it needs high light levels to look good. Videotape is not as sensitive as film. Therefore, when shooting video, it is a good general rule to make sure there is enough light available to create a good-looking image. Another factor of intensity that must be understood is the inverse square rule. This means that as the distance from the light source doubles, the effects of the light on the object are lowered to one fourth. Contrast is related to intensity, but it refers to the amount of white, gray, and black in the image. If the light is really intense, there is generally very little gray, but a lot of black and white (e.g., a single light shining on a face in a completely dark room). This is referred to as high-contrast lighting. Low contrast refers to the lack of bright highlights and dark shadows and a relatively even form of lighting. An example of low-contrast light would be a cloudy day. Without the direct light of the sun, there are no strong highlights or dark shadows. Contrast also determines meaning in your video image. The higher contrast the image, the more severe, stark, and

intense it is. The lower the contrast, the softer and less severe it is. Color temperature refers to the color of the light as it relates to sunlight. Color temperature is measured in degrees Kelvin, as seen in Color Plate 4. For example, photographically white light is 3,200 degrees Kelvin; sunlight is 6,600K. Color temperature can also be referred to as warmer or cooler light. Photographers often use early morning or late afternoon to shoot, because the color of the light is more desirable during those times of day. Light can also be colored. This is normally done with the use of acetate gels (e.g., during rock concerts). This type of light behaves the same way that RGB color does on the computer, and it has the same properties.

Direction is where the light is coming from. Is it coming from the front, side, below, or above? The direction of the light determines where the shadows will fall and the mood and feeling of the scene. Classic examples of light placement to deliver meaning are that light from above is often viewed as "angelic," whereas light from the bottom is viewed as "demonic." The quality or nature of light is a little bit harder to describe, but generally refers to the overall characteristics and effects of light on the particular scene. For example, soft lighting has the effect of producing a soft image, with fuzzy shadows and a warm feel to the image. Hard lighting is high in intensity and has strong highlights and hard shadows. The emotional component to this type of lighting is a cold and severe mood, rather than a warm and soft one.

Studio Lighting Techniques

Studio lighting is easier than location lighting. If you are really lucky, the studio you are shooting in already has a lighting setup in place. The general rule for video is to use a lot of light. Film is more sensitive and needs more care in setting up the lights. This is not to say that video lighting is not a challenge. It is an art. When approaching video lighting, the traditional approach of key, fill, and background light should be followed. The key light sets the tone, focuses the viewer's attention on the main subject. The fill light is used to soften shadows and to model the subject in a manner that supports the script and story line. The background light is used to give either unity or distance of the main subject from the set. If the actor is lit so that he or she stands out from the background, the viewer will pay more attention to the actor. In another scenario, a more even light tone will bring more prominence to the environment and its relationship to the actor. One of the best rules is to experiment and to test. Video affords the luxury of shooting a test scene and looking at the results. In concert with this, it is always a good idea to carefully document what the lighting setup was, so that if a reshoot is needed, you can duplicate what you had for the first shoot.

Location Lighting Techniques

Lighting techniques for video revolve around what we call the practical lighting considerations. Practical lights are the natural light sources. The concept behind good video lighting is to enhance and improve the practical lights. This will give you a good-quality picture. Good lighting directors also know how to enhance and improve the practical lighting situation. One important way to look at this is to understand that the shadows are just as important, if not more important, than the light. All of the aesthetic factors mentioned earlier all play into the development of the lighting.

For a videotape to look professional, it needs to have good lighting. Working only with available light is not recommended unless that is the effect that you are trying to achieve. Even a minimal amount of work on the lighting will make a major difference in how the final video will look.

Audio

The principles of audio for video are generally the same as those described in the chapter on audio. For most practical purposes (e.g., low-budget projects, student projects, etc.), there are several considerations to be looked at when recording audio during a live video shoot. These parameters are the audio capabilities of the recording device (i.e., video camera, camcorder, portable DAT, etc.). Microphones other than those on the camera should be used whenever possible and connected to a system that has mixing capabilities. The audio is then fed into the camera and the final quality of the audio will be superior to that of a camera microphone. Camera microphones are too far from the actor and tend to pick up too much noise from the environment.

Shooting Video

Now that we have talked about planning camera moves, lighting, and audio, it is finally time to talk about shooting. Camera people generally take their instructions from the director. The director works from the shooting script and knows exactly what needs to

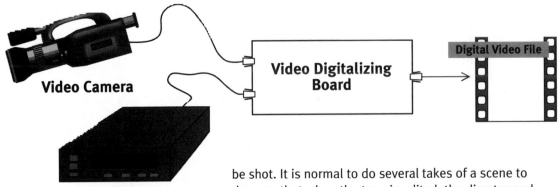

Video Camera

Video Deck

Video Digitalizing Board

Digital Video File

[8.6] How the video digitizing process works.

be shot. It is normal to do several takes of a scene to make sure that when the tape is edited, the director and editor have some choices. Every take has subtle elements that are not really evident until after they have been viewed several times. The general rule is to do three takes or to shoot until a good take is agreed upon. Usually after that, one more take is shot for good luck. Some directors videotape all the takes, including the rehearsals. Much of this depends on the director's style, the time available, and the temperament of the talent.

Covering a Scene

Another approach to shooting video is to cover the scene, or to take a wide range of shots. This includes long shots, medium shots, close-ups, zooms in and out, pans left and right, and so on. By shooting in this way, you are gathering a lot of footage and giving yourself a range of decisions once you reach the editing room. This type of shooting is generally not recommended when working with actors, since they will tire of doing too many takes. However, at the beginning of a shoot or at the end of a shoot, it is a good idea to shoot coverage. You never know when you are going to need extra footage, and it is always better to have too much video than too little. The minimal approach to shooting evolved out of film because of the high cost.

This approach to shooting evolved from video because videotape is relatively cheap compared to the cost of a crew and talent. The best approach is to combine the two methods and make sure that you have enough to create a good quality video when you arrive in the editing room.

Digitizing Video

Digitizing means converting video into a computer file (see Figure 8.6). There are many different kinds of digital video formats, and they all have advantages and disadvantages. There are two main factors to be considered when digitizing video. The first is the final resolution of the video. Will it be full screen or a small size (e.g., Quicktime for the Internet)? Using a lower resolution is one way to decrease the amount of data. For example, if an image is half screen, it takes half the amount of data, quarter screen, one fourth, and so on. The second area of concern is compression. There are many types of video compression, but the real issue is final quality. Uncompressed video is the best quality, but also requires the most memory. Uncompressed video is about 30 MB per second. A single frame of video takes about 1 MB. With typical Internet modem rates of 56k/sec, it is easy to see why compression is so important. Compression is usually looked at as a ratio (e.g., 3:1 or 6:1). When resolution and compression are combined, lower data rates can be more easily accomplished. For example, if we have an image that is one eighth of the screen, or 80 by 60, its uncompressed data rate would be about 4 MB per second or 1/8 of 30. Now if we compress this with a compression ratio of 10:1, we now have 400 k per second.

Practical Concerns When Digitizing Footage

[8.7] Even though digital video editing is becoming more common, window dubs are a very useful way to log and make notes about your footage. Most window dubs are done on VHS tape.

Once we have decided what the final size of the video image will be and what compression we are going to use, it is time to digitize the footage. The process of digitizing begins with the selection of the footage to be used. This can be done in several ways. In traditional video production, a window dub was made with the SMPTE time code burned into it (see Figure 8.7). A list was made of usable takes, and then a copy was made from these takes with time code burned in over the video. With digital nonlinear editing techniques, it is usually brought into the computer directly. It is important to leave a head and tail (extra footage) on each scene, so that dissolves and other effects can be added. Another point to remember when digitizing video footage is that it takes a lot of memory. Digitize only the scenes that you plan to use.

Editing

Once the scenes have been digitized, it is time to do the editing. The basic concept of editing is to put the scenes in the correct order. It sounds easy, but it is very complicated. Editing supports the structure of the story or narrative. When digitizing, you need to choose the scenes that best support the script. Although you should be editing to the script, you should also take into consideration what the final footage is. Editing is a creative process.

Your approach to editing should match the situation and budget. High-budget commercials are tightly scripted, storyboarded, and the end result is generally known in advance. Lower-budget projects normally have two approaches. One is that there is not enough money to have a really creative editing session. In this case, a lot of work must be done before you go into the editing room. Another low-budget scenario exists with music videos, student projects, and situations where the editing time is low cost and not a major factor. This also exists with nonlinear video editing on the desktop. We will talk about all three.

High-budget jobs are generally put together with a lot of preproduction. The shoot is usually expensive, and the director and client have a good idea of what the final product is to be. In these types of situations, this is normally the process followed. Once the final footage is shown, a selection reel is made. A selection reel is a collection of the best takes of all of the scenes. From the selection reel, a window dub, a copy of the original footage with visible SMPTE time code on it, is made. Window dubs are normally made onto VHS tape so that the client, director, editor, and those involved can look at the footage at home or in their studio. From the window dub, an edit decision list is made with the start and ending time codes of each scene. After this has been done, a rough edit is made using this footage in an off-line editing room, which is usually fairly inexpensive to rent. After a couple rough edits have been done, the project is moved into an on-line room and the time codes from the window dubs are used to assemble the original footage. The final edit is also done a few times before the final product is agreed upon.

Lower-budget jobs are done exactly the same way as the high-budget jobs, but more care is taken with the edit decision list and rough edits, so that the time in the on-line editing room is kept to a minimum. On-line editing rooms are very expensive.

The third scenario is generally the realm of student projects and people who use their own desktop computers for editing. This is becoming more common for a few reasons. One is that the hardware and software are becoming more affordable. An Apple G4 machine, with a lot of RAM and Apple Final Cut Pro software is an excellent cost-effective nonlinear editing system. For the price of a few on-line editing sessions, individuals can now purchase complete systems. Although having your own system does remove the restrictions of time, it is still a good idea to follow standard profes-

DIGITAL | Creativity

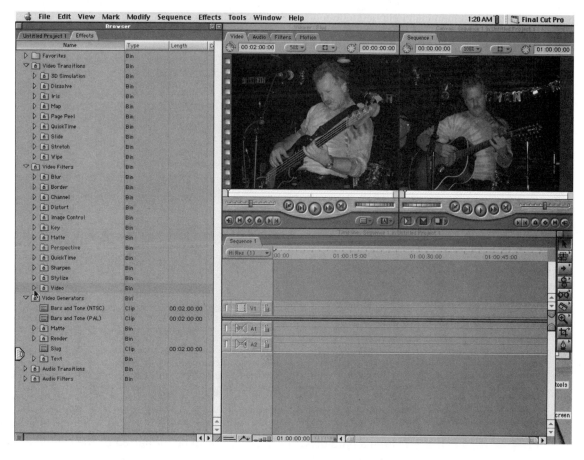

[8.8] Apple Final Cut Pro is gaining favor among many seasoned video professionals for its full range of features and ease of use.

sional practice. Careful viewing of window dubs, making a tight edit decision list, and following the practice of a rough edit followed by a final edit will definitely improve your final product.

In terms of the aesthetics of editing, there are a great many good books written on the subject. It is beyond the scope of this book to spend a lot of time on editing. Suffice it to say that the script and storyboard should really have told the story originally. Cuts, fades, dissolves, and special effects need to be placed in a narrative for a reason. Cuts do not imply a connection between scenes, but dissolves do. Fades start and end scenes as well as signify the passage of time. Like sound, editing should really be an invisible art. If you are noticing the editing and losing your involvement in the story, the editor has failed.

Chapter 8 • Video Production

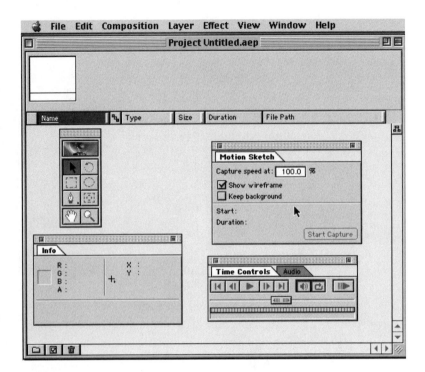

Video Output

Full-frame video output from the computer can be accomplished in a variety of ways. Although professional systems still use them, the days of specialized video boards are drawing to a close for low-priced systems. Firewire enables full-frame video to come directly from a hard disk. This video can also be formatted by the computer for the Internet.

Video for the Internet

There are several things to keep in mind when producing video for the Internet. The most important factor is the size of the image. Due to current bandwidth concerns, video for the Internet is usually low resolution, generally 320 by 240 or 160 by 120. At this size, it is important not to have too much detail in the image. Detail at this size gets lost. Video images for the Internet need to be shot in a clear and easy-to-see manner. Close-ups and medium shots are preferred. Also, large areas of flat color are better than patterns or textures that may vibrate or break up. When composing for the Internet, pay special attention to space and form in the image and use a graphic approach to shooting your content.

Streaming Media

Streaming media has gained enormous popularity recently. It enables video to travel over the Internet without downloading an entire file first. It also affords some copy protection for the copyright holder. The two most popular forms of streaming video are RealNetworks and Quicktime.

DVD

DVD is a growing standard. Although slow to catch on at first, the large storage capabilities of DVD make it an attractive medium. It is following the same course as the CD-ROM, and DVD disk recorders will fall in price in the near future. DVD allows for multiple streams of audio and video, as well as interactivity. Its large commercial appeal is the ability to store an entire feature film on a single disk. Although

[8.10] Media Cleaner Pro is the best software to use when processing video for the Internet and other digital video formats. A sample of the options available is visible on the left.

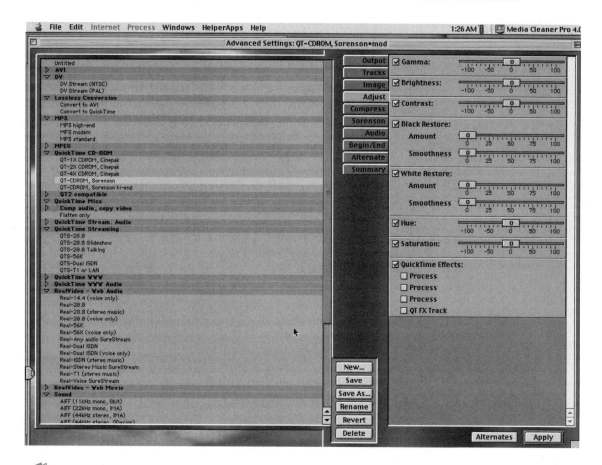

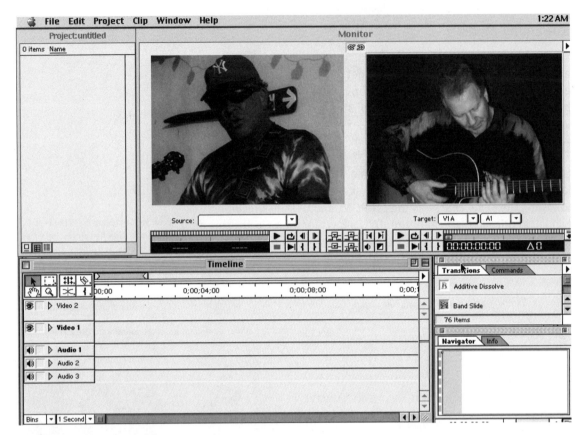

[8.11] Adobe Premiere was one of the first digital video applications. It is still popular.

VHS is still the largest user installed base for video playback, DVD will eventually replace it, although this will take several years.

Digital Video Software

There are several popular digital video software packages. One of the most up and coming is Apple Final Cut Pro™ (see Figure 8.8). This software has many of the features of the more expensive packages, and is a good all around digital video editing software. Adobe After Effects® is used for video special effects (see Figure 8.9). Terran Media Cleaner Pro™ is the preferred package for processing digital video for the Internet (see Figure 8.10). Adobe Premiere® is also popular. (see Figure 8.11).

Future Trends in Digital Video

Digital video will continue to develop at a rapid rate. Future developments will include full-frame video over the Internet. There is also development of MPEG video that will allow interactivity to be added to video. Analog video will become a thing of the past, the way that analog audio has. Video will become incorporated into PDAs and mobile phones. For now, small mini-DV cameras are very popular and yield good results for digital video and video for the Internet (see Figure 8.12). Another item to remember is that video is generally a team effort. Although digital tools allow for a one-person video team, a small video team consisting of a producer, director, camera person, lighting person, audio person, and editor is more common (see Figure 8.13).

[8.12] My Sony PC10 mini DV camera. It is small, very portable and takes great video, stills, and records stereo audio. I use it all the time.

Summary

In this chapter, we took a look at video from both an analog and digital viewpoint. The traditional video production process was reviewed and camera techniques, lighting fundamentals, and studio and location lighting techniques were explained. The process of shooting good video is to make sure a scene is covered, and that enough video is shot, so that the edit session will go smoothly. Careful planning always helps maximize the results of a shoot. Video is also rarely shot in sequence. The usual process is to break the script down into a shooting script, where all the exteriors are shot at once, then the interiors, etc. We then took a brief look at digitizing video, video for the Internet, and the future of digital video. The increased use of video on the Internet makes this field an important one for the future.

**Producer
Director
Camera person
Lighting person
Audio person
Editor**

[8.13] It is nearly impossible for one person to be an expert in everything, particularly video. For professional projects, a small team is usually assembled. Collaboration generally brings better results.

BIBLIOGRAPHY

Gerald Millerson, *Video Production Handbook,* second edition, Focal Press, Oxford, England, 1992.

This is an excellent overview of video production. It covers practical techniques, as well as some of the theory involved. It does not address digital video but is very worthwhile otherwise.

Trish and Chris Meyer, *Creating Motion Graphics with After Effects,* CMP Books, San Francisco, CA, 2000. www.cmpbooks.com

Trish and Chris are excellent speakers and authors. This is a real hands-on book full of tips and techniques. A must for anyone who is serious about Adobe After Effects.

Herbert Zettl, *Sight, Sound and Motion,* Wadsworth Publishing Company, Belmont, CA, 1999.

I have mentioned this book before. It is the best theory book on design for light, space, time/motion, and sound I have read. It does not address digital media specifically but is a great resource for content development. Zettl's *Television Production Handbook,* sixth edition is a classic in the field and highly recommended.

Kris Malkiewicz, *Film Lighting: Talks with Hollywood's Cinematographers and Gaffers,* Fireside Books, New York, NY, 1992.

This book is a combination of interviews and practical lighting techniques. Since lighting is so critical to delivering content, I definitely recommend it.

EXERCISES

 1. **Produce a short video documentary about a typical day in your life. Get a video camera and bring it everywhere you go for one day. Shoot scenes that have meaning to you. Do not worry about lighting, sounds, or having high production values. Focus on content. Do not edit the tape and try to shoot it between 5 and 10 minutes in length. Look at the final video and critique it yourself and have your classmates critique it. How well did your storytelling skills come through? Did you use a variety of techniques, such as long shots, medium shots, and close ups? How did you pace the shots? What did the in-camera editing look like? Digitize the video into the computer and edit it to improve it, or repeat the first exercise. This will train you how to think in terms of narrative storytelling and video production.**

 2. **Create a short digital video project for the Internet. Keep it simple or use special effects. Keep it between 15 seconds and 1 minute in length. Use digital video software (e.g., iMovie™, Adobe Premiere, and Adobe After Effects). Your content can be anything you like (e.g., a poem or a short music video), but you must finish a complete thought. Play it for other people and think about their reactions. This will give you experience in using digital tools and teach you the digital video production process.**

DIGITAL | Creativity

[Color Plate 1] This is a color view of the AVID keyboard. You can see that it is color coded and has graphic symbols on the keys for ease of use.

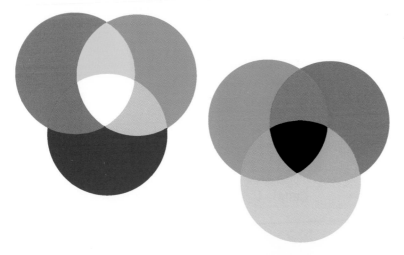

[Color Plate 2] (far left) How additive RGB color theory works. Red, green, and blue are the primary colors. Red and green together make yellow. Green and blue together make cyan. Blue and red together make magenta.

[Color Plate 3] (left) This shows how CMYK or subtractive color works. This is the system used for printing.

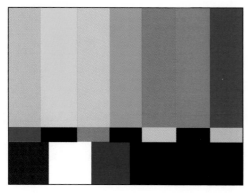

[Color Plate 4] These are video color bars. Color bars are used by video engineers to make sure that the signal played back from the videotape is accurate. They also are a standard by which to adjust a television or video monitor.

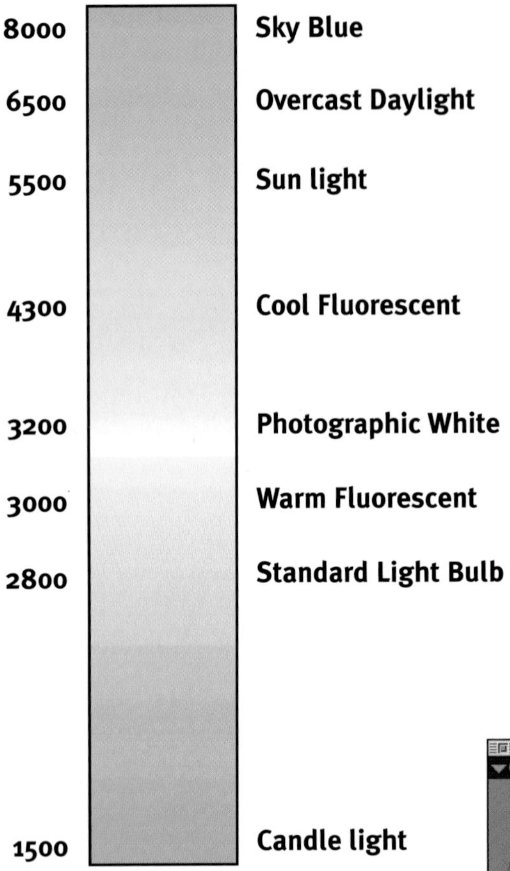

8000 — Sky Blue

6500 — Overcast Daylight

5500 — Sun light

4300 — Cool Fluorescent

3200 — Photographic White

3000 — Warm Fluorescent

2800 — Standard Light Bulb

1500 — Candle light

[Color Plate 5] A diagram of color temperature with degrees Kelvin. All light is not white. Candlelight and standard light bulbs have a yellowish tint to them. Fluorescent lights and the sky have a bluish tint. Color temperature is an important element in color photography and video production.

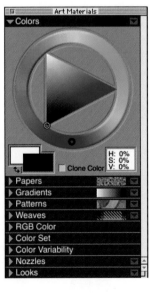

[Color Plate 6] (right) Metacreations Painter uses a circular interface for color selection.

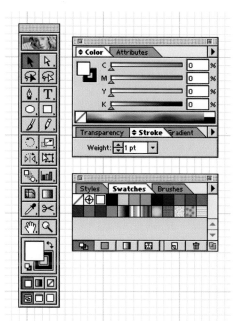

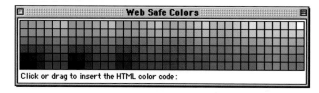

[Color Plate 7] (left) This diagram shows how Adobe Illustrator deals with colors. You can also store swatches of color for easy selection.

[Color Plate 8] (above) BBedit has a palette for Web-safe colors.

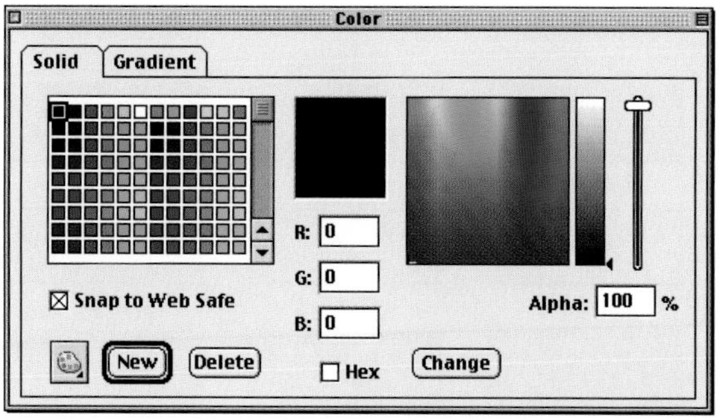

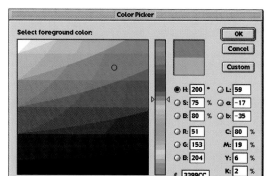

[Color Plate 9] Macromedia Flash has Web-safe colors and the ability to create colors using RGB.

[Color Plate 10] The Photoshop color picker can be set to allow only Web colors to be chosen. One can also input the hexadecimal color name, numbers, and percentages to create colors.

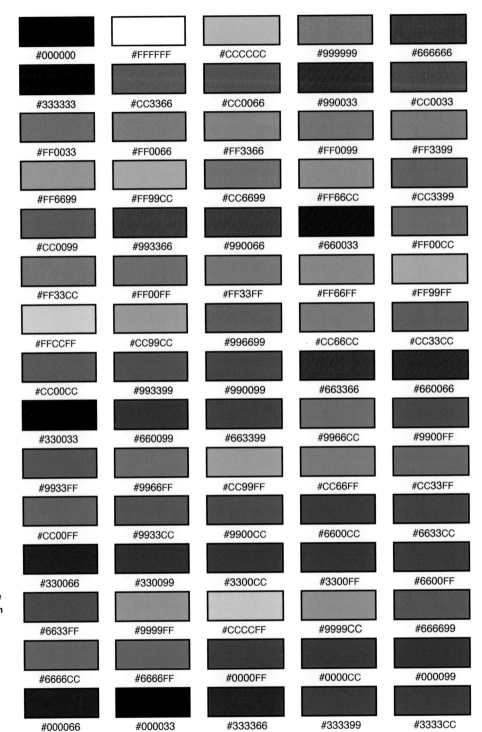

[Color Plates 11–13] These color plates show the Web Safe Color Palette. Underneath each color swatch is the hexadecimal code for the color. Use this palette to choose colors when you are designing a Web site. The Web safe color palette is normally viewed on a computer monitor and the RGB colors will look brighter on the screen.

#000000	#FFFFFF	#CCCCCC	#999999	#666666
#333333	#CC3366	#CC0066	#990033	#CC0033
#FF0033	#FF0066	#FF3366	#FF0099	#FF3399
#FF6699	#FF99CC	#CC6699	#FF66CC	#CC3399
#CC0099	#993366	#990066	#660033	#FF00CC
#FF33CC	#FF00FF	#FF33FF	#FF66FF	#FF99FF
#FFCCFF	#CC99CC	#996699	#CC66CC	#CC33CC
#CC00CC	#993399	#990099	#663366	#660066
#330033	#660099	#663399	#9966CC	#9900FF
#9933FF	#9966FF	#CC99FF	#CC66FF	#CC33FF
#CC00FF	#9933CC	#9900CC	#6600CC	#6633CC
#330066	#330099	#3300CC	#3300FF	#6600FF
#6633FF	#9999FF	#CCCCFF	#9999CC	#666699
#6666CC	#6666FF	#0000FF	#0000CC	#000099
#000066	#000033	#333366	#333399	#3333CC

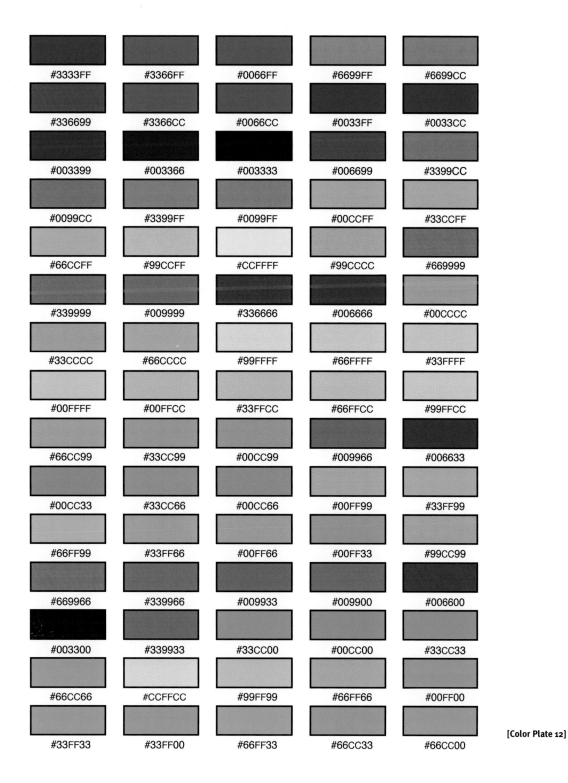

#3333FF	#3366FF	#0066FF	#6699FF	#6699CC
#336699	#3366CC	#0066CC	#0033FF	#0033CC
#003399	#003366	#003333	#006699	#3399CC
#0099CC	#3399FF	#0099FF	#00CCFF	#33CCFF
#66CCFF	#99CCFF	#CCFFFF	#99CCCC	#669999
#339999	#009999	#336666	#006666	#00CCCC
#33CCCC	#66CCCC	#99FFFF	#66FFFF	#33FFFF
#00FFFF	#00FFCC	#33FFCC	#66FFCC	#99FFCC
#66CC99	#33CC99	#00CC99	#009966	#006633
#00CC33	#33CC66	#00CC66	#00FF99	#33FF99
#66FF99	#33FF66	#00FF66	#00FF33	#99CC99
#669966	#339966	#009933	#009900	#006600
#003300	#339933	#33CC00	#00CC00	#33CC33
#66CC66	#CCFFCC	#99FF99	#66FF66	#00FF00
#33FF33	#33FF00	#66FF33	#66CC33	#66CC00

[Color Plate 12]

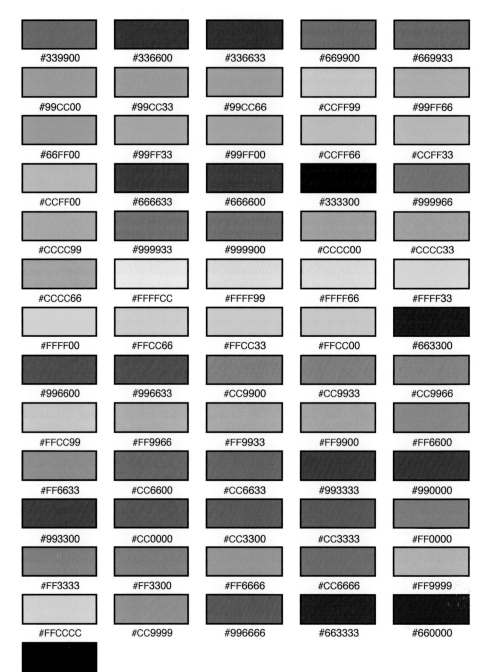

#339900	#336600	#336633	#669900	#669933
#99CC00	#99CC33	#99CC66	#CCFF99	#99FF66
#66FF00	#99FF33	#99FF00	#CCFF66	#CCFF33
#CCFF00	#666633	#666600	#333300	#999966
#CCCC99	#999933	#999900	#CCCC00	#CCCC33
#CCCC66	#FFFFCC	#FFFF99	#FFFF66	#FFFF33
#FFFF00	#FFCC66	#FFCC33	#FFCC00	#663300
#996600	#996633	#CC9900	#CC9933	#CC9966
#FFCC99	#FF9966	#FF9933	#FF9900	#FF6600
#FF6633	#CC6600	#CC6633	#993333	#990000
#993300	#CC0000	#CC3300	#CC3333	#FF0000
#FF3333	#FF3300	#FF6666	#CC6666	#FF9999
#FFCCCC	#CC9999	#996666	#663333	#660000
#330000				

[Color Plate 14] A better view of the audio portion of the studio.

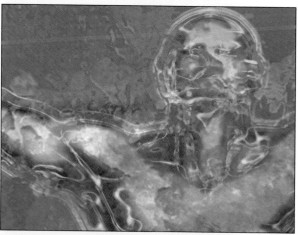

[Color Plate 15] This image was drawn directly on the computer using a graphics tablet and AT&T TARGA TIPS software. This image was designed by Troi Jackson as a backgound for one of my poems.

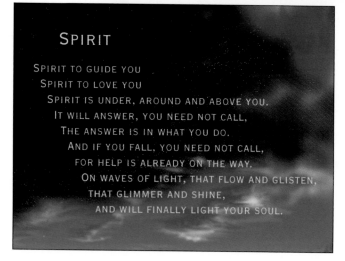

SPIRIT

SPIRIT TO GUIDE YOU
SPIRIT TO LOVE YOU
SPIRIT IS UNDER, AROUND AND ABOVE YOU.
IT WILL ANSWER, YOU NEED NOT CALL,
THE ANSWER IS IN WHAT YOU DO.
AND IF YOU FALL, YOU NEED NOT CALL,
FOR HELP IS ALREADY ON THE WAY.
ON WAVES OF LIGHT, THAT FLOW AND GLISTEN,
THAT GLIMMER AND SHINE,
AND WILL FINALLY LIGHT YOUR SOUL.

[Color Plate 16] This is a poem I wrote called "Spirit." It is an image from a series of interactive poems I create. The poems have voice and music as part of the interactive experience.

[Color Plate 17] This is a portrait I did of Silas Rhodes as part of a multi-portrait gift to Mr. Rhodes by faculty members on the 50th anniversary of the School of Visual Arts. The image represents his aura. It was produced from a scanned black-and-white photo and colors were layered over it in Photoshop. No physical drawing was involved.

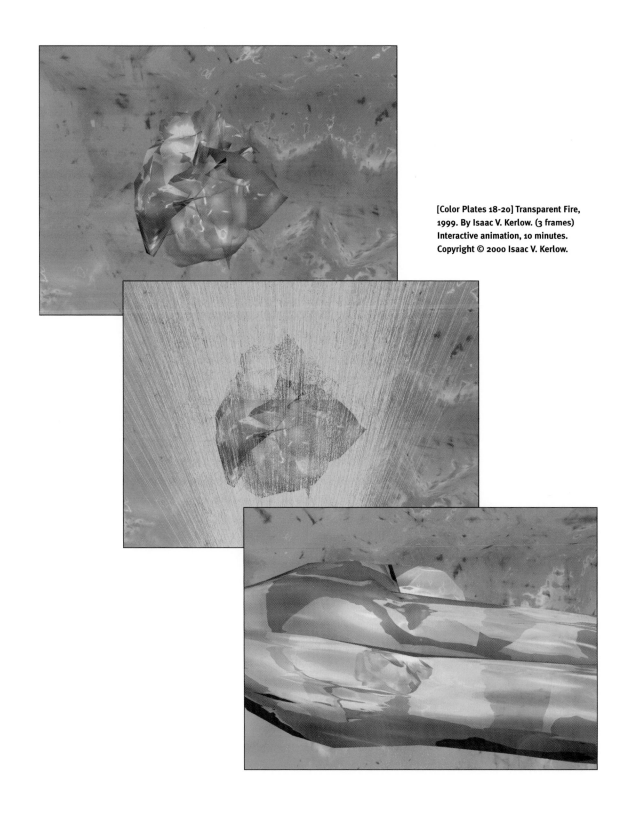

[Color Plates 18-20] Transparent Fire, 1999. By Isaac V. Kerlow. (3 frames) Interactive animation, 10 minutes. Copyright © 2000 Isaac V. Kerlow.

[Color Plate 21] Blue Pearl, 1998.
By Isaac V. Kerlow. Limited edition
digital inkjet print, 13 by 16 inches.
Copyright © 2000 Isaac Victor Kerlow.

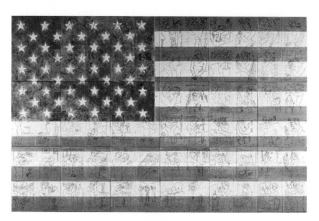

[Color Plate 22] (above) An image by Barbara Nessim that works with color and composition, as well as shape. Copyright © Barbara Nessim 2000.

[Color Plate 23] Within the flag are myraid figures. Copyright © Barbara Nessim 2000.

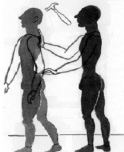

[Color Plates 24-25] These are four images from Barbara Nessim's sketchbooks. Copyright © Barbara Nessim 2000.

[Color Plate 26] (right) This is a variation of a realistic globe. I was trying to abstract the geography so that it did not look like Earth. A cloud layer was added for realism.

[Color Plate 27] (far right) At this point, I decided to experiment with color to see what results I could get.

[Color Plate 28] (right) Another color experiment.

[Color Plate 29] (far right) This image was a combination of working with the surface and color. At this point, I had the idea to create a series of these globes as a fine art exhibition. I had the thought to work with international flags and colors. For example, Japan's flag is white with a red circle and Brazil's flag has a blue globe with a yellow and green background.

[Color Plate 30] (right) By this time, I was happier with the color choice but not satisfied with the surface.

[Color Plate 31] (far right) This was the final globe I chose. It had dimension, I liked the colors, and it had the feeling of Earth, but was an abstraction of it. I then rendered it at 4,000 lines of resolution to get the highest quality image. The final image was 64 MB.

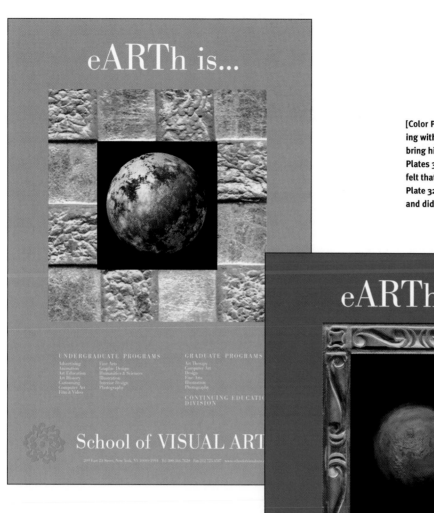

[Color Plates 32-33] I had another meeting with Silas Rhodes and decided to bring him three designs to choose from. Plates 32 and 33 were not chosen. We felt that the frame was too dominant in Plate 32 and that Plate 33 was too subtle and did not have enough strength.

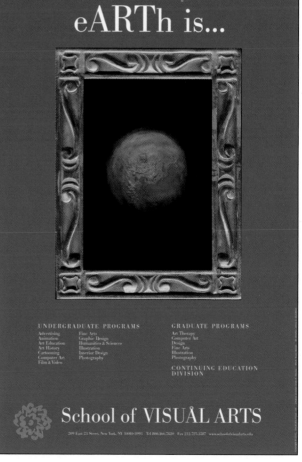

eARTh is...

UNDERGRADUATE PROGRAMS

Advertising Fine Arts
Animation Graphic Design
Art Education Humanities & Sciences
Art History Illustration
Cartooning Interior Design
Computer Art Photography
Film & Video

GRADUATE PROGRAMS

Art Therapy
Computer Art
Design
Fine Arts
Illustration
Photography

CONTINUING EDUCATION
DIVISION

School of VISUAL ARTS

209 East 23 Street, New York, NY 10010-3994 Tel 800.366.7820 Fax 212.725.3587 www.schoolofvisualarts.edu

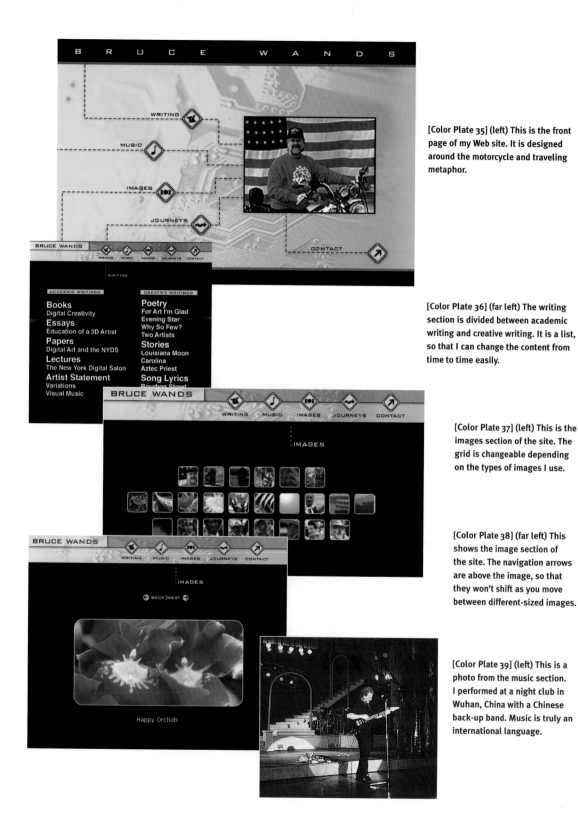

[Color Plate 35] (left) This is the front page of my Web site. It is designed around the motorcycle and traveling metaphor.

[Color Plate 36] (far left) The writing section is divided between academic writing and creative writing. It is a list, so that I can change the content from time to time easily.

[Color Plate 37] (left) This is the images section of the site. The grid is changeable depending on the types of images I use.

[Color Plate 38] (far left) This shows the image section of the site. The navigation arrows are above the image, so that they won't shift as you move between different-sized images.

[Color Plate 39] (left) This is a photo from the music section. I performed at a night club in Wuhan, China with a Chinese back-up band. Music is truly an international language.

Introduction

from here the user can access all screens. The user returns to this screen each time they click on 'sail home'.

[Color Plate 40] This is a color version of Jeremy Gardiner's site map. Courtesy of Jeremy Gardiner.

Map & Itinerary

the background map details various ports of call. When the user clicks on one of the names, such as 'Liverpool' text will be displayed on the left detailing when the Grand Turk will arrive and perhaps details on how to reach the port via walking, car or public transport.

Virtual Tour (a)

Virtual Tour (b)

when the user clicks on one of the 'bubbles' as detailed on the ship image in 'virtual tour (a) the screen will go to 'virtual tour (b) which houses the 'virtual tour'. To make another choice/to view another 'bubble' the user clicks on the small boat to return to the first 'virtual tour' screen – or the user can click on the 'sail home' icon to return to the introduction (choice) screen).

Maritime Artifacts (a)

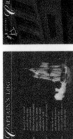

Maritime Artifacts (b)

maritime artefacts (a) has information on how to access the object movies for each of the 'artefacts'. When the user chooses an item to look at, maritime artefacts screen (b) appears. This screen allows the user to view the chosen image/object in 360 degrees. Information relating to the 'artefact' appears on the left hand side and changes for as appropriate to the object being viewed.

Crew & Activities

At the moment this screen contains no information or interactivity. It may be that this page features several 'crew members' with a brief outline of the activities that the visitor to the Grand Turk may expect to find and perhaps take part in.

Captain's Log

This page will probably be the most text heavy with updates on where the Grand Turk it and its crew have been up to. This may be partly fun (as in cannon firing) or totally practical - schedule updates etc., This has yet to be finalised. It may be that data from previous days is also accessible in which case some form of 'backwards/forwards' navigation control will be need to be included.

Credits

The 'Coast Show' logo concludes the website visit. This page simple gives details of those people who have worked on this site, i.e. picture taking/gathering, design, sound, programming etc.,

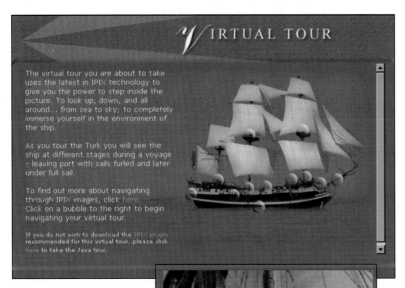

VIRTUAL TOUR

The virtual tour you are about to take uses the latest in IPIX technology to give you the power to step inside the picture. To look up, down, and all around... from sea to sky; to completely immerse yourself in the environment of the ship.

As you tour the Turk you will see the ship at different stages during a voyage - leaving port with sails furled and later under full sail.

To find out more about navigating through IPIX images, click here. Click on a bubble to the right to begin navigating your virtual tour.

If you do not wish to download the IPIX plugin recommended for this virtual tour, please click here to take the Java tour.

[Color Plate 41] The virtual tour used IPIX technology and gave a realistic feeling of where you were on the ship. This was supplemented by audio clips recorded in the same location as the VR images. Courtesy of Jeremy Gardiner.

[Color Plate 42] (left) This is a view of how the VR tour looks. As you move the mouse, the view changes interactively. Courtesy of Jeremy Gardiner.

[Color Plate 43] (bottom left) The Web site included a section on the crew. You can click on a photo and get a brief biography of what that person did. Courtesy of Jeremy Gardiner.

[Color Plate 44] (below) The section of Maritime Artefacts allowed you to view them in three dimentions. Courtesy of Jeremy Gardiner.

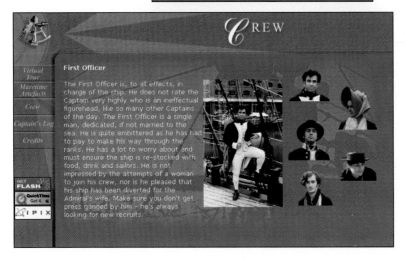

CREW

Virtual Tour
Maritime Artefacts
Crew
Captain's Log
Credits

First Officer

The First Officer is, to all effects, in charge of the ship. He does not rate the Captain very highly who is an ineffectual figurehead, like so many other Captains of the day. The First Officer is a single man, dedicated, if not married to the sea. He is quite embittered as he has had to pay to make his way through the ranks. He has a lot to worry about and must ensure the ship is re-stocked with food, drink and sailors. He is not impressed by the attempts of a woman to join his crew, nor is he pleased that his ship has been diverted for the Admiral's wife. Make sure you don't get press ganged by him – he's always looking for new recruits.

[Color Plate 45] (right) The front page of Rich Borge's site. It is clean, straightforward, and gives you a good idea of his style right away. © 2000 Richard Borge.

[Color Plates 46–48] (below and opposite) These are some examples of Rich Borge's unique illustration style. © 2000 Richard Borge.

[Color Plate 46]

[Color Plate 47 (left)]

[Color Plate 48] (left below)

[Color Plate 49] (below)
This is the welcome screen
for Pamela Hobbs' Web site.
© Pamela Hobbs
pam@pamorama.com.

[Color Plate 50] (bottom)
The interface for stock art
has a section of editorial
illustrations, icons, and kids
images. © Pamela Hobbs
pam@pamorama.com.

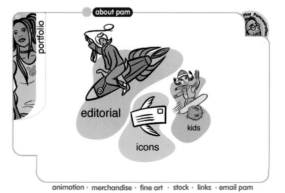

[Color Plate 51] This is additional illustration work from Pamela Hobbs. This is a poster for Tori Amos. © Pamela Hobbs pam@pamorama.com.

[Color Plate 52]
(above right) A poster
for the Red Herring
by Pamela Hobbs.
© Pamela Hobbs
pam@pamorama.com.

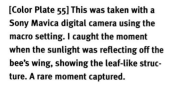

[Color Plate 53] (above) The cover of
the Black Book by Pamela Hobbs.
© Pamela Hobbs pam@pamorama.com.

[Color Plate 54] (above right) A poster
for the Rolling Stones by Pamela Hobbs.
© Pamela Hobbs. pam@pamorama.com

[Color Plate 55] This was taken with a
Sony Mavica digital camera using the
macro setting. I caught the moment
when the sunlight was reflecting off the
bee's wing, showing the leaf-like structure. A rare moment captured.

[Color Plate 56]
This photograph
of orchids uses
repetition and
symmetry to
make its point.

[Color Plate 57] (above) A still video
image taken with a Sony PC10 mini DV
camera. Photoshop was used to adjust
the color, brightness, and contrast to get
a more abstract image.

[Color Plate 58] (left) This image uses
the overlapping landscape as the focus
of attention.

[Color Plate 59] This is one of my favorite images. I took it on a motorcycle trip to the Outer Banks of North Carolina. It is a view from the Cape Hatteras light house. What makes this image work for me are the several levels that it contains. The composition has an enhanced perspective and balance between the water and the land. The myriad figures on both the beach and the water provide a subplot for the viewer to experience. For this image to be successful, it must be printed in a large format.

[Color Plate 60] Pattern is the main element of this photograph. The color green dominates the image and forces one to look at the pattern, since the image is monochromatic.

[Color Plate 61] Another example of pattern. The similarity of the boats leads the eye from right to left.

[Color Plate 62] This photograph works with composition and balance. The quiet blue of the water contrasts with the lilies and the over-lapping petals.

[Color Plate 63] This photograph works with light. It isolates the leaves by showing their transparent nature. The aperture was open on this image, blurring the background and emphasizing the foreground.

[Color Plate 64] This image is about density. The sheer number of leaves keeps the eye busy and moving around the image. The blue in the water was the reflection of the sky.

[Color Plate 65] (below left) I was motorcycling on the Blue Ridge Parkway in Virginia when I took this photograph. I waited for the right lookout point to stop at and took at least 15 images to get this one. I used different focal lengths, exposures and apertures to give myself a selection. It is always better to shoot too many images than to miss the one you wanted.

[Color Plate 66] (below right) My most successful self-portrait. This was done as a promotional photograph of my motorcycle travels.

[Color Plate 67] Taken from the Star Ferry terminal in Hong Kong. This image contrasts the old with the new.

[Color Plate 68] (left) This image has a predominant color blue and plays off the symmetry of sky and water. The clouds and reflections in the water give it interest.

[Color Plate 69] (below left) An example of a time exposure. The motion of the water is captured by the long exposure.

[Color Plate 70] (below right) An example of foreground, middleground and background. The dimensional nature of the image draws you into it.

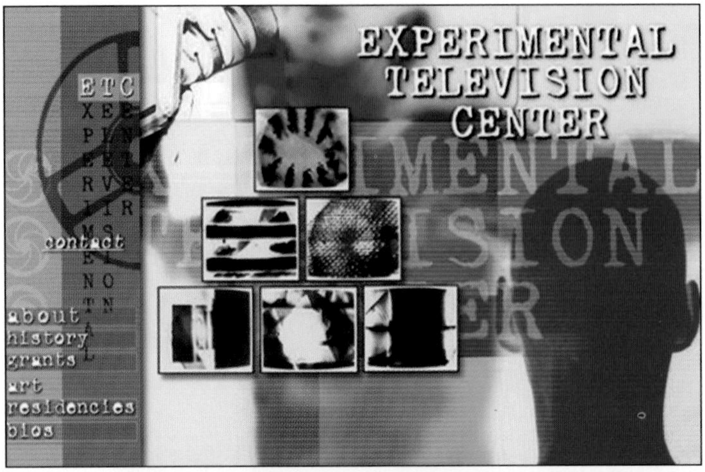

[Color Plate 71] Experimental Television Center. Screen capture from a website created for the Experimental Television Center by Black Hammer Productions, Inc. Design Direction by Pauliina Raitosola. The Experimental Television Center was created in 1970 by Ralph Hocking to support electronic media art.

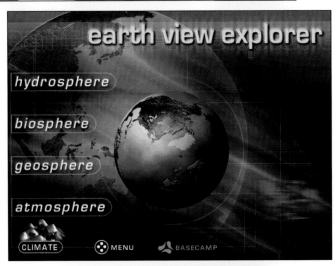

[Color Plate 72] Earth View Explorer. Screen capture from a CD-ROM created for Lamont-Doherty Earth Observatory of Columbia University by Black Hammer Productions, Inc. Design Direction by Pauliina Raitosola. Earth View Explorer is an educational product intended to aid in the instruction of earth science and was funded by the National Science Foundation.

[Color Plate 73] A piece G. H. Hovagimyian put together with Peter Sinclair called "Soap Opera for Laptops." The computer robots interact with each other with AI software that recognizes speech and pitch. Courtesy of G. H. Hovagimyan.

©1999 Andy Lackow

[Color Plates 74-78] Wide range of work by Andy Lackow. Andy's style combines 3D, science fiction, and classic airbrush looks executed in a digital environment. © Andy Lackow.

[Color Plate 79] The Lacemaker. This was exhibited at the SIGGRAPH 25th Anniversary Pioneers Art Show and was featured in "The Story of Computer Graphics." © 2000 Victor Acevedo.

[Color Plate 80] (below left) Suit on the Phone. © 2000 Victor Acevedo.

[Color Plate 81] (below right) Ectoplasmic Kitchen. © 2000 Victor Acevedo.

[Color Plate 82] (bottom left) Cynthia De Moss. © 2000 Victor Acevedo.

[Color Plate 83] (bottom right) Axis. © 2000 Victor Acevedo.

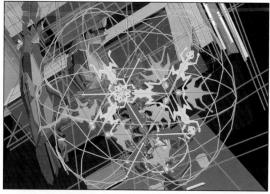

[Color Plates 84-85] These two images are 3D visualizations of an interactive music installation I exhibited at the Museum het Toreke in Tienen Belgium in 2001. Inside each cube is a CD player and a speaker. When you lift a sphere off of a tube, you hear music, poetry, or other sounds. People can change the overall sound they hear by moving different spheres on and off the tubes. For this piece, I created four tracks of music. The piece is modular, so that I add or subtract modules, as well as change the audio on the CDs. I plan to explore this idea further, since it combines my interest in art and music. The images were created in Alias/Wavefront Maya™ by Yaron Canetti and Sheng-Fang Chen.

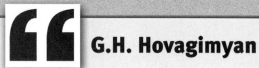

G.H. Hovagimyan

INTERVIEW

Cross-Media Digital Artist

G.H. Hovagimyan started using computers in 1993. What fascinated him was the "otherness" of online and digital culture. Before that he was a punk conceptual artist creating video, performance, installation, rock music, word pieces (not poetry), and photography. He started producing audio and visual works for the Internet in 1994, and produced one of the first Webcast shows, "Art Dirt," for www.pseudo.com. He has exhibited his work in France at the Gallerie Aldebaran, Avigono Electronique, and Musee d'Art Contemporain. He has exhibited in the United States at Postmasters Gallery, New Museum of Contemporary Art, PS1 Contemporary Art Center, the Soho Arts Festival in New York, and the Massachusetts Institute of Technology. He has also shown his work on the Internet at ThingNet, ArtNetWeb, and the Walker Art Center. He has performed at the New York Digital Salon, Ars Electronica, and Les Musiques '98. See Color Plate 73 for an example of his work.

What is your creative process?

For me the creative process is several things. It is a liberation, an affirmation of my existence, a congealing of disparate sensations knocking around in my psyche. I think of art as a discussion about humanity and a discourse about the world of art ideas. When I start a new media project it's with the express desire of enlarging the scope of what is called "art." I have little or no desire to create a refined product. The best part of working in new media is the necessity to collaborate with other people. It allows for new discoveries and points of view not available to the lone studio artist. It's also just plain fun. The constraints or challenges of working in new media have to do with what I see as a struggle between the creative propensities of coders and artists as opposed to the forces of business, advertising and intellectual property. I believe that creativity is winning this round.

What are you working on now?

What I'm working on at the moment has several interlocking aspects. I've just begun to explore the Linux OS. I've loaded this onto a Power Mac platform. I'm very excited about building a multiuser environment and a home server that also has a robust development environment. My intention is to liberate myself from the constraints of working with software vendors' tool sets. I and a few other artists are talking about creating an alternative Web that is postbrowser. I am particularly interested in XML (extensible markup language). This seems to be a way to define my own aesthetic parameters (control designators). I'm interested in VoxML (voice markup language) as a potential area for extending my use of text-to-speech and voice recognition. I'm trying to build a fluid computing system that is attuned to the needs of the type of experimental art in which I am engaged. On another front, my main collaborative partner, Peter Sinclair and I are working on an installation piece. The work is a 5-m round table enclosed in an igloo made of cement block. Embedded in the walls are six loud speakers to create sound spatialization. A video eyeball camera placed on the floor will survey the table surface. People will be invited to place figurines on the table. When a figure is placed on the surface, the camera recognizes it and triggers a text-to-speech file. If the person moves the figure, the voice will move to the corresponding sound spatialized location. If another figure is placed on the table, it will trigger a voice. If the figures are placed near each other they will converse or interact in some manner. My position in the collaboration is to write all the text/song/raps and interlock them in a quasi-musical structure that makes sense but is nonlinear. This piece is being funded by the National Center for Experimental Music of France and will be exhibited sometime in the Fall of 2000. My other main concern is an ongoing streamed video talk show I do over the Web called *Collider* and a more recent video free-form jam show called *10001-1101* that are streamed and archived on The Thing's Web site (http://bbs.thing.net).

What software do you use?

I'm using MKLinux OS (DR3), Yellow Dog Linux, and various Linux APis, emacs, GNOME, Apple OS, Macintalk, Opcode Max, Sound Edit

16, RealMedia, Quicktime video and audio, Steim's bigeye, GMEM's sound spatialization software, and Netscape because it's open source.

What advice do you have for students entering the new media field?

My main advice for artists is to work with the open source structures. In this way you can create the world for yourself free from the dictates of software vendors. This is an unprecedented intersection of creative science and creative art that can free you from the cycle of constant upgrade. Spend as much time on the Internet as possible, it's all there. The Mac OS is still the preferred platform for artists. Although it's less and less a developer's platform there are thousands of freeware and shareware apps that were developed for artists. In particular, MIT has a great Mac archive. Apple has also joined the open source movement and has released a free license APLS that allows you to hack the whole OS. What is most lacking in the education of new media students are experimental courses about exploring creativity using the computer without necessarily producing a finished product or learning a set of marketable skills.

What do you think about the Web?

The Web is only one part of the Internet, which came to exist because of HTML and the Mosaic browser. I believe we are moving into a postbrowser Internet. The way to resolve cross-platform conflicts is to use open source platforms and software. *Kill your browser*. In terms of the Internet's affect on other media, I feel we are moving beyond playback culture and into a postmedia information environment. In this information environment there are three main areas:

1. Push. This most resembles traditional media.
2. Two-way. This area is wide open and can be a whole lot more than interactive TV.
3. Virtual object. This is the most interesting because it points to nonreproducible art forms that *live* in digital space.

What are your favorite URLs?

http://www.netomat.net
http://artnetweb.com
http://bbs.thing.net
http://www.walkerart.org
http://mklinux.com
http://www.gnu.org
http://www.thing.net/~homestudio/

How important is audio?

One of the areas I work in is sound art. In new media this is a way to get beyond the linear idea of and sameness of recording and playback. Using text-to-speech, the voice synthesizers "sing" the text. Putting in random structure programming allows for permutations that make any work nonlinear. The key here is that the sound is generated rather than recorded.

Is programming important?

Programming is part of the work done by a digital artist as is scripting and markup language. I would like to collaborate with engineers and programmers, but I'm not sure how one goes about this. I am, after all, a fine artist.

Where do you see digital fine art heading?

Obviously that's what I'm involved in. I feel that the next ten years will see the gallery and museum structures change to incorporate digital fine art. This is tremendously exciting because the structures are just being worked out. No one knows how it will be augmented. My favorite computer artists are Maciej Wisniewski, John Simon, Jr., Robbin Murphy, Prema Murthy, John Klima, Perry Hoberman, Ricardo Dominguez, Jarryd Lowder, Carey Peppermint, Tim Whidden, Wolfgang Staehle, Floodnet, Etoys, Jerome Joy, Alexi Shulgin, The Thing, Simon Biggs, Takuji KOGO, Paul Garrin, Christina Mohamed, Yael Kanerek, Zhang Ga, Tina La Porta. I'm sure I left some people out.

What does the future hold?

I think that new media and the Internet will expand in importance and overshadow traditional media. This is already happening. What is not as clear is the form it will take. What I think is most interesting is everything other than what business thinks will succeed. Right now I'm setting up a home server; one of the potentials is to have a shared music source that is reprogrammed by several artists and distributed over the net. A collective music project that is always generating. There will be a divide between the physical object art world and the virtual object art world. Future emerging technologies that I believe will achieve importance are wireless Internet, digital movies distributed to theaters by satellite, building-sized programmable LED display fabric, embedded chip technology, artificial intelligence linked with voice synthesis.

Antoinette LaFarge

Founder and Director of the Museum of Forgery (www.forger.com)
Director of the Plaintext Players

Trained as a fine artist, Antoinette LaFarge is also a writer, editor, Internet and performance artist, as well as an educator. Her interests lie in the ephemeral, virtual, and evolving aspects of digital media. She has been published in *Gnosis* and *Wired* magazine. Before she moved to California, she was actively involved with the New York Digital Salon as a writer, artist, and guest editor of the Leonardo issue, which served as the exhibition's catalog. She is an Assistant Professor at the University of California at Irvine and formerly taught in the MFA Computer Art and MFA Photography and Related Media departments at the School of Visual Arts. She received her undergraduate degree magna cum laude from Harvard University.

INTERVIEW

When did you enter the digital realm?

The first computer I worked on was an Alphatype Multiset typesetting system back in the early 1980s. Digital editing and typesetting in turn got me interested in the desktop publishing revolution and that prompted me to get my first computer, a used Apple Macintosh 512k (which I quickly traded in for a IIsi).

What was your background prior to your entry into the field of new media?

I was trained as a fine artist in a broad range of traditional media—drawing, printmaking, photography, painting—and I also worked as a set designer for choreographers. In addition, I am a writer, and I've worked as a book editor, a book reviewer, and a journalist.

What made you decide to work with new media?

I have a particularly strong interest in the ephemeral, the virtual, and the evolving, and computers facilitate working along those lines. Unlike many artists, I feel more hindered than rewarded by the refractoriness of tactile media—the demands imposed by paint drying times, paper absorbencies, and so on—and find that I work faster and better with computers.

What aspect of your background have you found most helpful in your transition to new media?

Two things: I learn new information and skills fast, which turns out to be important in the ever-changing world of software; and I don't feel wedded to a single medium, so I find it natural to think about moving ideas and data back and forth among different types of software.

Who has influenced you most within the field of new media art?

Grahame Weinbren, whose *Sonata* overwhelmed me as a powerful new form of immersive storytelling. Pavel Curtis, who created and freely distributed a new kind of virtual world (MOO) with its own programming language that encouraged thousands of virtual strangers to collaborate on building worlds together.

What are the major constraints you have encountered in working with new technology?

Money. Computers, peripherals, and software are still very expensive for individuals when you add up all the parts, and there is a continuous pull to upgrade. And output of digital media in any form more sophisticated than inkjet or laser printers remains expensive. Categories and assumptions. Digital art still often has problems being recognized as art unless it fits into an already accepted category, like "digital print," so you have to spend as much time explaining the medium as the artwork.

Bandwidth. One's ideas are still often ahead of what is readily feasible. One wants to work with large files without enough storage or RAM to do so or design a Web site that would require T1 speeds when most people still have 28.8 modems.

Technology is a rapidly changing and complex medium. Because of the diverse skill sets required to work in the field it is often necessary to collaborate. What effect does this have on the creative process?

It moves the process towards the models already familiar from theater, television, and film with the same rewards and penalties that apply to those fields—you can do more ambitious projects when working in teams, but they also tend to cost more, they take longer, and not everyone has the skills and temperament to work collaboratively.

Many artists will still work with traditional media and then translate it into a digital format. What implications does this have on your creative process?

I think that this kind of direct translation is the least interesting thing one can do with digital media and has almost no effect on the creative process. Only when one starts to think in terms of the new medium does one's creative process change fundamentally.

What are you working on now?

Currently I am working on a project called "The Roman Forum," which is a series of on-line and off-line performances scheduled to take place in Los Angeles during the week of the Democratic National Convention (2000). It is part of a larger national project called "Democracy: The Last Campaign" (D-TLC) that focuses on the upcoming presidential election. D-TLC (organized by artists Jon Winet and Margaret Crane) is being sponsored by a number of venues across the country, including UC-Irvine; the Walker Art Center and Intermedia Arts in Minneapolis; San Francisco Camerawork; and Hallwalls in Buffalo, New York. "The Roman Forum" builds on the idea that we are still Roman in our heads, especially when it comes to politics—our notions of civic virtue, the particular types of corruption our system is prey to; our imperial attitude toward the rest of the world. Imagine bringing to life half a dozen of the more colorful figures from the Rome of 2000 years ago. This group of talking heads will be embodied by six on-line performers and six theater actors.

Please describe the creative process as it relates to this project.

The key to "The Roman Forum" is the idea that there are two parallel and related persistent worlds that communicate back and forth, one of which is on-line and other of which is off-line (real-world theater). We begin with six characters who will exist in both worlds and yet be embodied by different performers in each world. We use these characters to unfold a story; we do not write or even outline the story first. The story must emerge organically from the truth of the characters. For the on-line characters, there is a long developmental period that takes place in a MOO [a Multiuser Object-Oriented environment—an Internet-accessible, text-mediated virtual environment] during which the characters learn who they are, what their relationship to each other is, what their goals are, and so on. The process is similar to an actor's development of an individual variation on a stock *commedia dell'arte* character, except in this case it all takes place through text, so that it bears at least as much affinity to writing as to theater. At the same time, it is more collaborative than traditional writing in that each character writes itself. At the end of this development period, the virtual Romans will perform public improvisations on set themes having to do with the 2000 elections. They will be aware that everything they say and do—the script they create—will be taken up later the same day by their six real-world

alter egos, who will work together to reimagine this material in the terms of physical theater. The language of virtuality collides with and sparks physical reality, and out of this comes yet another kind of performance. And the next day, the cycle starts over. Video clips of the stage Romans go up on the Internet, "evidence" of the interest 2000-year-old Romans have in our present-day elections. The virtual Romans learn what their real-world (stage) counterparts have been up to, and this information becomes part of their reality and is another factor driving the story forward.

Describe your most recent commercial project.

My current commercial project is the design of various graphical and typographical elements for a computer game now in development. Among the elements I'm designing are typefaces in several languages, linguistic structures and histories, and interface elements. I can't say much more about the project at this stage.

What software do you use?

On any given day, I use between three and ten different pieces of software, and probably close to two dozen on a regular basis. These include writing apps (MS Word, SimpleText), Internet apps (Netscape, Explorer, Eudora, Telnet, Fetch, BBEdit, Dreamweaver, UnStuffIt, TurboGopher, HTML Color Picker, RealPlayer, Microphone, LambdaMOO, pine, pico), graphics and DTP apps (Photoshop®, ImageReady®, Illustrator®, QuarkXpress™, Fontographer™, PageMaker®, FreeHand™), interactivity apps (Director, SoundEdit, Premiere, Linker), and utilities (Stuffit, MacZIP, DeBabelizer, Slideshow, Norton Utilities), not to mention games.

What hardware do you use?

My preferred platform by far is Macintosh, but I also work on PCs running Windows or NT and on SGI and SUN Unix boxes.

What advice would you offer to people entering the field of new media and technology?

Avoid the tendency to think that learning software is the key. It's only the first step, just as learning English doesn't of itself make someone a writer. With all of the rapid developments in the technology, it is virtually impossible to know all of the software packages, programming, video, and audio skills.

How important is it for a new media artist to know everything? Where should students focus their attention?

It's not important at all. Artists should learn the skills that most appeal to them, however strange the mix. You always do your best work when you play from your strengths. Artists who just try to learn the package that they think will get them a good job are likely to become white-collar wage slaves and burn out after a few years of being little more than skilled producers of other people's work.

What is most lacking in the education of design and new media students?

An understanding and appreciation of the fundamental differences between art and design. An understanding that experimentation is as important as craft. Solid grounding in the history of traditional media.

How do you think the Web has changed traditional design?

It has made it more visually flexible in that any design has to accommodate differently shaped and sized browsers and different type-size defaults. It has brought back the miniature as a thing of beauty and importance in Western art, since small images work so much better than large ones on the bandwidth-limited net. It has shifted design from being something essentially visually static to something dynamic-responsive, evolving, participatory, open.

Where do you see Web design heading?

There will be increasing use of time-based and programming-driven material, including animations, sound, interactivity (buttons), and programmed variations, changes, and responses (e.g., use of randomized material).

Where do you see the Internet heading?

I see an eventual convergence between large parts of the net and role-playing games. Corporations will set up RPGS like virtual theme parks to entice people in to both play and shop.

What do you see as the most limiting aspects of the present technology, and how do you expect this to change in the future?

The biggest limitation is that programming today is essentially inaccessible to nonprogrammers. This limits the majority of artists to collaborating with programmers or foreswearing programming altogether. I foresee more user-friendly programming interfaces aimed at nonprogrammers. For certain types of things that many people want to program, like games, I foresee new kinds of design software with much of the needed programming already accessible as built-ins or libraries—not unlike how advanced Web design software now makes the most common Javascript functions easy to use.

How do you compare the Internet with the gallery system as a venue for artists?

The gallery system has two functions: publicity and sales. The Internet is rapidly becoming a better way to publicize yourself, and for individuals it will shortly become a better place to manage sales as well. I think galleries are on a long road to obsolescence—even as places to see objects they have severe limitations, and much of the most interesting object-based work has already left the gallery for other public spaces.

What emerging technologies will become important?

Wireless computing, Open Source software, massively multiplayer games, e-money, micro-money, and e-cash (untraceable transactions).

Chapter Nine

DIGITAL Creativity

`00:02:13:11`

Audio

I n this chapter, the focus will be on developing a working

knowledge of creating audio for digital media and the

Internet. Basic audio theory will be reviewed as it relates to

digital audio. The basic concepts of frequency, amplitude, and

other basic audio terminology will be taught. Sample rates and

bit depths are covered. Techniques of audio recording, including

microphones, mixers, recorders, and special effects will be cov-

ered. Sources of sound for digital media will be shown, including

stock music, sound effects, sample libraries, and MIDI files. The

theory and practice of sound design will be explained by using

professional examples. This will include live action, as well as

sound design for the Internet.

The Nature of Sound

Sound is becoming increasingly important when designing for new media and the Internet. Most computers are now capable of CD quality sound and progress with compression has made audio an increasing component of Web sites. You do not have to be a musician to be a sound designer, but familiarity with all types of audio is important. In this chapter, we will start with some of the basics of understanding how sound works, both in the analog and digital domain, and then describe the audio production process.

Analog and Digital Audio Theory

Sound is composed of a complex set of waves. These waves vibrate at different frequencies. On a very basic level, high frequencies are defined and controlled by the treble knob on your amplifier, and the low frequencies are controlled by the bass knob. Sound is more complicated than that, so let's start with some of the basic definitions. Analog means that the sound has been recorded on an analog medium, most likely tape. Analog also means that each copy is not going to be equal to the original. When you make a copy of analog tape, you lose a generation each time a copy is made. This adds noise and hiss, and it changes the frequency response of the original material. The great advantage of digital sound is that each copy is equal to the original, and there is no generation loss. This is why the music business moved to CDs. Although you will most probably deal with analog sound at some time in your career, for practical purposes, we will discuss digital audio in this chapter, with reference to analog sound when it is necessary.

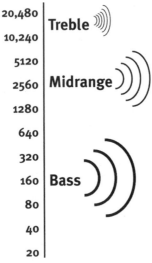

20,480 — Treble
10,240
5120
2560 — Midrange
1280
640
320
160 — Bass
80
40
20

Frequency (Hz)

[9.1] The range of sound for human hearing. Sound is generally divided into three ranges, treble, midrange, and bass. The human voice falls in the midrange category.

Frequency Range

One of the most important aspects of sound is the frequency range with which it is recorded and played back. For most professional applications, it is desirable to record the original sound in as high a quality as possible and then sample it down (this will be described later). The normal range of human hearing is 20 to

20,000 Hertz, or cycles per second (see Figure 9.1). Only very high quality sound systems and headphones are capable of reproducing this range. Small computer speakers are capable of reproducing a more limited range of frequencies. When creating an audio project, it is important to consider what the final medium will be. For CD or digital video, it should be the highest quality possible. For the Internet and CD-ROM applications, the size of the final file is often the more important determining factor.

Dynamic Range

Dynamic range is the degree to which the sound gets louder and softer. The wider the dynamic range, the more natural a sound appears and the greater the emotional impact. Most recording systems seek to have the widest dynamic range possible. A typical dynamic range for a CD quality recording is 95 decibels (dB). To make a sound seem louder, compression is often used. Compression squeezes the sound into a narrower dynamic range. This technique is often used for commercial recordings, so that when the sounds are played back on a variety of equipment, the quality is fairly consistent. If a sound is created only to be played on a very expensive sound system, it will not sound the same on an inexpensive system, and vice versa. Compromises have to be made depending on the playback medium. Compression is used a lot in television and radio, where most of the speakers are not of a very high quality.

Sample Rates

The sample rate is the number of times per second a sample is made of the particular sound. The sample rate used for audio CDs is 44.1 kHz. There are higher sample rates, up to 96 kHz, and lower sample rates, the most common being 22 and 11 kHz. Each time you increase or decrease the sample rate, the size of the file goes up or down. A typical song on a CD takes about 20 to 30 MB of disk space. An MP3 file takes about 3 to 4 MB. File size is generally synonymous with sound quality. However, if the original recording was not made well, no amount of digital manipulation will improve it.

Bit Depth

The bit depth refers to the number of bits assigned to each sample. The CD bit depth is 16. Some professional recording formats use 24-bit, and 8-bit is used for the Internet and CD-ROMs when smaller files sizes are necessary.

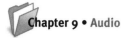

Formats

Sound used to come in only two media, tape and vinyl. Now, myriad formats are available, including CD, Minidisk, and others that are based on the type of computer you use and the way that you play back your sound. Some common formats are MP3, AIFF, WAV, and Sound Resource.

MIDI

In addition to the digital audio format, which is actual sound data, there is MIDI, which stands for Musical Instrument Digital Interface and was developed in the mid-1980s as means to allow keyboard synthesizers talk to each other. It revolutionized the writing and recording process for musicians. If you are serious about becoming an audio specialist, you need to have a thorough understanding of MIDI.

MIDI parameters are the various elements assigned to a MIDI file. They relate to the MIDI notes and how they are played back. MIDI generates MIDI time code as it is recording, and this defines the timing of the music. MIDI Time Code divides each second into discreet segments smaller than the resolution of the human ear. When a performance is recorded with MIDI and played back, it sounds like an exact reproduction of the actual performance. Note On is the exact time a note is struck and Note Off is the exact time the note ends. Velocity is the hardness or softness with which the note was struck. Aftertouch is the way that the note was let go, quickly or slowly. There are additional MIDI parameters, such as Pitch, Control Change, Pitch Bend Change, Program Change, and others. MIDI can also be used to control mixing consoles and recording equipment.

Audio on the Internet

Audio is a growing part of the Internet. The MP3 phenomenon is proof of that. MP3 is a technology that created its own industry. Fueled mainly by college students, MP3 was a quick way to exchange and share music over the Internet. The technology had outstripped the ability of the recording industry and copyright lawyers to keep up with it. The Naspster case was a landmark, in that a cottage industry developed around this technology and there were no legal controls in place. The large amount of time that people spend on the Internet has made audio very important, since it is a very effective form of communication and entertainment.

When creating audio for the Internet, it is important to know who your audience is so you can choose an appropriate format. PCs and Macintoshes use different audio software and methods.

Audio Internet Formats

There are many different formats for audio on the Internet, but five of them are the most common.

MP3

MP3 is probably the most popular audio file format on the Internet. It is widely used to for exchange music files. It has a good compression scheme, and a typical file size for a song is about 3 to 4 MB. MP3 is not really a true audiophile format, but for listening to music on your computer and for portable MP3 players, it is fine. The advantage of MP3 is that there is a huge user base and almost any song can be located in MP3 format. Although the legal issues are still being worked out, MP3 is here to stay.

RealAudio

RealAudio is a subset of the RealNetworks technology and software that uses the RealPlayer plug-in. The advantage of this is that it is streaming media. You do not have to wait for a download, as you do with MP3 or AIFF. RealAudio and RealVideo are in very wide use.

Windows™ Media Player

Windows Media Player has a lot of features and competes head to head with RealNetworks. RealNetworks was the first to appear, so it has a larger user base.

Quicktime

Quicktime recently converted to a streaming format. Before that, you had to download Quicktime files. Now that Quicktime is streaming, it will see an increase in use for audio and video on the Internet. Quicktime audio files are simply files that do not have video content.

AIFF and WAV

AIFF stands for Audio Interchange File Format, and WAV files are called "wave" files. Both are high-quality audio files, and both require a lot of memory. If you want CD-quality sound, AIFF or WAV will deliver it.

Digital Audio Production

The design and production of audio follows the same process of preproduction, production, and postproduction as the other digital media follow (see Figure 9.2).

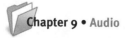

Audio Preproduction

This stage normally begins once the development stage has started. During this process, the types of sounds and music for the particular project have been roughly defined. This usually takes the form of sample music that has been taken from commercially available CDs. There may also have been a choice of a narrator and character voices. For example, the client may ask for a James Bond type of voice or a Bette Midler type of voice. These can be for a voice-over narration or for the voices of characters. Although sound designers are rarely brought in during the development stage, their involvement in preproduction is critical. Budgets for music can be considerable, especially when recordings by major recording acts, such as the Rolling Stones, are licensed.

The job of the sound designer generally begins once the audio needs have been assessed and script has been written. One of the first stages is to analyze the script and production book. The sound designer makes a list of all places in the project where sound is to be used. This can include music, narration, sound effects, and character's voices. Another task is to go through the script or navigational diagram and determine all of the sound effects needed. The third decision to be made is whether to use original music, license the music, or use stock music. Once this has been done, the sound designer has a clear idea of how much sound needs to be produced and by whom. At this point, a review of the budget for the audio portion of the project has been allocated. Soundtracks can be created for as little as a few thousand dollars but for large projects may go into the tens of thousands of dollars. Key elements in this decision are generally the choice of music and narrators. Music licensing fees can vary widely and will be discussed later in detail. Good professional narrators are paid about $250 per hour, and celebrities are much more expensive. Sound effects are normally not very expensive. Once these factors have been determined, a total budget is created.

Audio Production

The production process is normally divided into several stages, including locating the sounds/music, recording/digitizing, editing,

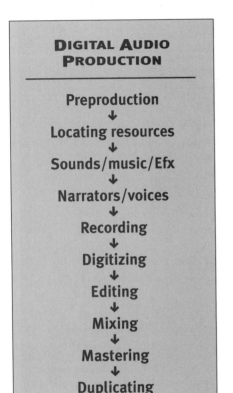

DIGITAL AUDIO PRODUCTION

Preproduction
↓
Locating resources
↓
Sounds/music/Efx
↓
Narrators/voices
↓
Recording
↓
Digitizing
↓
Editing
↓
Mixing
↓
Mastering
↓
Duplicating

[9.2] The production process for digital audio. Use it as a guide when you are producing sound tracks and audio.

DIGITAL | Creativity

mixing, and mastering. The process can be simplified immensely if a recording studio is involved. Most studios have almost everything needed to produce a reasonably priced soundtrack. The only items that can be variable are the choice of narrator, original music, and nonstandard sound effects.

Locating Sounds/Music

This phase of the process is not as complicated as it may appear on the surface. During the preproduction phase, the sound designer makes a list of all the sounds/music needed for the production. The choice has already been made regarding using prerecorded music or original music. Sound effects libraries are available in most recording studios. These studios also generally have a box full of professional narrators' audition tapes.

Narrators

As mentioned earlier, a wide range of narrators is available. If you cannot locate one from the demo tapes, local television and radio stations are good sources. On-air personalities generally do this type of freelance work on the side. Hourly rates for narrators can be high, but remember that these are professionals who are familiar with the recording environment and who know how to use a microphone. If a narration script has been prepared, the time involved for using a narrator is generally short. Narrators cannot be expected to read a script through from beginning to end without making a mistake, but you will not need to pay them for the time spent editing. You pay them only for the time they are in the studio recording. The sound designer is also responsible for coaching the narrator on the tone and style of delivery expected. For example, a commercial has a very different delivery type than a dramatic reading.

An important note for animators: it is now standard practice to videotape a narrator/actor when they are recording the voice of an animated character. The nuances of the vocal performance are generally acted out when they are reading the lines. It is particularly helpful for animators who are going to have lip sync along with the animation. The way actors contort their faces is critical in getting a believable performance from animated characters. It is also important to try to get the whole performance in one recording session. Although there is a certain amount of standardization in most recording studios, the humidity, time of day, and health of narrators contribute to the unique sound of their voices. it is extremely diffi-

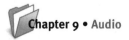

cult to get precisely the same sound when multiple recording sessions are used. Also, the cost of the narration will be higher because there will be multiple set-up charges. The result of this process is a collection of takes of the narration. This is now put in the hands of the editor, who assembles the final voice sound track.

Sound Effects

Most sound effects are drawn from a sound effects library. Any good record store will have a sound effects section. More comprehensive, and expensive, sound effects libraries can be purchased. In fact, most of the complete sound effects libraries from the major film studios are available for purchase. These generally cost several hundred dollars. When sound effects CDs are purchased, the purchase price normally includes an unlimited license for the use of these effects in various projects, so there are usually no copyright issues.

The role of the sound designer is to assemble the digital files of the effects from the list made from the script of navigation begin. There are usually several different effects for any particular sound, and the sound designer chooses the best one for the circumstance. This can be a rather lengthy process. There are several software packages available that allow for the digital copying of files from a CD onto a hard disk. If original sound effects are needed, a portable DAT recorder or a digital video camera can be used to gather them.

Music

As mentioned earlier, music can be prerecorded or original. Music is intellectual property, so there are always copyright and licensing issues to be dealt with.

The least expensive type of music is called stock music. Several companies produce general-purpose music. These are pieces of varying length and moods that can be easily edited to fit almost any situation. This type of music is usually inexpensive, but it may not fit the mood of the work exactly and the audience may have heard it before in a different context.

Licensing prerecorded music can vary widely in cost. For example, a musical group or composer may want to get wide exposure for their music and may not charge a lot of money if the project will bring them more recognition and business. Music that is used for broadcast or feature films is generally fairly expensive. Several agencies license music. The two largest are ASCAP and BMI. The

Harry Fox Agency is also widely used. These agencies are in the process of converting their music libraries to digital formats that can be auditioned and licensed over the Internet. A few years down the road, this will be very common, and choosing and licensing music will be as easy as logging onto their Web site and entering a credit card number. Several classification schemes will evolve so that you can quickly find the music you are looking for. For example, an artificial intelligence program might be written so that you can give it samples of music you like and it will locate music similar to what you have provided.

There are several types of licenses, and some usage is protected by the fair use clause in the U.S. Copyright Act. If the work is not being exhibited publicly or used for profit, generally no licensing fee is required. This would apply to student assignments. However, if the assignment is put on the Internet or sent to a film festival, a licensing agreement is required. Other types are per-use licenses, where a one-time usage fee is paid. There are also licenses for the annual use of music and unlimited use of music.

A final option is to commission original music. This can be very expensive. Again, the type of project, its budget, and public exposure all factor into this equation. A well-known Hollywood composer makes tens of thousands of dollars on a feature film soundtrack, plus royalties. A new composer looking for exposure may charge a very reasonable fee for composing music for a project. Again, most recording studios have a list of composers and copies of their demo tapes.

Choosing Music

Now that you know where to find the music, the real challenge is to choose the right music. On feature films, this task is left to music supervisors. It is their job to pick the right music, to arrange for the rights to the use the music, and have all of this fall within the budget.

If you do not have a music supervisor handy, there is another, less expensive way. Many music and bookstores now have headphones and a selection of CDs to listen to before you buy, and the Internet has an almost unlimited amount of music that can be researched. When choosing music, there is one major rule to follow. The music must support and not overshadow the visuals. If a project is audio only, there is no problem. However, if you are watching a film and start listening to the music and stop paying attention to the dialog

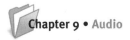

and action, there is a problem. The function of music is to enhance the mood and ambience of a scene, game, or environment. The easiest way to work with this is to try a wide range of music until something clicks.

The Recording Process

Now that we understand the different types of sound and where to get them, let's talk about the process of collecting sounds. There are many methods for doing this, but they generally fall into two categories: using a microphone or using electronic methods. Electronic methods include recording a source directly from an instrument or synthesizer or transferring sound effects from a CD. This is a rather straightforward process and will be explained in detail later. The use of microphones is a more complicated process and often very critical.

Types of Microphones

All microphones fall into two basic categories: dynamic and condenser. Dynamic microphones have a small diaphragm in them that vibrates when sound is detected. They do not require batteries. Condenser microphones use electrical current to create the sound and need batteries. Dynamic microphones are more common and less expensive. Condenser microphones are more expensive and are usually found in recording studios, although they are also used for location recording.

[9.3] The Shure SM58 microphone. This is the workhorse of the performing musician. It is a great live vocal microphone.

Choosing a Microphone

Using the right microphone for recording is as important as using the right color when painting a picture. The word *color* is appropriate, because all microphones add color to the original sound. Microphones are often described as "bright" or "warm." There are several hundred types of microphones; the easy rule is to use the best microphone you have access to or can afford. Microphones used for Hollywood sound tracks or top recording artists, like the Neumann U87, cost several thousand dollars. The Shure SM 57 and 58 are used by many musicians and cost about $100 (see Figure 9.3).

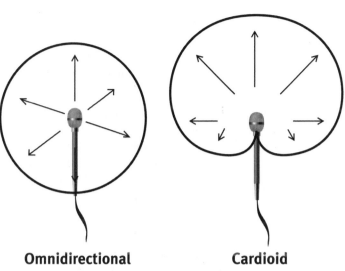

Omnidirectional   **Cardioid**   **Unidirectional**

[9.4] These are the three main types
of microphones and their patterns.

Omnidirectional Microphones

Omnidirectional microphones record sound coming from all directions (see Figure 9.4). They are generally used to record sound effects or musical performances where you want to get the sound of the room in addition to the sound of the instruments.

Cardioid Microphones

Cardioid microphones have a heart-shaped pattern and are used for voices. Singers like to use cardioid microphones because they can move around the microphone. Figure 9.5 is an Audio Technica 4050, which can use multiple patterns. Omnidirectional microphones are not good for singing because they also pick up what is behind the microphone in addition to the singer's voice.

Unidirectional Microphones

Unidirectional microphones are also called directional microphones. They have a narrow pattern and are used for sounds coming from a particular direction, sound effects, and voices. Cardioid microphones are preferred for voices, since unidirectional microphones have a more specific angle pattern and if you move out of the pattern, the level of the sound drops dramatically. Shotgun microphones are a specific type of unidirectional microphone with a very narrow pattern of a only a few degrees. Since the pattern is so narrow, they are often used to record sounds from a long distance away and must be

[9.5] An Audio Technica 4050 microphone. This is a very good quality large-diaphragm condenser microphone I use in my studio for vocals, acoustic instruments, and other applications.

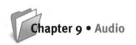

carefully aimed. They are often put on tripods to keep them focused on the sound source. They are also widely used in location recording for film, where the microphone needs to be away from the actors and not visible in the camera.

Lavalier Microphones

Lavalier microphones are small microphones that are either worn around the neck or clipped to a lapel. They are also called lapel mikes. They are used for television, documentaries, and interviews. They are inconspicuous and therefore used in video applications. They can also be made wireless and used by actors in film and video location shoots.

Camcorder Microphones

Camcorder microphones are probably one of the most widely used microphones because they are attached to video cameras. However, they are low-quality microphones and their location on the camera makes them less than ideal for recording sound. They are good for reference and for recording the sound as it is heard by the camera person. For professional applications, camera microphones are not recommended. It is generally best to have an external microphone attached to the camera with a long cable so the microphone can be near the sound source.

Location Sound

When recording sound on location, it is important to get the best possible sounds at the moment, because very often you do not have a second chance. There are simple ways to record location sound, and there are very complex ones. It all depends on your budget. For a low-budget project, plugging a good quality microphone into a camcorder will work, but there are some limitations. Most camcorders have built-in limiters and compressors, which will raise or lower the sound level. They work automatically, which takes some of the control away from the person doing the recording, but sound effects can be recorded this way, because they generally have a single level of sound. Sounds that get louder and softer are difficult to record with this process. If all you have is a camcorder and a good-quality mike, be sure to use a lavalier microphone as close to the person's mouth as possible or a shotgun microphone pointed at the person's mouth.

Other tips for recording location sound are to have several minutes of the sound of the environment, so that when you are editing the sound, you can add this in, rather than have an awkward silence. Also, use headphones to monitor and check the sound as you are recording. The few minutes spent checking the sound while you are recording it will be paid back by the time saved in the studio or the time wasted by going back and having to record the sound again. Many things can happen on location—there may be wind noise from the microphone, a bad cable, an annoying sound in the background that you don't notice. Always monitor the sound with headphones to test it while you are recording location sound.

Mixing

Microphones are not generally plugged directly into a recorder. They are usually plugged into a mixer, which allows the sound engineer to vary the levels of each input, so that the final recording can be adjusted. Some location set-ups include a mixer.

Mixing generally refers to the blending of several tracks of sound, dialog, sound effects, music, and so on, into a final stereo recording. Mixing is an art, and there are people who spend their careers as mixing engineers.

Mixing is to audio as editing is to film. By combining all of the elements in the right way, you can create very realistic sonic environments that add significant impact to the visual element of your project.

The process of mixing starts with bringing all of the elements together into a multitrack recorder or multitrack digital audio software. Many digital audio software packages combine MIDI with the digital audio and have the capability to play a Quicktime movie along with the audio. This is very important when synchronizing sound effects or music to the visuals.

Once all of the elements have been recorded and are put in the proper sequence, the mixing process begins.

The most basic multitrack mixing process might be to have the voice, music, and some sound effects. When approaching this type of mix, the first thing to do is to focus on the voice. Assemble all of the best takes of the voice, sequence them together, and then adjust the tone controls to get the voice to sound as good as possible. If appropriate, add echo or reverb to match the voice with the environment.

Once the voice is finished, you can concentrate on the sound effects. Make sure they are the right duration and synchronize per-

fectly with the visuals. Aligning sound effects is tricky and even a frame or two matters.

Once you have finished aligning and pacing the sound effects, work on the music, For this example, we will assume that you already have a stereo mix. When placing music, make sure that there is enough on the head and tail to allow for fade ins and fade outs. Music also needs to be placed in the project at the appropriate moments. Once this has been done, you will have several channels labeled with each of the character's voices, two channels for the stereo music, and one or more channels for the effects. This is when the final mixing begins.

A rough mix is done first. This is a run-through during which the basic levels are set and the engineer gets a feel for what sound level changes need to be made when. Most digital software packages have automated mixing capabilities that will record the movements of the faders and allow the engineer to go back in to tweak them. This is a preferred method of mixing, since you do not have to perform the mix live each time. If you do not have automated mixing, you need to raise and lower the different channels as needed while the tape is playing and recording. When engineers do this, they normally record several mixes and choose the one they like the best. When working with automated mixes, the engineer tweaks and perfects the original mix.

Having a good mix really depends on having a good engineer and producer. A good mix is characterized by a smooth level of the sound, voices that can be easily understood, and music that supports the voices and does not overwhelm them. A good way to test a mix is to play it back in the final format on the equipment that will be used—for example, a TV set with a VCR attached or computer speakers over the Internet. Hearing the sound on the final medium will tell you a lot about the mix.

Mastering

Mastering is the last step before mass duplication. Mastering engineers are some of the most sought-after people in the recording business. They are the unknown stars of the industry. Bob Ludwig is one of these people. People wait months for him to master their projects. Mastering often involves compression and equalization. The art of mastering is to provide a master tape that, when duplicated, sounds as good as it possibly can. This requires an intimate understanding of the duplication process and what a CD or video-tape will sound like.

Duplicating

Once the master recording is completed, it is then sent to be duplicated, either onto CD, audio/videotape, or uploaded to the Internet. Commercial duplicators can produce large numbers of CDs for a very reasonable price. You need to supply them with the master tape, either on CD or DAT, and all the files for the graphics.

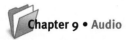

CASE STUDY

"Louisiana Moon" by Bruce Wands

I'd like to take a minute to talk about the recording and writing process behind my song "Louisiana Moon." I'll start with a quick tip. Figure 9.6 is a tuning machine. I use a 12-string Guild guitar, and it is very difficult to tune by ear. A tuning machine makes it easy. Also, since recording time is precious, a tuning machine will always let you know that you are recording an instrument in tune. Wasting an entire recording session because an instrument was out of tune is a painful experience.

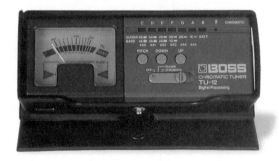

[9.6] A Boss Chromatic Tuner. Every musician playing a stringed instrument should have a tuning machine. It makes keeping the guitar in tune easy and resolves any questions in the recording studio about an instrument being in tune.

The basic tracks for "Louisiana Moon" were recorded in my studio and then taken to a local recording studio to add drums and other instruments. I wrote the chord progression first. I wanted to write a song about someone walking through Louisiana at night with the moon above. The phrase "under Louisiana Moon" was to be the main approach to the song. I worked out the chord progression first and tried to get an ambling rhythm to the song. Once I had the chord progression worked out (Am Em G Am), I began to refine the chorus, and from there worked on the lyrics. It took several passes through the song to finalize the lyrics. Once I was close to where I wanted it to be, I brought Jeff McGowan, a piano player I have worked with over the years, into the studio to lay down a basic keyboard track for the song. Figure 9.7 shows that track. It is a work track, so all the audio (my guitar and voice) is on Audio 1, and the MIDI signal from Jeff's piano is on MIDI 1. ProTools has a really great interface and

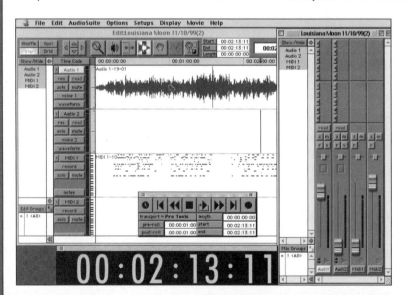

[9.7] A screen view of the ProTools interface.

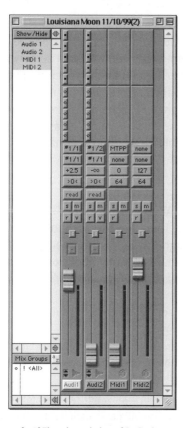

[9.8] The mixer window of ProTools.

is the professional standard for digital audio. I run it on a Macintosh G3 with 320 MB of RAM and an Ultra SCSI III card with a Seagate 10,000 RPM hard drive for the music files. This allows me to work with 32 tracks of audio. Figure 9.8 shows the mixer window of ProTools. I use my studio for as much as I can and then use local studios with compatible equipment for drums, other musicians, outboard gear, and a variety of other things. Most professional digital studios have ProTools, so I do not lose any generations when I bring my tracks into these studios.

To finish the song, I overdubbed a new vocal track, bass track, rhythm guitar track, and added studio musicians to the final song. Hopefully, this will give you a little insight into how I approach my music. I find that writing music is an evolutionary process. I start by roughing out a song and adding some musical tracks to it. Then I listen to that version over and over, refine the words and get a better idea of how I want the song to be arranged. After this, I record all of the tracks I can do on my own (i.e., vocals, bass, rhythm guitar) and then use studio musicians for everything else.

Summary

The importance of sound cannot be overemphasized. Sound is a very powerful medium because of its emotional impact and the strong presence of audio in a room. When you look at a screen, the video or image is only in one place. Sound fills the space that you are in and has a greater impact. In this chapter we covered the theory of audio, as well as the wide range of techniques used to record, mix, and produce a final sound track. Audio is fast becoming a major force on the Internet and will be an important part of Web sites in the future.

BIBLIOGRAPHY

I have only listed two books here. Alten's book is really all that you will need as a supplementary text. There are a lot of books on audio and music production. Look through them and pick one that fits the style and area you are interested in. Also, many books on video and film production have good sections on audio production.

Stanley R. Alten, *Audio in Media,* fifth edition, Wadsworth Publishing Company, Belmont, CA, 1998.

 This is the best book I know of on audio. I highly recommend it. It is current and extremely comprehensive. If you can only afford one book on audio, buy this book. It is well worth it.

Bruce Fries, *The MP3 and Internet,* TeamCom Books, Burtonsville, MD, 2000.

 This book will bring you up to date on MP3 and audio for the Internet.

EXERCISES

 1. Create a simple, short audio-only project. Use a portable tape recorder or a camcorder and record location, as well as studio sounds. Don't worry too much about making the audio as high quality as possible, but focus on content. Use multiple tracks of sound, so that you have to mix them for the final project. Once it is mixed, convert it to a CD and critique the project. Although it won't be technically perfect, it will give you the experience of making an audio project from beginning to end.

2. Make a sound track for a short video (about 30 seconds). Use software like Adobe Premiere® or ProTools®. This time, focus on making the project sound as professional as possible. Use prerecorded music from a CD and the highest quality microphones you can get to record voices, sound effects, and location sounds. Digitize the sound and mix it in the computer. Use headphones to get the best final result you can.

DIGITAL | Creativity

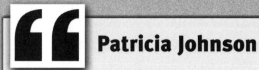

Patricia Johnson

INTERVIEW

Digital Artist, Writer, Educator, Founder of the SIGGRAPH Guerilla Gallery

Patricia Johnson's involvement with computer art dates back to 1986, when she started studying at the School of Visual Arts, receiving her MFA degree in Computer Art in 1989. She has gone on to make a major contribution to the computer graphics industry as an artist, lecturer, and evangelist of digital art. Her fine art has been exhibited internationally since 1989. As founder of the SIGGRAPH Guerilla Gallery, she brought considerable awareness to the needs of digital fine art printmakers. She has been an active participant in many conferences, including SIGGRAPH, the 3D Conference, and MacWorld. As an educator, she has taught at a variety of institutions including the Pratt Institute and the Kodak Center for Creative Imaging, and she has served as the Co-Chair of Computer Arts at the Academy of Art College.

What was your background prior to your entry into the field of new media?

Fine art, theater arts, education, hi-tech marketing.

What aspect of your background have you found most helpful in your transition to new media?

Both the exposure to high tech in the marketplace and my fine art and theater backgrounds, which have facilitated both 2D and 3D digital work.

Who has influenced you most within the field of new media art?

I started getting into this arena when the first fine artists to enter the field were hot news. The first and most significant exposure I had to this side of the industry was at the Digital Visions exhibit at the IBM Gallery in New York where I worked as a guide, walking the general populace through their first exposure to technology in the arts. I loved the works of these early pioneers: Mark Wilson, David Em, Harold Cohen, Manfred Moore, Jeane Pierre Hebert, Collette Bangert, and others who are now known as The Algorists. These artists reached down into the guts of computer code to produce rhythmic, mysterious, precise images that to me fully represent the capacity to raise the use of technology to the level of the sublime. I have since worked with Roman Verotsko and the late Robert Mallory. Later, the works of the early digital photographers who were a part of the Studio 2000, an experiment sponsored by *Photo District News* at the School of Visual Arts in New York, led me to the opportunity to explore this new media as a teacher at the Kodak Center for Creative Imaging. These were exciting times. Recently my work has focused more on 3D, where I join the ranks of all who are entertained and amazed by the productions coming from all the big studios. Of these, I feel the most magical was *What Dreams May Come* because it combined artistry and cinematography with an astonishingly creative application programming, harnessing the power of digital code to produce painterly effects.

What do you see as the important milestones in the development of new media?

A few years ago I would have said the Wacom tablet because it offered a tool akin to the paint brush and reduced the effects of repetitive motion injury that plagues all digital professionals. Second to this was the advent of high-quality digital printing because it stretches the tool into the realm of other traditional print mediums. As far as pure computing power, the more powerful personal computing systems have been the magic wand that enabled the most recent wave of creativity. In the future, I see the extensive use of reconfigurable computing using Field Programmable Gate Array (FPGA) technology as the next significant wave of development.

Describe your creative process.

I use the computer to create statements about how technology has changed the face of the country, focusing on the rural landscape where I was raised and locations where other families once lived, such as Silicon Valley. Digital technology allows me to create powerful imagery that would not be possible in any other medium and to use technology to make a statement about technology.

How do you begin a new media project?

In my personal work I combine source materials, scans of my great grandmother's quilts, photos, letters; things I could not fully utilize in my paintings. These I print digitally and then ultimately digitally color-separate and convert to silk screen prints.

How have the use of new media and the use of the computer affected this process?

As an artist I have long been obsessed with the concept of reproduction. Traditional print media was exciting but tedious and did not allow for some of the intricate collaging and effects I wished to create in images I wished to edition. Digital printing has been a breakthrough for me.

What are the major constraints you have encountered in working with new technology?

When digital prints first made their way to the mass market, they were scoffed at and scorned by the traditional art market as cheap, valueless copies that could be mass-produced and were therefore worthless. However, as storage media and software become obsolete, these early editions are suddenly very difficult to reproduce and have taken on a new value, which I find gratifying.

Technology is a rapidly changing and complex medium. Because of the diverse skill sets required to work in the field it is often necessary to collaborate. What effect does this have on the creative process?

I have said for several years now that this is a new Renaissance, enabling and requiring a studio system not seen since the great masters.

Many artists still work with traditional media and then translate it into a digital format.

What implications does this have on your creative process?

Technology has expanded my thinking process and provided opportunity to stretch my visual ideas into a wider range. I still prefer that the final step be converted back to traditional media, however.

Describe your most recent fine arts/personal project.

My most recent printed works, *Harvest Home* and *Rattlesnake* were exhibited in San Francisco, and in one of the first digital exhibits in Rome and Paris. I am now preparing an animation using moving layers of similar imagery to tell the story of the displacement of the Japanese farm families from the West Coast to prison camps during World War II.

What software do you use?

Photoshop®, After Effects®, Lightwave™, Painter™, Deneba™, Quark™, Illustrator®, Power Point™, Persuasion™, Premiere, and Flint™.

What hardware do you use?

Mac, PC, SGI, Speed Razor, SonyDV camera, Wacom tablet.

What advice would you offer to people entering the field of new media and technology?

Dive in fearlessly and always begin learning new tools and techniques by finding the similarities between what you are learning and what you already know.

How important is it for a new media artist to know everything?

Find what you need and use it as you wish.

Where they should focus their attention?

Focus on your area of strongest interest.

What is most lacking in the education of design and new media students?

Traditional art training.

What are the important elements of a new media portfolio?

Content.

How do you think the Web has changed traditional design?

Squeezed it, popularized it, and expanded it again.

Where do you see the Internet heading?

To the universe and beyond.

How do you see the Web affecting other media, for example, print/news, traditional art, TV, movies, animation, galleries?

Expanded, popularized, and to some extent watered them down.

What are your favorite Web sites/URLs?

Fine art sites, Itheo, NewMonet, 911, Bock Gallery.

How important are traditional animation skills?

Critical!

How important is programming in the work you do?

It is just important for me to understand how programming works and to be able to communicate the need to incorporate it and where.

What do you see as the most limiting aspects of the present technology, and how do you expect this to change in the future?

Rendering power is the limitation. Reconfigurable computing is the answer.

What is the future of digital fine art?

It will evolve as did Dada and Pop Art.

Catherine Benante

INTERVIEW

Computer Artist, Electronic Arts, Redwood CA

Cathy graduated from the School of Visual Arts in 1980 with a BFA in Graphic Design. Prior to discovering the computer as an art tool, she worked as a typesetter, a graphic designer for books, and as a designer of children's clothing in NYC's garment district. In 1987, she began taking computer art classes. The rest is history. She is now a computer artist with one of the largest video game companies in the world, Electronic Arts. Although she has specialized in creating color palettes for digital video, her latest project was handling motion capture data for the 3D characters in Tiger Wood's CyberTiger game for the Sony Playstation. Prior to her stint at Electronic Arts, Cathy worked as a Visual Effects Artist on the feature film, *Spawn*.

What made you decide to work with new media?

Creating artwork on a computer was absolutely fascinating to me. The difference in work methods and the endless possibilities it offered completely hooked me. I remember feeling as if I was seeing the future in production and design, and I wanted to be a part of it.

What aspect of your background have you found most helpful in your transition to new media?

I was already comfortable with the idea of type and text as elements of art . . . the sense of precision and placement of objects on the page transferred well to a computer screen.

Who has influenced you most within the field of new media art?

I love the work of John Lasseter. His mastery of animation is beautifully showcased in the films he's directed (*Toy Story I* and *II, A Bug's Life*) and the computer animation shorts he's helped create since the 1980s.

What do you see as the important milestones in the development of new media?

Creation of desktop computers, for starters, the graphical user interface, Photoshop's creation by John and Thomas Knoll, the creation of numerous software packages that address creative instead of business needs, the Internet, the continuing drop in price of computers while their speed and power increases.

How do you begin a new media project?

I work on a team that includes 12 other artists. We are broken into groups that address the user interface of a game, the creation of the in-game artwork (the environment), and the animation of the characters that will appear in the game. There are numerous meetings between management, the artists, and the programmers that help determine the look we want and how to technically produce it.

How has the use of new media and the use of the computer affected this process?

There wouldn't be computer games without it! Our industry is driven by the technological advances around us—the creation of game consoles like the Dreamcast and Sony Playstation 2 systems, and the move of gaming to on-line sources through the Internet.

What are the major constraints you have encountered in working with new technology?

Trying to put large amounts of information into rather small containers. A CD can hold 650 MB of data, which is not much when you are trying to create the illusion of a world. Technology is a rapidly changing and complex medium. Because of the diverse skill sets required to work in the field it is often necessary to collaborate.

What effect does this have on the creative process?

I have worked in a collaborative process for several years now, and it makes you approach your work differently. You know you'll have to explain your ideas to people who may not even be trained in the arts, so you find yourself carefully considering the merits of what you want, you fight for your ideas sometimes, you learn to compromise, you learn to listen and to be articulate. All this may not sound like it's part of a creative process, but it is. It helps you focus on your artwork and it helps you produce closer to your own vision, because you've learned what's important to you and how to get close to it. New media incorporates the elements of video, sound, interactivity and navigation. Because I make computer games, all these elements are an integral part to what I do. Many artists will still work with traditional media and then translate it into a digital format.

What implications does this have on your creative process?

I love that artists do this. They're using the computer as an additional tool for their expression, not as the sole source of interest in their work. I don't want "this was done on a computer" screaming at me when I look at another artist's work. I want to be introduced to their images and, hopefully, be caught up in their world.

What are you working on now?

The next generation of games for the Sony Playstation (I can't be more specific than this right now.)

Describe your most recent commercial project.

My most recent commercial project was handling the motion capture data for the 3D characters in a Playstation game Electronic Arts made called CyberTiger. It was Tiger Woods' golf game for little kids. We created six characters at three different stages of their lives (child, teen, and adult). As the player advanced in the game, they could power-up to the next level and play as an older character, and the game increased in difficulty as they powered-up. It was a fun project. We got to address a younger audience, and we created colorful courses and characters.

What software do you use?

Alias Wavefront's Maya™ for animation, Photoshop for textures, AfterEffects for video work.

What hardware do you use?

Dell Dimension Pentium III 800 mHz with a GeForce video card, and lots of RAM.

What advice would you offer to people entering the field of new media and technology?

Focus—don't get lost and learn a little of this and that, without having a strong area you can point to as your specialty. And try not to get too caught up in the minutia of the field you do enter. The industry changes constantly; be as flexible as you can and be open to the next big wave, because it's always right around the corner.

With all of the rapid developments in the technology, it is virtually impossible to know all of the software packages, programming, video and audio skills. How important is it for a new media artist to know everything?

You're never going to know everything, because as soon as you do, a newer version of the software will come out and they'll have changed the entire interface on you! My best advice is, again, to focus on what you really care about and let it become your winning card.

Where they should focus their attention?

On what they love to do most . . . for instance, if they're fabulous in Photoshop, learn to make the best textures ever made. The ability to map the texture onto a figure in a 3D program will come with time, but being able to show expertise in a particular area of the field they want to enter will help land a job that could teach them more advanced skills.

What is most lacking in the education of design and new media students?

Presentation skills and confidence . . . things that are hard to teach. I've interviewed technically strong people and they've brought their work rolled up in a messy pile, and then they apologize for the mess. Don't ever go into an interview telling us all the things you can't do. I've seen too many people do this. Focus on what you want and believe it when you say it.

What are the important elements of a new media portfolio?

Again, a strong presentation of what the artist feels they are best at. We also like to see traditional drawing skills—pencil sketches of the figure and so on. It can be just a few drawings toward the back of the book, but it helps us understand how the artist sees things.

How important are traditional animation skills?

They are very, very important. You will be using them in ways you can't even guess at now . . . they will appear in your dreams when you're trying to figure out how to move that 800-pound object across the screen. Most animators study movement for the rest of their lives. It becomes a part of how you see things. Studying the animation classics to become familiar with the older methods will hone your skills and give you a base of knowledge that's quite valuable.

Bandwidth issues have limited 3D implementation on the Web. What impact will this have on the field on 3D animation?

It's all changing. Broader bandwidth is up and coming, and already we are seeing some very interesting animations on the Web. It's only a matter of time before the post-VRML crew starts creating good 3D animations that can really move.

How important is programming in the work you do?

Programming is the guts of the game. We wouldn't have interaction with the player or game movement without it; it's extremely important.

How do you see the collaboration between engineers and artists affecting the use of the media?

If the engineers and artists can't work cooperatively, a game will not get made. Each group completely needs the other. It's a relationship that can foster innovative and exciting approaches to the medium, but it can be uncomfortably close at times. The skills and training for each discipline brings a diverse group of people together, and there are many stories, both good and bad, or how well this blending of talents works. I will say it often makes for an interesting work day, and one that can bring very impressive games to the market.

What is the outlook for the future of digital media?

It's bright. It's a strong field, with a high demand for good artists. Technically, software is continually being modified to give the artist more control and creative capabilities. I'm sure what we consider cutting edge now will look very quaint in a few years.

What careers will be important?

The people who can integrate their technical know-how with strong creative skills will be in demand, as they have been from the start. There is a very strong move onto the Internet for advertising and games, and I'm sure it will continue. A particular focus will be on global applications of what many of us in the United States have become accustomed to, as far as Internet communication and content are concerned. Wireless and cable-driven technologies are just beginning to be introduced into other regions of the world. It's exciting to think about how we will be expressing our ideas in this global context.

What emerging technologies will become important?

Wireless everything.

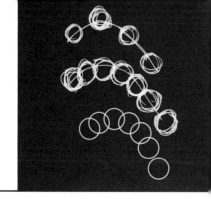

2D Animation

Traditional into Digital

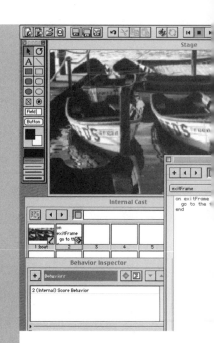

The purpose of this chapter is to give readers a glimpse into the traditional process of animation and to describe the techniques that have made animation such a vital art form. Animation differs from a still image in two major ways. First, it can move and change in three dimensions. Although the image is two dimensional, the camera can move in three dimensions. Beyond that, the image can change form and become alive. We will start with a review of the history of animation. The creative process of traditional animation is then covered from concept to completion, including the basics of script, storyboard, and animatic. The role of the animation director in breaking down a script, making exposure sheets, and planning camera

moves, is explained. The fundamentals of motion, such as squash and stretch, overlapping action, and anticipation of action, are covered, as well as the animation process of drawing roughs, in-betweens, and clean-ups. Finally, traditional methods in which pencil drawings are inked, painted, and photographed are explained, as well as the current digital approach. It is hoped that by understanding these ideas, you can draw from the creative tradition, and incorporate this knowledge into your own projects.

It is important to understand how the computer has affected animation. In terms of hand-drawn animation, the process is exactly the same until the ink and paint and camera stages. Character animation for feature films and commercials is still drawn by hand, but now the cleaned up drawings are scanned into the computer to be inked, and painted, and the camera step is now handled digitally.

Animation that does not involve sequential drawing (i.e., objects pan left, right, etc.) is done totally in the computer. Common examples of this are Flash animations for the Internet.

History

The history of 2D animation will be traced from the beginning from a technical point of view so we can later on compare the traditional and the digital methods. Technical limitations were significant in the early days of animation, and animators drew heavily on their imagination and artistic skills to overcome them. One of the first animated film series was *Felix the Cat*. The creator of Felix, Otto Mesmer drew every frame by hand, including the character and the backgrounds. He had to animate the character, the camera moves, backgrounds, and all aspects of the action by hand. He would do as many as a thousand drawings a week. This early animation was done on white paper with a pen, brush, and India ink. Each drawing was then photographed individually with a motion picture camera that was completely stationary. The archetype of all animated films is *Steamboat Willie* by Walt Disney. This film sparked great public interest in animation.

The next step in the development of animation was two-fold. The first was the development of the peg registration system by Bray Studios and the second was the use of clear acetate cels. Early animation was done by individuals, but because of the sheer manpower needed to complete all of the drawings, it evolved into a studio environment with a division of roles. There were now animators, in-betweeners, inkers, painters, and cameramen. Pegs allowed many artists to work independently of each other and still have their artwork match perfectly when assembled. The director would plan the layouts and animation and then pass the animation on to the animators and the backgrounds on to the background artists. Further subdivision occurred when the animator would draw the key poses and an in-betweener would do the in-between animation. Meanwhile, the background artist, who was more often than not a traditional painter, would be illustrating the backgrounds.

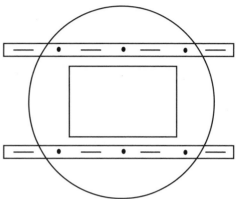

There were originally three types of peg systems: Oxberry, Acme, and Signal Corp. Signal Corp pegs were used during World War II. Oxberry pegs were developed for the Oxberry camera. They are more rectangular in shape. Acme pegs are thinner and longer. All peg registration systems are similar in that there is a center hole and two peg holes about two to three inches apart on either side. Pegs were placed on drawing boards with a light underneath to allow the animator to see through the paper as he drew. Animation disks were used by the animation director and the animators (see Figure 10.1). These disks had a dual set of pegs that matched the camera exactly. The director could plan camera moves for the cameraman this way and use the disk to create the animation. Different animation studios use different systems, but each studio generally stuck to one standard.

[10.1] A schematic diagram of an animation disk. The disk has dual sets of pegs on it, and there are subdivided inch markings on the sliding peg bars to plan motion. The center rectangle is opaque glass and allows light to come in from the bottom.

The development of clear acetate cels also revolutionized the animation process. Now animators did not have to redraw the background for every frame. They would overlay their drawings on the background and use up to four layers of clear cels. Any more than four layers of cels began to gray down the background and disturb the color of the final film.

In addition to technical developments that assisted the artist, advances were made in the design of cameras used to photograph animation. The Oxberry camera evolved as the standard. This camera was a large apparatus, about 12 feet tall, that allowed for precise control of the photography (see Figure 10.2). The camera contained the exact peg registration system that the artists used. It was

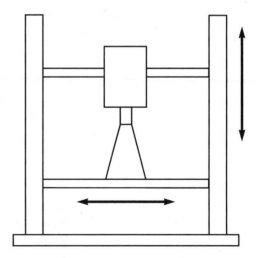

[10.2] A diagram of the Oxberry camera. The camera can move up and down and the compound, or flat area where the artwork is photographed can move right, left, forward, backward, and can even rotate.

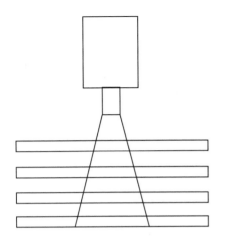

[10.3] The multiplane camera allowed for several levels of artwork. This allowed for more complex camera motions, as well as the addition of depth of field and variable focus controls.

mounted on two large columns, which allowed the camera to move up and down. The camera could then photograph a piece of artwork as large as 36 inches wide or as small as 2 inches wide. In addition to the upward and downward movement, the compound, or table upon which the artwork was placed, could move forward (north) and backward, (south), to the left (east), and to the right (west.). This system was known as the "field" system, and camera moves and positions were noted as a 5 field, 3 North and 6 West.

The compound also had movable peg bars on it, generally two on the top and two on the bottom. This would allow for independent motion of the background or cels while the animation stayed in one position. The table was also capable of 360 degrees of rotation.

These were the major technical developments made in the early days of animation. This system stayed in place for many years before the development of computer-assisted camera control. The only other major development was the multiplane camera by the Disney studios.

The multiplane camera was developed to allow for a greater sense of depth of field and the ability of the camera to move between cel levels and create a greater sense of realism (Figure 10.3). The Oxberry camera had the limitation of the cels and background being squeezed between a glass platen to eliminate reflections. The use of 12- or 16-field cels also limited the animation artwork to 12 to 16 inches in width.

Most animation studios used the Oxberry camera and worked with 12-field cels. This was for both economic and practical reasons. The multiplane camera required several people to operate it and was quite expensive. Also, the 12-field became the standard due to the higher cost of the 16-field cels. Since film projects at 24 frames per second, and 1,440 frames per minute, the sheer number of cels needed became an important factor in the costs of the production. This technology remained constant until the introduction of computer-assisted cameras, which became widespread in the early 1980s. Computer-controlled stepping motors were adapted to the Oxberry camera, which eliminated the tedious calculations which up to that point were done by hand. Once the calculations had been finished, the cameraman had to manually move each axis of the camera before each shot. This would limit a cameraman to how much he could shoot in one day. The computerized cameras now allowed for an order of magnitude increase in productivity. In addition, the camera could repeat moves precisely and created photographic effects previously impossible with manual photography.

Unfortunately, the final stage in the development of the animation camera was the elimination of it altogether. Although animation cameras are still in wide use, Oxberry has not manufactured any new cameras for many years. The scanner and digital ink and paint software are replacing the camera. The advantages of this new approach are many. Digital ink and paint is less expensive and quicker. Color correction does not require repainting all the cels. You do not have to wait for the paint to dry. The transparency of the digital image allows for almost unlimited cel levels. Camera moves can be more complex. Combining live action with animation is also easier. Thus, technology is giving animators more options and increasing the creative potential of the medium.

The Creative Process for 2D Animation

The creative process for traditional animation is shown in Figure 10.4, and it is very focused on the early stages of preproduction. Because traditional animation uses cels and is photographed on an Oxberry camera, the early parts of the process are the most creative, due to the great expense involved in the production phase. Most scenes consist of hundreds of painted cels. It is very expensive to change or redo any cel inking and painting. In addition, camera time, film, and processing are very expensive.

Given these parameters, traditional animation studios spend a great deal of time in the preproduction stage. The first part of this stage is the writing of the story and the script. Normally this is done before any animation drawing is started. However, it is common for some sketching to be done as the story is being written. This generally takes the form of inspirational sketches to define the mood and look of the story or characters.

The writing of a story for animation is a complex but well-documented process. Many books on scriptwriting are available.

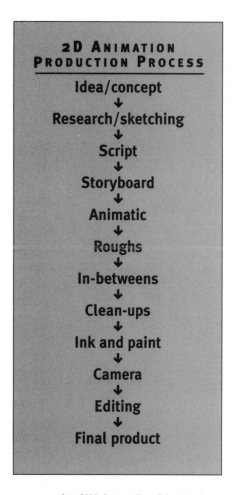

2D ANIMATION PRODUCTION PROCESS

Idea/concept
↓
Research/sketching
↓
Script
↓
Storyboard
↓
Animatic
↓
Roughs
↓
In-betweens
↓
Clean-ups
↓
Ink and paint
↓
Camera
↓
Editing
↓
Final product

[10.4] This is an outline of the 2D animation process. This is strictly followed by all 2D animation studios. Because of the time-consuming and expensive process of drawing the animation, considerable time is spent in the preproduction period.

One of the major items to consider when doing animation is whether something needs to be animated. Can it be done in live action? Who is the target audience? What is the budget and time frame for the production? Animation is a time-consuming and expensive process. If a story can be told and the goals met by live action, it may not be necessary or appropriate to use animation.

There are a variety of reasons for using animation. First and foremost, animation has universal appeal. By using hand-drawn art, the project takes on a timeless character. In addition, all things are possible with animation. The only limits to what is seen on the screen is the artist's imagination.

The purpose of this chapter is not to focus on the writing process, and we will assume that your story has been finished. One thing to remember is that the story needs to readapted and put into a form ready for the screen. This is the scriptwriting process. The narrative is broken down into its visual and audio elements.

Scriptwriting is a specialized process, and what follows is a very brief description of the process you must go through to format a script. Although there are several formats, most animation scripts use the two-column format. The one used for feature films is a stacked format, where camera and visual instructions are stacked above the dialog and sound. The two-column format for animation puts the video information in the left column and the audio in the right column. When a story is adapted for the screen, it is broken down into these two basic elements. Visual sequences are broken down into scenes, and each scene is numbered. Once this is done, a storyboard is made of each individual scene and each major key frame of that scene. This is when the animation director begins to take a major role in the development of a project.

The Role of the Animation Director

The animation director is responsible for making sure that the project is executed to his or her creative vision and standards. The animation director reports to the producer, who is responsible for overseeing the entire production from beginning to the end. The producer is also involved in the financial management of the project.

The director is usually brought in during the beginning stages when the script is being written and the initial process of visual development is being done. *Development* is the term used for the early stages of an animated film. Either before or during the time when the story and script are being written, the visual development phase begins. This is a period when artists are called in to visualize key elements of the film and to begin to develop a mood and visual style for the production. In some feature film companies, well-known artists, who are not necessarily animators, are commissioned to do ten or fifteen illustrations or paintings related to the story and script. This may even be done with several artists who have differing styles. This development stage is the most creative phase of the project. Dozens or even hundreds of sketches may be made to begin to define what the story and characters will look like. Very often, these sketches are matched to a musical composition or vocal narrative to give the producer and artists an idea of the stylistic direction the project will take.

It is during this time that the visual style and production value of the film is defined. Once this has been determined, the character model sheets are created as a reference for the animators and several group production meetings are held to give the entire crew an idea of what the production is about and where it is going.

At this point, a script is written and then a storyboard illustrating this script is prepared. Storyboards are quick thumbnail sketches that illustrate the basic action and purpose of a scene (see Figure 10.5). Storyboards are deliberately done quickly because they go through several generations of change as the story is perfected and changed. Story sessions are held with the writers and artist and they "pitch" their scenes by guiding people through a scene along with storyboards, acting out the action as they tell the story. Hundreds and even thousands of storyboards are drawn for feature films. They are pinned on 4-by-8-foot boards and reviewed countless times before they are approved.

The final stage of storyboard approval is done by preparing an animatic. An animatic is a matching of the storyboard with the soundtrack. It gives a feel of the pacing and dialogue, as well as the overall look of the film. Animatics are assembled into a story reel,

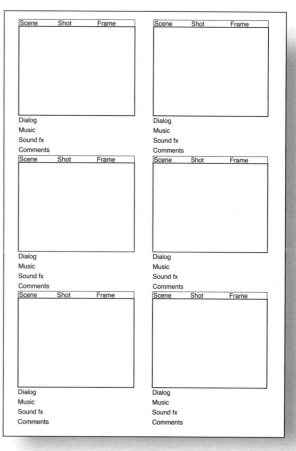

[10.5] A storyboard format. Enlarge and copy it and use it for your storyboards, or create your own form. This is the best way to plan animation, or video, since the sketches are quick and you can spend more time planning than drawing.

Production Sheet

Scene	Sequence	Title				Animator	Footage	Sheet No.

ACTION	DIAL	EXTRA	4	3	2	1	BKGD	CAMERA INSTRUCTIONS

[10.6] A blank exposure sheet. Each line represents a frame of film or video. Each drawing is entered into this, as well as the backgrounds and camera moves. The timing for the exposure sheet is taken from the track reading.

which is a full-length version of the final production, with the final dialog sound track. Large studios use the animatic as the backbone of the film. As pencil tests, clean-up tests, and final animation are completed, they are edited into this reel and reviewed by the director for approval. This method works very well, because you can get a general sense of the entire production and how individual scenes fit within it.

Breaking Down a Script

The process of breaking down a script begins when the script and storyboard have been approved and the dialog has been recorded. It is now the job of the animation director to prepare the scenes so that they can be clearly understood and animated. Folders are made for each scene. Inside each folder is a copy of the script and storyboard. Thumbnail sketches are made of the background and sequences of animation that must be done. The director also needs to decide what cel levels will be used for each character. Layouts are drawn at this stage to take the storyboards from their small size up to their final artwork size. Motion paths are laid out, and the technical steps in preparing the animation are done.

When a script is totally broken down, the director will have folders that can be given to the animators. Each folder contains a completely annotated exposure sheet, with dialog, layouts, backgrounds, cel levels, and camera moves. These folders are normally gone over with the animators in detail by the animation director.

Making Exposure Sheets

Exposure sheets are the road map from which the animators bring the film to life (see Figure 10.6). The dialog is always recorded before any animation is done. Today it is common practice to videotape the actors while their dialog is being recorded. This allows the animators to refer to and to exaggerate the gestures of the actors and to refine their performances into an animated performance. Once the dialog has been recorded, all the bad takes have been edited out, and the dialog has been paced for the final film, the track is "read."

The process of reading a soundtrack is a collaboration between the editor and the director. By this point in the production, the director is well along in developing a working script, which contains sketches, the script, and storyboards. Using the narration script, the typewritten script from which the actor(s) read their parts, the director marks it up with cue points for the editor to put in frame numbers.

Film plays at 24 frames per second. 16 mm film has 40 frames per foot and 35 mm film has 16 frames per foot. The final soundtrack is transferred from magnetic tape to a magnetic film stock, which is exactly like film, but it has iron oxide coating to record the sound on.

When the editor starts to read a track, he or she punches a hole in the first frame of the film and the counter on the synchronizer is set to 0000. As the film is pulled through the synchronizer, the sound head begins to play back the sound and the editor rocks the sound head back and forth. This is called "scrubbing," and it is done to find the location of every sound. The editor then marks the start and stop points on the script in feet and frames, which will enable the director to match the action with the sound accurately.

Reading a track is an art and a science. It is a very time-consuming process, and not every sound on the track must be read for every frame. If a character's dialog is not being spoken on screen, there is no need to read the track for that scene. If a camera move is meant to start at a particular word and end at the end of a sentence,

only two points need to be read. For dialogue, it is important to read the beginning and end of each word and then locate the particular sounds that relate to a particular mouth position. It is handy to have a mirror near by to mouth the dialog as you read it, to make sure you are getting the relevant visual references for the audio. Some animators actually put the mouth shapes on their exposure sheet when they read a track, to use as notes for when they animate.

Many editors and directors prefer to work with magnetic film because of its accuracy. The use of videotape and digital sound are also becoming widely used. Since it is difficult to scrub videotape, SMPTE time code is used for frame accurate reference. Digital audio software also has features to insert cue points and timing marks. Whether the process is done manually or digitally, it is vital that frame accuracy be maintained so that the picture will match the sound in the editing stage.

Once the track is read, it is transferred to exposure sheets by the director. Again, there are many differing methods for this, but commonly in traditional animation, an 80-column exposure sheet is used. The exposure sheet has a line for every frame, which indicates the camera position, background, and every cel level. Annotations on exposure sheets also tell the animator what the character is doing at any particular moment.

There are also some standard transitions used in animation. A fade indicates a beginning or ending. Back-to-back fades can signal the passage of time. A cut is a direct transition from scene to scene and does not imply a connection, but rather the progression of the narrative. A dissolve is when images blend between each other and usually implies a connection between the two images or scenes.

Image Sequencing

The most fundamental type of 2D animation is called image sequencing. It consists of images that follow each other one by one, almost the way a cartoon strip is laid out in a newspaper. The major difference is that animation is rarely seen as still art. It is projected on film or videotape or viewed over the Web. By putting images in a sequential format, the viewer will begin to see it as a linear set of images, rather than a static grouping. As the images speed up, persistence of vision takes over, and we begin to lose the sense of it being static and begin to view the images in a narrative form. Although this is the least expensive form of animation, because relatively few images are created, it is also the most primordial form. The process of moving from image sequencing to limited animation to full-character animation is seen in the number of drawings that are created and in the way that they are drawn. By its nature, an animatic, or motion storyboard, should tell the story as well as the final animation. However, viewer involvement is heightened as the number of images increases and the nature of the motion becomes more natural. This process is often used with photographs, and the term *photomation* is used to describe this process.

Limited Animation

Limited animation began as a reaction to the high costs of character animation. Early animations were either theatrical shorts or features. Both forms had relatively large budgets and long production schedules. The development of Saturday morning cartoons for television demanded a much quicker turnaround time and much longer running times. A typical television season is fifteen half-hour episodes. Given that a theatrical short is typically five minutes, and a feature is an hour and a half, new methods needed to be invented to produce seven and a half hours of animation for the fall television season each year.

Rather than have a complete drawing every frame or every other frame, limited animation animates only the basic elements of the characters. The most common example is a static head with a moving mouth. Another form of limited animation is to move a simple element over a background.

Character Animation

In character animation the entire character is usually redrawn every frame or two, allowing the character to act. When we speak, we normally do not stay stiff and only move our mouths. We use our bodies, hands, and arms to explain what we are saying. By having a character act, we can express emotions better, and the animation becomes more powerful and involving. This process is more time-consuming, since the number of drawings increases dramatically. This type of animation is also called Disney-style animation, after the studio that perfected it.

The Fundamentals of Motion

There is universal agreement that Disney-style animation has set the standard for classic character animation. No other studio in his-

tory has had as much success with their feature films. The following principles of animation are summarized from the book *The Illusion of Life* by Frank Thomas and Ollie Johnston.

The Disney Dozen

The "Disney Dozen" are the 12 most important elements that animation must contain. Without them, the animation seems lacking in some way. Try to incorporate these principles in your animation.

1. **Squash and Stretch**

   This principle encourages the animator to add flexibility and fluidity to their animation. A rigid shape is not natural when animated. A bouncing ball "stretches" when it is about to hit the ground and "squashes" when it hits the ground. It adds the feeling of weight to a character. Squash and stretch can be studied by looking at traditional animation in slow motion on a VCR. This is one of the best ways to learn how animation is drawn.

2. **Anticipation**

   It is important for an animator to let the audience know what is about to happen. When an action is signaled beforehand, the audience is ready to appreciate its effect. The wind-up of a pitcher in baseball is an example of anticipation. When people get out of chairs, they do not stand up directly, they prepare to stand up by leaning back and placing their hands of the sides of the chair.

3. **Staging**

   Because of the use of artwork, it is important that the desired reaction of the audience is incorporated into the composition of the background image. The composition, direction of the action, and ultimate result should be carefully planned. Camera angle, position, movement, and character behavior are all parts of staging a scene.

4. **Straight-Ahead and Pose-to-Pose**

   These are two techniques for animation. Straight-ahead animation means that the animator begins at the beginning of a scene, animates through it to the end. This is usually done by experienced animators. Pose-to-pose animation means that one sets up a variety of poses for the overall scene and then does the in-between animation. This is easier, since the extreme drawings provide a framework for the in-between drawings to be done.

5. **Follow Through and Overlapping Action**

   Not all action starts and stops at the same time. Follow through and overlapping action are necessary to give the illusion of true motion. When a car stops, it usually goes slightly beyond its stopping point and settles back.

6. **Ease In and Ease Out**

   This is the principle of acceleration and deceleration. Whenever an object starts to move its speed increases before it reaches its steady velocity. The same applies when an action is ending. Characters move in the same way. Cameras also ease in and out when they move, to prevent jarring when they stop (see Figure 10.7).

7. **Curves and Arcs**

   The principle described here relates to the fact that most motion occurs along a curve. Motion is generally smooth, not jerky. The motions of a robot are linear and appear to be stiff. To promote the notion of life, action must move along curves. It is helpful to draw the motion path first, before animating the character through it.

8. **Secondary Action**

   There is normally more than one thing going on in a scene. Secondary action refers to additional elements used to enhance the mood and believability of a scene. For instance, a character may be playing with a cat while he is talking to another character.

9. **Timing**

   Timing takes years to perfect. Seasoned animators can take a look at an action and know how many drawings it will take. The practice of counting "one thousand" will give the animator a rough count of 24 frames for film and 30 for video. Video cameras are often helpful for recording an action, studying it, and determining how many frames the action will take.

10. **Exaggeration**

    The 24 frames of film move too quickly for the eye to see each one of them. Exaggeration helps to infuse life into the drawings. Too much realism makes an action stiff. By taking exaggeration to the extreme in the key poses, the motions tends to look more believable. The exaggerated drawings may only last for a frame or two, but they add so much to the animation. If there is not enough exaggeration, the animation looks stiff.

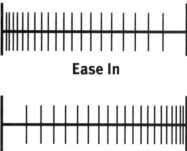

Ease In

Ease Out

[10.7] The principle of ease in and ease out. Accelerating at the beginning of a movement and slowing down before the end are natural ways to move an object or camera.

11. **Drawing**

I cannot say enough about drawing skills. Not only is drawing skill the way that an artist communicates, but bad drawing takes away from the message. Keep a sketchbook, and draw on a daily basis. Master figure drawing first. Figure drawing is the basis upon which all drawing is based. If you want to become an animator, begin to draw quick poses and focus on form, weight, and line, rather than rendering, detail, light, and shadow.

12. **Appeal**

Other words for appeal are composition, aesthetic value, form, and value. The viewer must become involved with your animation. Appeal is necessary for this to happen. It works on many levels, but the suspension of disbelief is the state of mind that most animators aim for. If your technique gets in the way, you are not getting your message across.

The Process of Animation Drawing

Animation drawing differs from traditional drawing in many ways. The style starts off very loose and is intended to capture motion, gesture, form, and weight. The initial drawings are done for the key frames, which are the extreme poses in the action. Classic animation uses a lot of circles and curves in their animated drawing style to give bounce and life to the drawings. Detail is generally added later. Animators work from the storyboard, character model sheets, exposure sheets, and the layouts to do a rough animation. The storyboard gives them an idea of the action that will occur during their animated sequence. The character model sheets gives them a reference from which to draw the character. In feature films, normally there is a lead animator who focuses on a particular character, but there are also several assistant animators, who must also maintain the consistent look of the character as put forward by the lead animator. The exposure sheet gives the animator a frame-by-frame guide of how long each action is to occur and what is happening during the scene in terms of audio. The layout provides the backdrop for the animation and will also indicate the camera position and moves.

Roughs

The first stage of the animation is drawing the roughs (see Figure 10.8). Roughs are very loose sketches of the initial blocking in of the action of the character. They are accompanied by timing marks, which indicate which frame the key pose is to fall on and the timing of the in-betweens, which will be drawn later. Normally, the cameraman will photograph the roughs in the frame sequence indicated so that the animator can get a feel for how the scene is unfolding. These and all subsequent photography done of pencil drawings are called pencil tests. Pencil tests are normally done for roughs, in-betweens, and clean-ups, before the art goes to the ink and paint department.

In-Betweens

Once the roughs have been approved, they are given to the in-betweener. Most apprentice animators start as in-betweeners and then work their way up to assistant animator and then animator. The process of in-betweening is to draw the in-between drawings, so that there is a drawing for every frame or two. Full-character animation is generally done on either "ones" or "twos." This means that there will be either one drawing per frame or one drawing per two frames. There is a large issue of economy involved in this decision. If a film is animated on ones, there will be 1440 drawings per minute. If it is animated on twos, there will be only 720 drawings per minute. It is obvious that time and money play an important part in this decision. For most animation, twos are sufficient, since the persistence of vision of the eye does not reveal a significant difference. However, for close-up dialog and rapid motion across the screen, ones are recommended. In-betweens are photographed the same way that the roughs are. They are looked at many times, corrected, and redrawn until they are perfect.

Clean-Ups

Once the in-betweens have been approved, the process of drawing the clean-up drawings is begun. Roughs and in-betweens are drawn loosely to perfect the motion. A clean-up is a single line drawing that provides the outline for the inking process. It must distill the multiple lines of the animation into a smooth fluid line. As with any art form, some artists excel as clean-up artists, just as there are those who excel as animators. A clean-up artist must be able to interpret the in-between drawings and make the line smooth and continuous, yet keep the feeling of motion, gesture, and form alive.

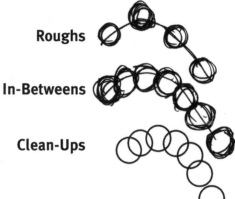

Roughs

In-Betweens

Clean-Ups

[10.8] An example of roughs, in-betweens, and clean-ups. Roughs are drawn for the key frames and are done more for the motion than for the finished look. Roughs are photographed and tested to make sure the motion is good, before the in-betweens are done. In-betweens are drawn from the roughs for each frame. They are again tested before the clean-up animation is produced. Once the clean-up animation has been tested, it is inked and painted.

Clean-up tests are also done. They are usually double-exposed with the layout to see if the animation is fluid and that the overall effect is what the director has intended. Clean-up tests are looked at very carefully because once they have been approved, the cels are inked, and if a scene is changes, there will be considerable expense involved.

Inking and Painting

Inking and painting are begun with the approved clean-up drawings. Clear acetate cels are laid over the clean-up drawings and a fine black or color line is traced from the clean-up. It must follow the drawings exactly. Very often, if multiple colors are used for the inks, style drawings or sample finished cels are made for the inkers to follow. Inking is done with a very fine brush or pen, and the artist normally wears white cotton gloves, so that no oil from their skin will get on the cels. Cels must be kept very clean, since even a small speck of dust or other imperfection will be magnified hundreds of times on the screen.

Once the cels have been inked, they are flipped over and painted from behind. The cel painters follow the sample cels provided by the director. Normally one color is done at a time. The technique of painting cels is to let the paint flow on and not to brush it on. Brush marks must not show on the final cel, or they will be noticed on film. There is a special paint for cels, which has a vinyl base and very opaque color.

The cels are then hung up to dry, and then reassembled in the scene and are ready for photography.

Before they are photographed, the cels are sent to a checker, who takes out the exposure sheet, background and goes through the "photography" process to make sure that all the cels are there, in the proper order, correctly numbered, and so on. Camera time, film, and processing are very expensive and the checker is there to make sure that a minimal number of takes are required by the photographer.

The ink and paint process is currently going through a rapid change. Large-scale animation projects are very rarely inked and painted in the United States. Most of the work is sent overseas to Korea, China, and other countries where labor is less expensive.

The new trend is digital ink and paint. This process uses a scanner for the clean-up drawings. Scenes are scanned in and then the colors are painted in electronically. Since video resolution is much lower than film, this process is becoming very popular for commercials and Saturday morning cartoons. Large feature film companies like Disney, Dream-works, and Warner Brothers are now using the digital ink and paint process.

Not only is it quicker, but it can offer many different ink colors, cel colors, and effects. In addition, image processing allows for the easy creation of soft edges, shadows, and so on. As the software becomes easier to use and less expensive, the use of digital ink and paint will continue to increase.

Animation Photography

Animation photography requires a lot of concentration and is a very exacting discipline. Film is very unforgiving, and if an animation cameraman makes a mistake three quarters of the way through a four-hour shoot, he must begin the shoot all over again.

A cameraman is given the checked scene to photograph. In the scene folder is a layout, the exposure sheets, the background and the cels. More often than not a copy of the storyboard and the script are included. It is important for the cameraman to understand what the scene is about before he begins to photograph it. The cameraman is normally not an artist and has had little to do with the preparation of the artwork. The director puts together the camera positions and moves (see Figure 10.9) and the exposure sheet; a background artist has rendered the backgrounds; and an animator, in-betweener, clean-up artist, inkers,

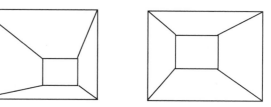

[10.9] Examples of how a camera move is planned. If it is a zoom in, small arrows are drawn on the lines to indicate that the camera is moving in, and vice versa.

and painters have done the animation and cels. Although the scene has been checked, it is important that this final stage of the animation process flow smoothly.

The exposure sheet is what the cameraman follows. It indicates which backgrounds are to be used, which cels will be on which level, and at what frame they must be shot.

The first thing a cameraman does is to center the camera by projecting a set of cross-hairs on the camera and matching them up with a field guide (see Figure 10.10). Once this is done, all of the counters on the camera are set to 0000. This gives a common starting point for all scenes. The next step is to photograph a slate, which has the date, scene number, take number, and any other relevant information on it. It usually has what is referred to as a "China

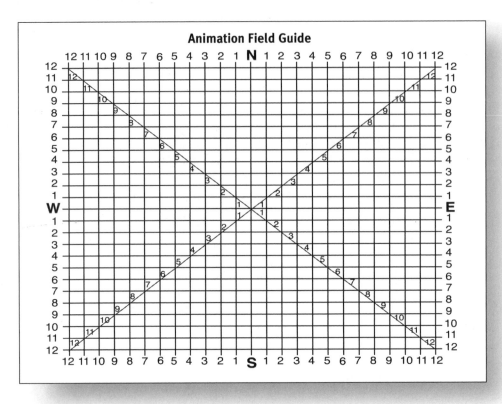

Animation Field Guide

[10.10] A field guide. It is used to plan camera moves and to frame the artwork. Locations are indicated by the location of the center of the frame and the size of the field. For example, 3F, 2N, 5S means that it is a 3 Field (3 inches wide) and the center of the field is at 2 North and 5 South.

Girl" on it, which is a photograph of a woman's face. Another technique is to use the Kodak color strip. These are references for the film lab timer, who color corrects the print for the dailies using either the woman's face or the color strip. Dailies are low-cost prints that are used to check the animation. The editor uses them to assemble the film. The original negative is normally never cut until the final film has been approved. Dailies and the original negative have edge numbers on the side of the film, which give a frame-by-frame reference when the final film is matched and cut. The slate is usually held for a foot of film.

After the slate, the layout is placed on the pegs, and the camera is aligned to the exact position as indicated by the director. These numbers are written on the exposure sheet. Any camera moves are then plotted. Once the camera moves have been plotted, all the information needed to shoot the scene has been collected. The cameraman will usually hold 60 frames of the first frame to allow for a dissolve or other effect and then go frame by frame through the animation, changing the camera position and cels. The old adage in the camera world is to "move and shoot." Once the scene has been photographed, the cameraman usually runs 60 frames of extra at the end and then sends it to the lab.

Digital 2D Animation

Oxberry stopped making cameras many years ago. The process of photographing animation is being replaced with both video methods and digital methods. For animation destined for video, you can take traditional art and capture it directly on video, thus eliminating the expensive film developing and film transfer process. You can use digital techniques to put the animation directly on videotape from the computer.

Taking this one step further, the animation can be scanned, inked, painted, and composited on the computer and then photographed directly onto film with a digital film recorder. Finally, animation used for the Internet can stay in its digital format. All of these processes are currently being used and are phasing out traditional animation photography.

There are a variety of reasons for this change. First and foremost is economics. Second, the vast majority of animation produced today is put on videotape or the Internet, and film is not needed. Most of the animation being put to film now is feature-length animation and high-budget commercials. Smaller studios still use traditional animation photography methods, but the major studios are now using the digital process. The reason for this is lower cost and more creative control. For example, if a color had to be changed on a thousand cels, every cell would have to be entirely redone and repainted. In the digital world, all that is needed is to change the files, which is a task that has been automated. Digital ink and paint also allows for unlimited layers. Cels are generally limited to four layers. Digital compositing makes combining 2D animation with 3D animation and live action much more manageable. It is easy to see why this new trend is taking the industry by storm and breathing new life into the animation industry.

Feature film companies and commercial production houses use high-end software packages like US Animation™ and Animo™ to produce 2D animation. For these types of software packages, once the clean-up drawings have been scanned in, the process is totally digital from there to the final videotape or film. Inking and painting and photography are done digitally, with all the advantages of the digital process.

Another example of digital 2D animation is how Flash™ is used on the Internet. Flash is a vector-based software package, which allows for low data rates. Most Flash animation is really what used to be called motion graphics; that is, graphic elements and text moving about the screen. Remember that every motion needs to have a reason. Don't move something just because you can. Also, when making a movement, take the time to make it really good, and use techniques like squash and stretch and easing in and easing out to polish it.

2D Animation for the Internet

Traditional animation principles all apply when creating animation for the Internet. The major limiting factor at the present time is bandwidth, but that will change as technology advances. Within a few years, it is reasonable to expect that full-screen animation will be possible over the Internet. Currently, the vast majority of animation is quarter screen or less in size. We will review the limitations first before examining the process for creating digital animation for the Internet.

The Internet is all about bandwidth, or the amount of data that can flow through the system at any one time. Typical speeds for the average user's modem are 56K, which means 56 kilobytes per second. Cable modems allow for much faster data rates of up to 300 kilobytes per second. To give some perspective on this data rate, uncompressed video, or the normal television signal is 1,000 kilobytes per second. Advances in video compression are allowing the amount of data needed to decrease, so that digital video or animation can run faster.

Another way to address the bandwidth issue is image size. The figures I just cited are for a full-screen image. If the animation traveling over the Internet is one fourth or one eighth of a screen, the data rate is reduced proportionally.

Frame rate is yet another way to save data and speed the animation process up. Film and video have fixed frame rates, 24 per second and 30 per second, respectively. In digital format, computer animation will play as quickly as the computer can process it, unless the frame rate has been frozen in some way (e.g., by using Quicktime). Thus, the less data in an animation, the faster it will play. This works well for most Internet animation, including animated logos or other moving Web site elements.

Quicktime

Quicktime is a cross-platform digital video standard originally developed by Apple. Its advantage is that it plays at a constant frame rate. This is particularly important when audio is used. Although visuals can be played a varying frame rates, audio cannot. The method by which Quicktime works is to play at a standard rate and when bandwidth issues intervene, it will drop frames to allow for maintaining its constant speed. This has the disadvantage of producing a video that may appear to be jerky or jump, but the time element remains constant. If audio and live video are an important part of your animation, consider using Quicktime.

Bit-mapped Animation

Bit-mapped animation refers to the use of pixel-based images. The most common form of this type of animation is animated GIF files. Many software programs can be used to create animated GIFs. One of the most popular is GIF Builder.™

Vector Animation

Vector animation for the Internet uses software that defines the geometry of the images, rather than using pixels. Its two advantages are speed and size. It runs more quickly because the execution of mathematical equations is generally faster than processing image files. The size of the files is also smaller because there is less data used. One of the most popular vector-based packages is Flash from Macromedia.

Programmed Animation

There are several ways to animate over the Internet using programs like Java or CGI scripts. As the amount of data decreases and the sophistication of the programming increases, the speed and flexibility of the animation capabilities increases. However, there is a steeper learning curve. This type of animation is generally done by people who have some knowledge of programming.

There are programming languages within software programs, as well. For example, Macromedia Director™ uses Lingo. This language can program animation, as well as interactivity (see Figure 10.11).

Creating an Animation for the Internet

So how do you go about producing an animation for the Internet or interactive multimedia? The answer is to spend a significant amount of time in preproduction and to gather as much information as possible before starting the actual production. In simple terms, you

[10.11] A view of the behavior script window of Macromedia Director. The advantage of digital 2D animation is that one can tweak and control the animation with programming, as well as having tight numerical control over the motion.

should follow the traditional process all the way up to the point of actually producing the artwork and images. The other major item to consider is the final output medium and the constraints that are placed on the final form (e.g., it must be a Quicktime movie at 160 by 120 pixel resolution).

Once the technical parameters have been defined, the process of creating the storyboard, making an animatic, synchronizing it with the soundtrack (if there is one) all come into play. Some animators prefer to do the animation in pencil first and then scan it in, and others work directly on the computer. A wide range of software can be used to create 2D animation. On a basic level, drawings can be produced by hand and then scanned into the computer using Photoshop®. These images can then be imported into a software like Macromedia Director, Premiere™, or After Effects™, which puts them in sequential order and allows the animation to be viewed and perfected. Once the animation is colored and finished, it is then converted either into a Quicktime movie or a series of animated GIF files.

Summary

Traditional animation is alive and well. It is being seamlessly integrated with live action and 3D animation. Major advances in digital technology and software have all but eliminated the traditional photography of animation and opened new doors for the creative use of traditional techniques. By studying the history of animation and the methods used in its production, contemporary animators can gain insight into how traditional animators rose above their limitations. This understanding will allow the current generation of animators to take the digital art of animation to new heights.

BIBLIOGRAPHY

You will notice that this bibliography does not contain any books on 2D computer animation. Most of this information is contained in software manuals or books on the software. For example, the Adobe Premiere *Classroom in a Book* and most Flash books cover 2D computer animation techniques extensively. The focus of this chapter was to provide you with a thorough understanding of traditional animation. Once you have achieved that, applying what you have learned to digital methods is a straightforward process.

Frank Thomas and Ollie Johnston, *Disney Animation: The Illusion of Life,* Abbeville Press, New York, NY, 1984. www.abbeville.com.

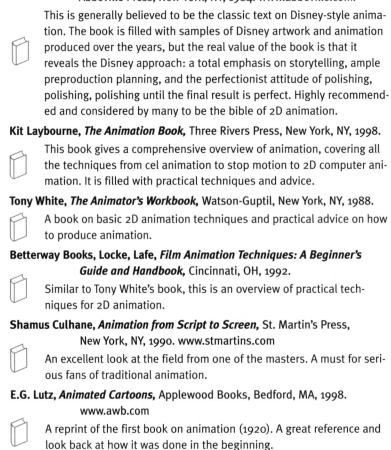

This is generally believed to be the classic text on Disney-style animation. The book is filled with samples of Disney artwork and animation produced over the years, but the real value of the book is that it reveals the Disney approach: a total emphasis on storytelling, ample preproduction planning, and the perfectionist attitude of polishing, polishing, polishing until the final result is perfect. Highly recommended and considered by many to be the bible of 2D animation.

Kit Laybourne, *The Animation Book,* Three Rivers Press, New York, NY, 1998.

This book gives a comprehensive overview of animation, covering all the techniques from cel animation to stop motion to 2D computer animation. It is filled with practical techniques and advice.

Tony White, *The Animator's Workbook,* Watson-Guptil, New York, NY, 1988.

A book on basic 2D animation techniques and practical advice on how to produce animation.

Betterway Books, Locke, Lafe, *Film Animation Techniques: A Beginner's Guide and Handbook,* Cincinnati, OH, 1992.

Similar to Tony White's book, this is an overview of practical techniques for 2D animation.

Shamus Culhane, *Animation from Script to Screen,* St. Martin's Press, New York, NY, 1990. www.stmartins.com

An excellent look at the field from one of the masters. A must for serious fans of traditional animation.

E.G. Lutz, *Animated Cartoons,* Applewood Books, Bedford, MA, 1998. www.awb.com

A reprint of the first book on animation (1920). A great reference and look back at how it was done in the beginning.

DIGITAL | Creativity

1. Make a flip book. A flip book is a collection of 3 by 5 cards with a series of drawings on them. When you put the cards together and flip them, the drawings take on motion and life. Flip books are one of the classic learning tools for animation. Once you are happy with your flip book, scan the images in and bring them into a software like Macromedia Director or Adobe Premiere and make a Quicktime movie of them.

2. Learning traditional animation usually starts by drawing a bouncing ball going up and down, followed by doing a flag waving test, and then a walk cycle. This process is usually a full semester class. The bouncing ball test can be done rather easily with software. Using software like Macromedia Director, animate a ball that bounces up and down a few times and then either moves across the frame or eventually bounces to a stop. Don't add anything extra to this test, just animate it as if you dropped a ball and it bounces to a stop or across the frame. To help you get the timing right, you can videotape a pink rubber ball and note the frame counts. Add squash and stretch to the ball, so that it "looks animated" rather than realistic. The ball can eventually become a character using its round shape as the body of the character. If you have the energy and ambition, animate a flag waving and a walk cycle.

EXERCISES

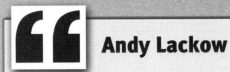

Andy Lackow

INTERVIEW

Digital Illustrator and Interactive Designer

Andy has been a professional artist for 25 years. Born in New York City, he began his career there in 1975 after attending Rhode Island School of Design and the School of Visual Arts. Using airbrush, he produced illustrations for many magazines and book and record companies, and won several awards. He moved on from editorial illustration to more lucrative advertising work. After 18 years of airbrush, he turned to the Mac. His concentration was on 3D digital illustration for print. He has since begun transitioning his talents toward the Web. Color Plates 74–78 show the wide range of work by Andy Lackow. Andy's style combines 3D, science fiction, and classic airbrush looks executed in a digital environment.

How do you define your illustration style?

Fantasy/realism/retro.

What is your creative process?

I am either given a concept or design by my client or asked to come up with my own. Then I usually do a very rough thumbnail and go right to 3D modeling on the computer.

For animation and interactive pieces, I create a rough storyboard and then go straight to the digital process. I have plenty of reference material to use as a jumping-off point in creating my models and interactive pieces. For instance, I have many architecture books that I use as reference for my cityscapes. I watch films for inspiration for my animation/interactive scripts, lighting, camera angles, editing, sound, and so on.

You combine traditional and digital imagery in your work. How did that style evolve?

I try to find a happy medium between making things look like they weren't done on a computer and giving certain elements that techno-electronic feel. Aside from "letting the computer do the work" in 3D programs (perfect perspective, automatic highlights and shadows, etc.), I like to use the airbrush tool in Photoshop to paint certain elements (like skies). Before I went digital I was an airbrush illustrator.

What advice would you give to aspiring illustrators?

The obvious: Learn how to draw well. Concentrate on traditional art skills instead of rushing straight to letting a computer to do the work for you. Develop an individual style. If you don't take these measures, your artwork will look like the rest of the clones.

How has the Web influenced your career?

The print illustration business has been decimated by art directors using underpriced stock illustration, image manipulation, and in-house artwork. The Web is where the future of professional artists lie. I am making the transition by learning new, Web-oriented skill sets.

What are your favorite Web sites?

The ones that entertain as well as inform. Since the Web will eventually replace TV, it needs to offer content that does something, rather than remain static, and draws you in. One of my favorite sites is http://hotwired.lycos.com/animation/. It has a lot of off-the-wall animations and video clips.

How do you see illustration evolving in the future?

The Web. Interactive CD-ROMs. Multimedia. Print is still alive and well, but the other venues I mentioned offer limitless opportunities now and in in the future.

What software do you use?

Photoshop®, Illustrator, Lightwave™, Electric Image™, Strata™, GoLive™, Flash, Premiere, Cubase™, and Acid Music.™

How do you see the balance between traditional and digital skills?

I have a traditional art background and still think the way I did when using traditional media in regard to composition, color, lighting, mood, and draughtmanship. Basically my goal as an artist, both traditional and digital, has been to manipulate the viewer's experience to elicit a particular reaction.

What is your advice for students studying digital media?

Don't let the technology take the place of your own creativity. Once again, get a traditional art background, whether it's in illustration, painting, animation, sculpture, film, or animation. It all applies to the digital counterpart of each discipline.

Describe one of your favorite projects.

My favorite projects are usually the ones I make up for myself, my promotional pieces. Occasionally I get a plum assignment where I have creative free reign and an intelligent art director without any ego/power issues.

Who are some of your favorite illustrators/ fine artists?

Too many to list here. Favorite American painters: Edward Hopper, Thomas Hart Benton, Stuart Davis, Georgia O'Keefe. All of the Renaissance Masters: Leonardo, Michelangelo. Europeans: Picasso, Van Gogh, Dali, Cézanne. Historic illustrators: Maxfield Parrish, Rockwell, Vargas. Contemporary illustrators: Todd Schorr, Michael Doret, Lou Brooks, Roger Huyyson, Gary Baseman, Robert Rodriguez, Nancy Stahl, Dan Pelavin, Jeff Seaver, Bill Mayer, Mark Frederickson, Henk Dawson, and Mark Matcho.

How did you get involved in 3D?

It seemed a natural progression from airbrush realism. Instant chrome! I'm a techie as well as an artist; I like the numerical precision. I find 3D fascinating and dense. There's so much to learn, it's never boring. I also like making things that look real that couldn't possibly exist in reality. It's like playing God—especially if you use Maya.

Your background is as an airbrush artist. How did you make the transition to the digital world?

I was going through a midcareer crisis. I hated the airbrush: the constant cleaning, the paint splatters (no "undo"), the endless friskets, the tedium. I was desperate for a change. I resisted getting into computer art at first, partly due to the high cost of hardware and software and partly out of fear. Then a Mac advocate friend of mine found a deal for me. Someone he worked with was selling a used Mac IIx, monitor, and software for a good price. That was seven years ago. I took to the Mac like a fish to water. I was hooked. I now use both Mac and Windows platforms. A lot of 3D and Web design programs are available only on Windows. Whether you like it or not, it's a cross-platform world out there.

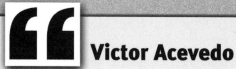

Victor Acevedo

INTERVIEW

Digital Artist

Victor Acevedo is a digital artist who has shown his work in over 77 exhibitions worldwide, including Podgallery@Spectra NYC 1999 and 2000, SIGGRAPH 98, NY Digital Salon 1996 and 1994, ISEA 1993, and Prix Ars Electronica 1991. In 1998 he was invited to show his work in the exhibition at the M.C. Escher Centennial Congress in Rome, Italy. In 1999 his piece *The Lacemaker* was featured in the ACM/SIGGRAPH documentary *The Story of Computer Graphics*. As a founding member of the Digilantes in conjunction with EZTV CyberSpace Gallery, he helped organize seven noteworthy "underground" digital art shows, including Silent Partners 1992, Digital Salon Des Independents 1993, Digital Site 1995, and L.A. Digilantes 1997. In acknowledgment of this record, Acevedo's work was included in the exhibition celebrating the 20th anniversary of EZTV/Cyber-Space Gallery, which was held at the American Film Institute in Los Angeles. Acevedo currently resides in New York City where he lectures on digital fine art at the School of Visual Arts. Acevedo attended Art Center College of Design in the early 1980s. Influenced by M.C. Escher, Salvador Dali, and later R. Buckminster Fuller, he produced a significant body of work in traditional media, primarily painting and drawing during the years 1977–1985. He made his last oil painting in 1984 and then adopted computer graphics as his primary medium. Acevedo's ongoing interest in geometrical structure, periodic space division, and polyhedra has continued to be an integral part of his digital work.

His recent work is at http://www.podgallery.com. Color Plates 79–84 show the range of Victor Acevedo's work. *Suit on the Phone* (see Color Plate 80) was the image through which I met Victor. It was accepted into the New York Digital Salon, a show I curated. Acevedo's other images show his use of photography with 3D geometry.

Please describe your work.

Although my work uses photography, it is computer based, as the final images are created and developed in the digital realm. The images' characteristic "pseudo-molecular-model" overlay, which connects and interpenetrates figure and ground, acts as a metaphor for domains of electromagnetic and metadimensional resonance. The overlay is also a visualization of a scene's universal substrate turned up in the mix—a metaphorical aggregate of the ocean of being. Which is an energetic domain that paradoxically oscillates between eternal emptiness and the fullness of an all-pervasive potentiality. This is sometimes called the void-matrix. This graphic metaphor can be sourced to Acevedo's synthesis of concept from Frijof Capra's book *The Tao of Physics* (1975) combined with aspects of R. Buckminster Fuller's *Synergetics* (1975–1979). Highly relevant to the visual arts is Fuller's geometry, based on triangulation and sphericity. It suggests a graphic language that is noncubist and noncubical. For example, Fuller's *Synergetics* promulgates mathematician Leonhard Euler's polyhedral topology of visual experience, which consists of a phenomenology of line, crossings, and windows (i.e., edges, vertices, and faces). This nicely updates the culminating nineteenth century's conceptual Cezannic toolset of cylinder, sphere, and cone and its resultant legacy—the twentieth century's traditional-media lexicon of graphical abstraction based on Cubism.

What was your background prior to your entry into the field of digital art?

I started drawing spontaneously at the age of four and took off from there. My father, who is a civil engineer, taught me one- and two-point perspective at the age of nine, which perhaps planted a seed for my interest in an underlying graphical structure in images. As an adult, I took up traditional painting and drawing in 1977 while attending the University of New Mexico in Albuquerque. Later returning to Los Angeles, I attended Art Center College of Design, majoring in traditional media fine art.

When did you enter the digital realm?

I was introduced to computer graphics in 1980 by Gene Youngblood, the author of the book *Expanded Cinema* at Art Center College of Design. He was teaching a lecture-survey class on the new developments in electronic imaging for both still and time-based imagery. He showed work by Ed Emshwiller and Woody and Steina Vysulka, as well as various early experiments in computer graphics being conducted at the New York Institute of Technology. The NYIT experiments took several forms, from early light-pen paint systems to 3D solid model rendering. I also recall a discussion of the now very famous West Coast collaboration between James Blinn and David Em.

What made you decide to work with digital media?

At the time that I was taking Youngblood's class, I was heavily involved in the geometric work of M.C. Escher, so the connection between his use of periodic space-division and computer graphics was clear and profound. I had seen the future, and that's where I wanted to go. However, not having a clue as to where to get access and still working with traditional media, I carried on with oil painting and graphite drawing for another three or four years. However, I gradually morphed into a full-on digital artist over years 1983–1986. During this time, I joined the local L.A. SIG-GRAPH chapter, took the odd workshop here and there, and then eventually got employed in the field. I produced my first digital prints for exhibition in 1987. (*The Ectoplasmic Kitchen* series, Cibachromes from slide output via film recorder)

What aspect of your background have you found most helpful in your transition to digital art?

I suppose a natural ability to draw and a certain design sense, which was later refined with art school training. Another thing I believe was helpful was a few years of playing guitar as a hobbyist and then as a semi-pro. Playing chords and chord progressions, in a visual sense, was extensive exercise with pattern and pattern transformation. Thinking about the guitar's fret board as a small Cartesian grid and chord progressions as sequential arrays of point constellations. All this lent itself later to a particular approach to pattern design and then later animation.

Describe your creative process. How do you begin a new digital work?

For a start, just walking around the city or sitting waiting for a subway train, having insights, or episodes of "heightened seeing" kind of sets the stage to begin a piece. I look through the many hundreds of photographs I've taken over the years to find a point of departure. Concurrent to this, on the computer, using SoftImage, I build new geometry or look through old geometry I've already built. Bringing the scanned photograph and the com-

puter-generated geometry into Photoshop, I composite the two together. I sort of play around with various positionings, sort of jam with the images to find the right spot for each. Thus a trail of iterations is produced. The final is the one that clicks in as the most satisfying juxtaposition. Also very important to the process is the interaction between extended production sessions working in the flow and then getting away from it, getting a change in scene and then coming back fresh to rework my ideas.

What are your thoughts on digital fine art?

I define digital fine art as the production of artifacts, performances, environments, and so on, designed to generate aesthetic experiences that heighten our perception, awareness, or insight—products made with fine-art intent as opposed to art for advertisement. This can be produced on a spectrum of platforms, everything from VR to digital prints. It includes of course, animation, digital video, and desktop, Web-based or environmental interactive work.

How do you compare the Internet and on-line galleries with the traditional gallery system as a venue for artists?

On-line galleries are becoming more and more prominent as the world economy is moving more and more toward e-commerce business models. As Internet bandwidth and interactive throughput moves closer to real-time, on-line galleries as venues to view, experience, and acquire fine art work will seem very natural. In the near future, art galleries that exist as both a real, physical walk-in space in a major cultural center like New York City, and on-line, will most likely continue to have a special and compelling experiential resonance for the serious art collector.

Who are your favorite computer artists?

Just off the top of my head, I like David Em's early work. Some other favorites are certain pieces by Stewart McSherry, Char Davies, and William Latham. Of course, there's a lot of excellent work out there. I usually see great new work every year at the SIGGRAPH Art Show and at the NY Digital Salon.

Who has influenced you the most within the field of digital art?

I still find that traditional media mentors like Salvador Dali, M.C. Escher, and R. Buckminster Fuller are highly relevant conceptually to digital media. On a technical or operational level, peers like Stewart McSherry, whom I happened to work with in 1991, and more recently, informal dialogues with Kevin Mutch of PODgallery, have been influential.

Who has influenced you most within the field of time-based digital art?

Videos by the creative group called Hexstatic, some of the digital video and animations I saw on MTV's *Amp* were very exciting. Much of that also appears in the Cinema Electronica category in the annual RESFEST screenings.

What is the future of digital art?

Most likely within ten years, any fine art that is not digital or digitally mediated will seem frightfully old-fashioned and quaint. Some of it will be valued and revered, but for the most part contemporary culture will focus on fine and popular arts that are digital and dynamically operating across a spectrum that embodies a synthesis of virtuality or the phenomenologically metaphysical and the so-called real world.

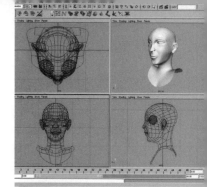

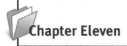

Chapter Eleven

DIGITAL Creativity

3D Animation

3D animation software has advanced so much over the past several years that the use of 3D images, graphics, and animation has penetrated most digital media. The most widely noticed use of 3D animation is for feature films, video games, and commercials. Other uses for 3D animation include broadcast design, corporate presentations and training programs, educational media, CD-ROMs, architectural renderings and walkthroughs, scientific visualization, virtual reality, and the Web. This chapter will provide the reader with a basic understanding 3D models, images, and animation. The process of creating 3D is divided into several distinct steps, beginning with creating the models or actors and objects in a 3D scene. Once the models have been

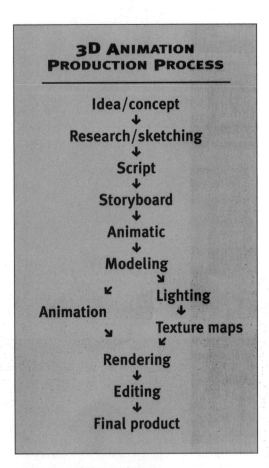

3D ANIMATION PRODUCTION PROCESS

Idea/concept
↓
Research/sketching
↓
Script
↓
Storyboard
↓
Animatic
↓
Modeling
↘
Lighting
↙
Animation
↓
↘
Texture maps
↙
Rendering
↓
Editing
↓
Final product

[11.1] The 3D animation process. As you can see, the first part is similar to 2D animation and video production. Also, there is a split after the modeling has been completed. The reason for this is the division of labor in the 3D production process. While the technical director is working on the lighting and surfaces, the animator is working on the motion. There is a lot of testing involved during this process. Technical directors also oversee the rendering and compositing of the final images.

created, they are assigned colors and surface properties. Lights are then added to the scene, a camera is positioned, and it is either rendered as a still image or into an animated sequence.

3D animation production is usually a team effort. Although 3D artists in small studios are involved in the entire process, large studios generally divide their staff into three main groups: modelers, animators, and technical directors. Modelers are responsible for creating the objects, actors and 3D environment in which the story takes place. Animators focus on making the characters come alive and telling the story. Technical directors generally handle everything else, from creating the lighting, surfaces, and texture maps, to rendering and compositing the final animation. In feature film studios, these teams are further broken down into very specialized roles.

The 3D Animation Process

Designing for 3D animation requires the ability to think in four dimensions: the three dimensions of space and the fourth dimension of time. One of the easiest ways to think of 3D animation is to compare it to a television studio environment. In this live-action environment, there are actors, lights, and a camera. In the 3D environment, the actors are the mathematically created objects and characters, and there are digitally simulated lights and a digitally simulated camera. When Hollywood films are made using live action and 3D animation, a mathematical model of the live-action set is created in the computer and the two are perfectly matched, so that when the 3D animation and special effects are created, they will blend seamlessly with the live action. The production process diagram shows the steps for 3D animation (see Figure 11.1)

The 3D World Space and Navigating Through It

The 3D space within which the objects are contained and the images and animation are produced is usually called the world space. It is defined by three planes or axes, *x, y,* and *z.* the normal position for these axes are *y* being up and down, *x* being left and

right, and *z* being in and out. Each axis is divided into units. These units can be feet, inches, meters, or simply units. It is called the Cartesian coordinate system (see Figure 11.2). An object's position in space is determined by three numbers, the *x, y,* and *z* location of the object relative to the origin, which is the intersection of all three axes. The origin is labeled as 0,0,0. If an object is at the origin, a light in front, above, and to the right could be labeled as 100,125,150. A camera directly in from of the object could be labeled as 0,0,100. It is in this way that objects are located in 3D space. Most 3D software packages have an interface where you can see a wire-frame depiction of the space, and they also have a way to mathematically locate and position objects. By positioning objects in 3D space, we have a way to see them and their position.

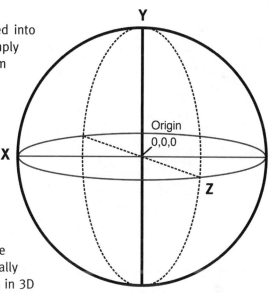

[11.2] A rendering of the Cartesian coordinate system. It is a 3D space that can be defined in its size, units, and orientation.

Because 3D databases, or files, can be very large, most software packages have a wide range of features to facilitate positioning, viewing, and working with objects. These include using grids, making objects visible and invisible, locking objects, and making objects active and inactive.

3D software also has an interface with which you can see your scenes and objects in a variety of ways. These are called windows, and they are normally set up so that you can see the top view, front view, side view, and perspective or camera view. The top, front, and side views are called orthographic projections (see Figure 11.3). That is, all the lines are straight, and no calculations are done for perspective. Orthographic projections are used to position objects and build models. The camera view is drawn by the computer in perspective. This gives the user an idea of how the final image will look. A mathematical camera is used to create this view and the center of the image is called the look-at point.

The Pyramid of Vision

Understanding the pyramid of vision is essential to working with any 3D software (see Figure 11.4). It explains the relationship between the final image generated and the 3D scene, or database. The pyramid starts with the eye of the user looking at the screen. The screen of the computer represents what is called the image plane. The image plane is what the final image or animation will

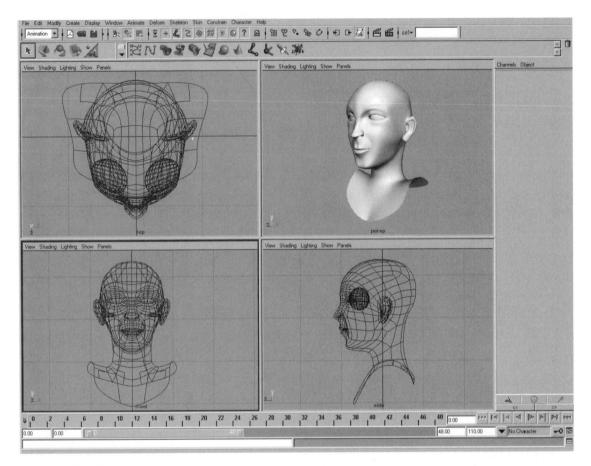

[11.3] A view of windows in Maya software. The Top, Front, Side, and Perspective windows are visible.

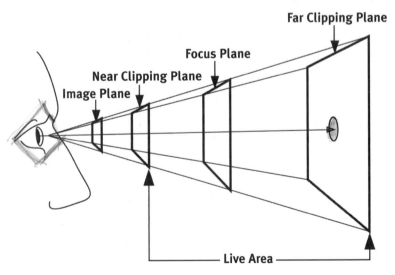

Far Clipping Plane

Focus Plane

Near Clipping Plane

Image Plane

Live Area

[11.4] Once you understand the Pyramid of Vision, you will be able to wrap your mind around 3D space. What gets rendered is the image plane.

DIGITAL Creativity

look like. Although it is seen on the screen, it is also a file. It is the rendering the computer makes of the 3D database. This image has a screen resolution, (e.g., SVGA, 800 by 600) and color, most commonly 24-bit or photographic quality. It also has a resolution, which, for film, is normally 2,000 lines. For Web sites, it can be 640 by 480 or smaller. Quicktime movies are generally rendered at 320 by 240 and 160 by 120.

The eye point and the image plane form the initial part of the pyramid of vision. This space is the actual 3D region defined by the software. The next plane to be encountered is the near-clipping plane. The near-clipping plane defines the front border of the database. Any objects that exist in front of this clipping plane do not get rendered, and any objects that exist behind it do get rendered. Clipping planes are used to define the dimensions of the 3D space used by a particular file. By eliminating unnecessary data from the file, the computer can render it more quickly.

The final plane to be encountered is the far clipping plane. It functions exactly like the near clipping but in reverse. Anything in front of the far clipping plane will be rendered, and anything behind it will not. The area between the clipping planes is where all of the cameras, objects, lights, and animation occur.

Transformations

Another fundamental 3D concept that needs explaining is transformation. Transformations allow actions to take place within the 3D world. The three basic transformations are translation, rotation, and scaling (see Figure 11.5). Transformations are calculated using x, y, z data and numerical values. In translation an object is moved in space in an $x, y,$ or z direction. Rotation can be around the $x, y,$ or z axis, or it can be around the center, or pivot point, of an object. When an object is created, it is given a center point, or pivot point. Most are created at the origin, so 0,0,0 is generally the first pivot point. Scaling means to enlarge or reduce the size of an object. Scaling can be proportional or nonproportional. Proportional scaling makes an object large and maintains its shape. Nonproportional scaling squashes or stretches an object.

Translation
Rotation
Scaling

[11.5] Translation, rotation, and scaling are the three fundamental transformations. They apply to modeling and animation.

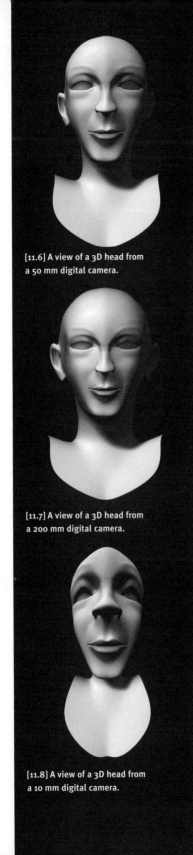

[11.6] A view of a 3D head from a 50 mm digital camera.

[11.7] A view of a 3D head from a 200 mm digital camera.

[11.8] A view of a 3D head from a 10 mm digital camera.

3D Cameras

Now that we have defined the 3D space where the animation will occur, we need to have a way to see it. This is accomplished by a mathematical camera. 3D cameras provide a way to look at the 3D space inside the computer. You are not limited to a single camera and several cameras can be positioned and pointed.

Cameras are placed in 3D space by their *x, y, z,* position, and this is normally defined as the eye point. The next parameter to consider when placing a camera is the look-at point, or where the camera is pointing. The camera position and look-at point create a line. When the eye point is moved, the camera moves but continues to look at the look-at point. When the look-at point moves, the camera follows it. Look-at points can be linked to objects or characters, so that the camera can automatically track them.

The field of view is the angle that defines what the camera sees. This angle has an important effect on how the perspective is drawn by the computer. It is a numerical value and can range from 0 to 360, degrees, but most fields of view range from 10 degrees to 90 degrees. When you create a camera, it is important to check what field of view the camera is using. Picking a field of view is very much like a photographer or filmmaker picking a lens. The choice depends on what the scene is about and how to best visualize it. There are three main types of field of view: normal, wide angle, and telephoto. They can also be defined in millimeters (mm). Figures 11.5-11.7 show how a face can be distorted by just using field of view. The normal head is 50 mm (see Figure 11.5). The flattened head is 200 mm, and the exaggerated head is 10 mm (see Figures 11.6, 11.7, and 11.8).

Normal

This field of view resembles the normal view of the human eye. It ranges from 30 to 60 degrees, corresponding to a 50 mm lens on a 35 mm camera. The vast majority of shots are done with this field of view.

Wide Angle

A wide angle field of view is generally 60 to 90 degrees. A wide angle field of view includes a large amount of the scene into the camera's view. It is used when the director wants the viewer to have an overall view of a scene or environment. This type of view exaggerates the perspective. It causes near objects to look larger, and far objects to look smaller. The most common example of this is a face, where the nose appears disproportionately large, and the ears appear to be very small. An extreme case of a wide angle lens is called the fish eye effect.

Telephoto

The telephoto field of view is a narrow field of view. Typical ranges for this view are 10 to 20 degrees. A telephoto field of view allows the camera to be very distant from the object. It also flattens the perspective and forces the viewer to focus on the object or character the camera is pointed at, since the object is generally separated visually from the background. Telephoto lenses are generally used for portraits or close-ups.

Twist or Roll

The degree to which the camera twists or rolls around the axis between the camera position and the look-at point is also controllable. It can be used to simulate the change of view, for example, of riding a motorcycle or flying airplane.

Point, Lines, and Curves

Points, lines, and cures are the fundamental elements of 3D objects and animation. Once you understand them, this knowledge can be applied to all aspects of 3D, particularly modeling and animation. Surfaces and objects are defined by curves and motion is calculated using curves.

As mentioned above, all objects are located in 3D space by an x, y, z location. A point in space is called a vertex, and several points are called vertices. 3D calculations are time consuming, so it is a good rule to use as few points as possible. This speeds up the calculation process and defines surfaces and motion in a more elegant manner. By using the least amount of points possible it is easier to make changes.

Before we talk about the different kinds of lines and curves, there are a few terms we need to define. One is curve density. This refers to the number of points that are used to define a curve. The higher the curve density, the more points there are. Subdivision is used to define how smoothly the curves are drawn. A low subdivision draws a linear line between each point, and a high subdivision draws a very smooth curve. This becomes important later, when surfaces have

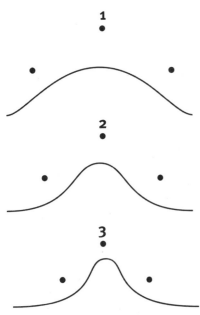

1

2

3

[11.9] As the weighting of the point is increased from 1 to 3, the curve is "pulled" toward the vertex.

been defined. Subdivision surfaces allow for the creation of a simple mathematical object, which generally looks that way. High subdivision allows for more detail to be included in a surface and a more realistic-looking object.

Points can also have a weight attached to them. Weighting is similar to a magnetic effect, that is, the higher the weight, the closer the curve is pulled to the point (see Figure 11.9).

Now that we have defined points, let's see how they can be connected into curves, and later into surfaces. There are five basic types of curves. Not all software packages use every type of curve. Simpler packages use fewer types of curves and vice versa. 3D software packages are generally referred to as either polygonal or spline-based system. Polygons render more quickly and have a lot of other advantages. Spline- (or curve-) based systems offer more sophisticated controls over modeling and animation but take longer to render and require more powerful computers.

Curves are the building blocks of surfaces. When lines and curves are connected, they form a surface. The more complex the curve, the more control you have over the surface. Before we discuss surfaces, it is important to understand the five basic kinds of curves: polyline, cardinal spline, bezier curve, b-spline, and nurb.

The first type of curve is actually not a curve at all, but a straight line drawn between two points. It is often referred to as a polyline. It is used to define the edge of a polygon, the fundamental unit of 3D surfaces. Triangles are the simplest polygons and are preferred because of their mathematical properties.

The second type of curve is referred to as a cardinal spline. In the cardinal spline, the curve passes through the control points. A bezier curve is similar to a cardinal spline, but it has control handles on it that give added control over the curve. A b-spline is an approximating curve that allows for the creation of curved 3D surfaces called bicubic patches. The final type of curve is called a NURB, for nonuniform rational b-spline. NURBS have both control points and edit points on the curve. The control points also have controllable weighting. Now that we have a basic understanding of curves, let's look at modeling. The process starts with points that are connected by lines of curves, which are then connected to create surfaces that compose the 3D model.

DIGITAL | Creativity

Modeling

Modeling is the creation of a 3D mathematical database that, when rendered or drawn by the computer, resembles the desired object. Building a model can be complicated or simple depending on the underlying geometry of an object. To build a model means to create a mathematical database composed of points, lines, curves, and surfaces. Simple objects, like a table, are easy to construct. Organic shapes and complex objects take much longer.

One of the fundamental rules of 3D is to keep the size of your files as small as possible. This reduces the number of calculations required, and in the end it will make your project easier to finish. Think of it this way. There are 30 frames in each second of video, and 1,800 frames in each minute of video. If it takes the computer 2 minutes to render each frame, it will take 3,600 minutes, or 60 hours to render your entire animation. If it takes 20 minutes to render each frame, it will take ten times as long (600 hours) to render

[11.10] A view of the different types of primitives: cone, torus, sphere, cube, and cylinder.

your complete animation. That's a little over 2 days compared to more than 20 days. Now you understand the importance of efficiency. Hollywood production studios have hundreds of processors to complete their 3D animation and special effects. These processors run 24 hours a day, 7 days a week.

The fundamental building blocks of objects are called primitives (see Figure 11.10). Primitives are simple mathematical shapes that can be modified into looking like real or fantastic objects. Sample primitives are spheres, cones, cubes, planes, and toruses. Primitives are fairly simple mathematical equations, so using them to model is recommended whenever possible. Almost anything can be built from primitives. A table can be easily constructed from cubes. Imagine how you could build a simple table. A table can be constructed out of modified cubes. You can flatten the cube and enlarge it to make the top of the table. You can stretch out the cubes and make them thin to make the legs. Faces, heads, and bodies are usually built from a polygonal sphere by pulling the points into the shape you want. If you create a sphere with a lot of points on it, you can pull the points out to make the face, nose, and ears. You can move the points to make the mouth. Small spheres can be used to make the eyes. The use of polygonal models has the advantage of creating continuous surfaces with low polygon counts.

Besides modifying primitives, there are several other ways to model. The most common ones are extrusion, rotation, and building with cross sections. In addition, there are advanced modeling techniques, such as patches, boundary curves, and birail surfaces.

Extrusion works with a polygon that describes an edge or side of an object. It is given dimension by being pulled, or extruded, along a path or curve. For example, if you were to model a key, you would draw the outline of the key and extrude it a short distance to give it depth.

Another way to model is to use to use rotation. Rotation works like a lathe. A shape is revolved around an axis to create an object that has rotational symmetry. A martini glass can be created by rotating the object shown in Figure 11.11 around the y axis. A spring can be created by adding a y displacement for every rotation.

One of the most prevalent approaches to modeling is to use polygons. This is different than using NURBs or curved surfaces. Polygons offer speed when rendering, and for simple models complex surfaces are not really needed. More advanced modeling uses complex curves and surfaces. The approach for advanced modeling

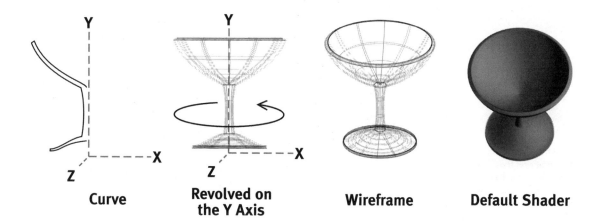

| Curve | Revolved on the Y Axis | Wireframe | Default Shader |

[11.11] A depiction of how to build a martini glass. Learning how to model takes a certain mindset. You need to start looking at objects as their mathematical counterpart. www.viewpoint.com is a great source for models and their catalog is a great reference for how to build them by looking at their structure.

is to connect these complex curves into cross sections, dividing the object vertically or horizontally depending on the shape of the object. With more advanced modeling techniques, you can add or remove cross sections and create more complicated surfaces to get more organic-looking models.

In addition to these kinds of modeling, there are advanced surfaces called procedural surfaces. These are equations that define a complex surface. For example, a cork or a piece of Swiss cheese can be described mathematically rather than building it.

3D Scanning

New technologies have made the use of 3D scanning practical. New software enables you to specify the amount of detail you want when scanning a model. These technologies use laser and infrared methods of inputting data. A small maquette, or sculpture, of the desired object is made and then placed on the scanner. Lasers track the depth information of the object and create a 3D database it. One problem with this method is that the models generally need to be worked on to reduce the number of points, so that they can be animated more easily.

Surfaces

Once a mesh model has been made of an object, it is time to give the object a surface. Surfaces are defined by polygons or curved surfaces that define the area bordered by the points, lines, and

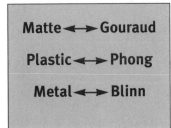

[11.12] The three basic shading models are named after the people who invented them, Gouraud defined a matte surface, Phong defined a plastic surface, and Blinn defined a metallic surface using mathematical descriptions.

curves. Here, triangles are the polygons of choice. Triangles are always planar, so rendering problems are avoided.

Shading Models

Once the surfaces have been defined, they need to be assigned surface properties. Surface properties give the model color, highlights, texture, and so on. Most software packages have libraries of surfaces already defined. Although using these libraries can be a time-saving process, the work will not look unique. It is recommended that one start with a standard library and then modify it for the current project. This will give the animation or illustration a more custom and personal look.

The first step in defining a surface is to give it a shading model. This defines the type of surface that it describes. There are three major types of shading models, with a few other variations (see Figure 11.12). When you look at the object, you try to define the surface and assign it a shading model that most accurately describes that surface.

Flat

Flat shading means that the polygon has a single color. That color is defined by the RGB values assigned to the surface and its interaction with the light source. This type of surface usually looks faceted.

Gouraud

This type of shading gives a matte or dull surface. There are no distinct highlights or a gouraud surface. Examples of a gouraud surface would be felt, carpet, and other dull surfaces.

[11.13] A view of the three shading models. The ball on the left is Blinn, the ball in the middle is Phong, and the ball on the right is Gouraud.

DIGITAL | Creativity

Phong

The word used most frequently to define phong shading is *plastic*. It is very shiny. It can be best described by saying that the surface is a defined color, and the highlight is the color of the light. Cue balls or any shiny plastic appliance are examples of phong surfaces.

Blinn

Blinn shading is best described as a metallic surface. Blinn gives a slightly softer-looking surface, like brushed metal. The highlight is the color of the surface.

The shading model is the most important decision made once a model is complete (see Figure 11.13). After this, there are many parameters and techniques by which a surface can be modified and changed. Some artists work with the surface properties, some work with the color, and others can even describe the surface mathematically, giving fractal surfaces similar to mountains or waters.

Color

The simplest of all surface descriptions is color. There are usually 256 levels of red, green, and blue assigned to surfaces, which gives 16.7 million potential colors. These are generally given as a string of three numbers r, g, b; for example 255, 255, 255 being white.

Surface Properties

A wide range of surface properties can me modified. A list of common surface properties follows (see Figure 11.14).

Specularity

Defines how shiny a surface is. The shinier the surface, the more intense the highlight and effect of light on the surface.

Gloss

Generally used to describe the size of the highlight on an object. A light bulb will give a very small, intense highlight on an object, whereas diffuse light coming in from a window will give a larger and softer highlight.

Diffusion

Defines the amount of light that is reflected back at you. For example, a white sheet will send a large amount of light back from its surface. A spherical surface will not reflect a lot of light.

Reflectivity

Used to describe how much of the reflection map is replacing the color of the surface. A low level of reflectivity will give a hint that the object is reflecting a surface. A high level will give the

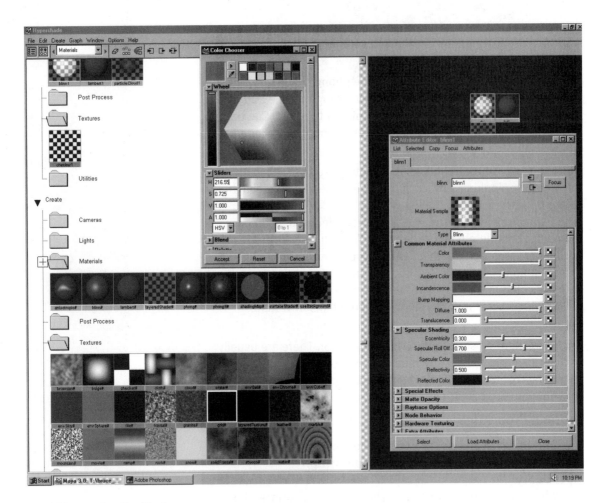

[11.14] This screen from Maya™ software shows the different controls used to modify surfaces.

surface an almost mirror-like effect, where most of the color of the object is replaced with the reflection map.

Transparency

Determines the degree to which an object can be seen through.

Textures

Textures are used extensively in 3D computer graphics. Simple colors are very often inadequate when trying to describe an object. The nature of most objects is that they have a more complex color composition. Images can be applied to objects or to model or modify the surface.

DIGITAL Creativity

Image Maps

Image maps replace the RGB color value of a pixel with the RGB value of an image that has been mapped, or adjusted, to a particular surface. For example, a brown plank can be made to look like wood by scanning a wood pattern and mapping it to the plank. This is the same principle that is used for all maps (see Figure 11.15).

U and *v* values determine how an image is mapped to a surface. The *u* is the direction of the curve and the *v* is the direction of the surface. These values are read when a texture map is compared to a surface and the image can be modified by the *u* and *v* values. For example, an image can be scaled larger or smaller, as in the case of placing a label of a bottle. The map can be moved along the *u* and the *v* direction, as well as being stretched, rotated, and repeated. This gives the artist a great deal of control.

Bump Maps

Bump maps work with the surface normal of a polygon. A surface normal is a vector that is perpendicular to the polygon's surface. By changing the position of the surface normal, you can modify a surface to look as if it had bumps, grooves and may other surface disturbances. A bump map is a normally an 8-bit image with 256 levels of gray. These levels of gray help to turn the surface normal

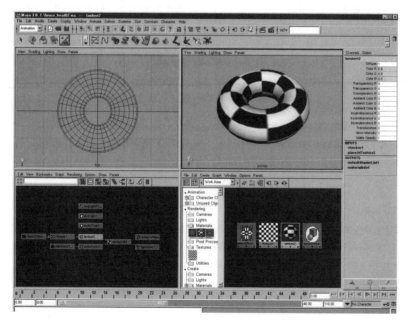

[11.15] This screen refers to the texture-mapping process.

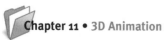

either toward or away from the light source. One way of looking at it is that the bump map is creating artificial "shapes" on the surface. The surface of a golf ball or potato are irregular. By having a bump map that mimics the pattern, when rendered, it will give the illusion of having depth.

Displacement Maps

This technique allows the actual geometry of an object to be modified by an image. For example, an indented logo can easily made by applying a black-and-white displacement map to a polygon mesh.

Opacity Maps

Opacity maps use the color value of an object to determine if the pixel is transparent or opaque. For an irregular surface, an opacity map can be applied, and the areas without color will not be rendered.

Transparency Maps

Transparency maps work in a variety of ways. The first is that they add transparency to an object. However, this transparency can be modified in many ways. For example, if you have a green bottle but want to place a label on it, a transparency map can be used. Another example of a transparency map is placing a reflection onto a surface.

Reflection and Environmental Maps

There are several types of environmental maps. Reflection maps are usually single images. A reflection map is used to give the idea that a surface is reflective (e.g., a chrome logo flying over a surface). Environmental maps add realism to a shiny object when it is moving through space. Raytracing is a rendering process that emulates the natural bouncing of light. Unfortunately, it takes a very long time to render, since there are a lot of additional calculations. One way to simulate ray tracing is to use a cubic environmental map. This map represents the top, bottom, and sides of an environment. The images are the mapped onto the surface of an object to give it a more realistic look. Chrome is the most notable example of this. When looking at a chrome reflection, the top is blue, because it is reflecting the sky. The middle of the reflection would depend on the environment the object is in, and the bottom might be black, to reflect the color of the road. As an object passes through this cubic environment, moving reflections are created, giving the illusion of reality and ray tracing.

Lighting

Lighting is just as important as the surface properties in determining the quality and production value of an image. If the end desire is realism, careful creation of textures and attention to lighting will add much to a scene. The fundamentals of lighting transfer from cinema and television to the 3D digital environment. Before we describe techniques of lighting in a 3D environment, let's look at the different types of lights.

Color and Color Temperature

As with surfaces, lights can be given any color. Examples, like theatrical lights, neon signs, and Christmas lights are easy. However, the concept of color temperature must be understood to fully understand lighting. Our eyes adjust to lighting to compensate for any variations. For example, right when you put on or take off sunglasses, you notice a distinct change in how things look, but shortly thereafter, the world returns to normal.

Types of Lights

There are several types of digital lights. Not all software packages have them, but the following lights are fairly common (see Figure 11.16).

Ambient

Normally, there is an overall level of illumination (e.g., morning, afternoon, and evening). This is usually described as the ambient light level in a 3D software. Once the ambient light level has been defined, it is important to get believable and realistic lighting effects.

Point Light

An omnilight is sometimes called a point light. It radiates light in all directions in a spherical manner. There is normally what is called intensity, or near value, and within this range, the light has a constant level. The fall off, or far level, indicates when the effect of light tapers off until it has no effect. The size of the sphere depends on the intensity of the light. For example, a candle would have a small sphere of influence, whereas the sun has an enormous sphere of influence. Point lights do not cast shadows.

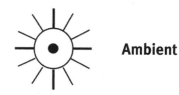
Ambient

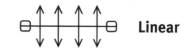
Spot

Linear

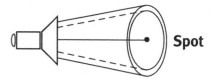
Volumetric

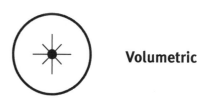
Area

Directional

Point

[11.16] Symbols for the different types of lights. The names and symbols are not the same for all 3D software packages, but the lights do function in a similar way. For example, a point light might be called an omni light.

Spot

A spot light is the kind of light you would see in a rock concert or a Broadway play. It is conical. Spot lights in some ways resemble a camera; that is, the spotlight has a look-at point and the size of the cone of light resembles the field of view of the camera. Spotlights for theatrical applications in concerts have a very narrow cone, ranging from 2 to 10 degrees. One of the important elements of a spot light is that they can cast shadows because the light has a specific direction. Therefore, spot lights are used very often in 3D animation.

Directional Lights

Directional lights emit light in which the rays of the light are parallel. Direction lights are used to illuminate a large area and give the effect of even illumination.

Linear Lights

Some software packages have linear lights. The most common example of this would be the fluorescent light.

Lighting Techniques

When creating light in a 3D scene, there are many things to take into consideration. One of the best ways to start lighting a scene is to adjust the ambient light level to where you think it would be best. Then place the key light, or main light, in position and turn it on and off to see what effect it has on the scene. Take cues from the storyboard and production sketches. These often have a specific lighting scenario in mind. Next, add fill lights to add detail to the shadows.

When working with lights, it is important to pay attention to the color of light, both from the highlight and from the shadow point of view. Very often shadows have color. They are not always gray.

Animation

Animation is intimately related to the storytelling of the animation you are working on. Text, logos, and other object animation are more mathematical in nature. The goal of character animation is for the viewer to see the character as alive and almost forget that it is a computer image. This is the real goal of character animation: to make it come alive. References for character animation come from videotape or storyboards. Animators also use a mirror to act the scenes out for reference. It is now standard procedure for Hollywood animated film to videotape the actors as they record their voices of the characters. These videotapes become reference performances, whereby the animator can add nuances of character from the actor into the acting of the character. Excellent examples are Robin Williams in *Alladin* and Woody Allen in *Antz*. The physical behavior of the characters mimics that of the actors who supplied their voices.

Planning Animation

Most beginning 3D animators tend to go to the computer too early, before the animation is planned and thought through. In an educational environment, this is very easy to do, since machine time is not carefully controlled. In the real world of commercials and feature animation, most of the planning is finished before a computer animator even sees an assignment. We've discussed the production pipeline in detail previously, but let's review what a computer animator would receive.

In a small studio, the person doing the animation is often involved in many of the other preproduction tasks. In a large studio, a computer animator only does that: animate. In the first scenario, the minimal amount of material an animator would receive would be the storyboards and a sound track. The storyboards tell the animator what is expected during a scene and the soundtrack will give the timing of the animation. This is particularly important with lip sync.

Timing and Exposure Sheets

Timing and the making of exposure sheets is generally the task of the director, assistant director, or in some cases the sound editor. Timing is something that takes a lifetime to develop. Making a character animate to the point of it actually feeling alive is what all animators strive for. The more experience you have, the better you are at it. One good way of figuring out timing is to use a video camera. Although you may not look like the character you are animating, if you act out the motions live, you will then have a series of frame counts that can be applied to the motion you are seeking. Another method is to do a really tight animatic, so that the action is well timed during this part of the preproduction process. Once the motion is transferred into the computer, you can see the data in graphs and further refine it mathematically (see Figure 11.17).

Layout and Camera Composition

Layout begins when the storyboards have been approved, the models have been built, and the basic lighting has been created. The process of layout is to provide a more precise and exact view of each scene. This is done by manipulating the camera to the proper position, focal length, and viewpoint.

The 3D camera acts very much like a typical video camera, except that the director has total control over all of the parameters of the camera. The only thing that a computer-created camera lacks is a glass lens. Otherwise, it behaves just like a physical camera. There are several parameters to consider when using a computer-created camera. The first is position. When a 3D scene is created, there are

[11.17] This screen grab shows animation curves. By changing these curves, you can modify the motion of the objects.

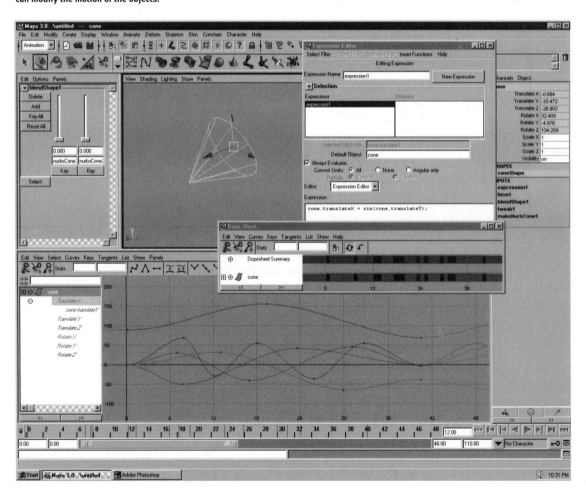

DIGITAL | Creativity

generally two approaches, depending on the budget and the type of project being created. The first and more time-consuming is to build the entire 3D database or environment within which the camera will operate and then decide where to place the camera. The second approach is to do more planning during the preproduction phase and build only the models and environments that the camera is going to see. This is reminiscent of the old western films, where only the fronts of the buildings were built.

Character Animation

The process of character animation for 3D animation is similar to the 2D process only in the beginning stages. Once the character is designed, the process is much different. In 2D character animation, everything is drawn by hand and the computer is used only for the scanning, painting, and production of the final movie. For 3D animation, the character is animated within the computer and nothing is drawn by hand, expect the texture maps and possibly the backgrounds.

Design

Design of 3D characters requires an intimate understanding of the capability of the software package you are using. Simple characters can be made from primitives. More complex characters require more sophisticated modeling techniques. For feature films and special effects, detailed sculptures of the characters are made and then scanned into the computer using 3D scanning techniques. These scans are then manipulated to reduce the point count and make them more easily animated and rendered.

No matter what techniques you are using, your characters must be believable. There are several factors to consider when creating a 3D character. What is their role in the story or animation? What level of detail is required? Start by drawing your characters in different poses. Then focus on key moments in the story. Character design is an art that takes many years to perfect.

Advanced Animation Techniques

Advanced techniques are beyond the scope of this book, but three commonly used methods are hierarchical animation, inverse kinematics, and particle systems.

Hierarchical Animation

Hierarchies allow you to link objects together so that they can be animated both as a group and independently. For example, a body is a

hierarchy. The body is generally at the top, so that when it moves, all the limbs and head move with it. But since the arms are below the body, they can be animated independently, then the forearm, then the hand, then the fingers.

Inverse Kinematics

A variation of hierarchical animation is inverse kinematics. Instead of the animation happening from the top down, it happens in reverse, from the bottom up. For inverse kinematics to work properly, limits and precise movements of the parts need to be defined mathematically before the animation starts. For example, a head may rotate only a few degrees, rather than spinning in a total circle. By defining the limits in advance, when you do choose to move the hand, the arm and body will move along with it.

Both hierarchical animation and inverse kinematics have specific applications. There are also times when you must break the hierarchy to get the animation to work the way you want it to. The general rule of computer animation is to plan it carefully, design your environments and characters so that they can be animated easily, and take every short cut and trick you know to get it done. Being a purist in the 3D animation world will often get you into corners that are difficult to get out of. Animation is a problem-solving process, not a purely mathematical one. The desired result is to make the technology transparent and have the audience believe that your character has a personality and emotions. You want them to forget that they are watching computer animation and become involved with the character and the story.

Particle Systems

Particle systems are used for a variety of purposes. One of the best things about particle systems is that they generate their own geometry. For example, if you want to simulate rain in a 3D animation system, it would be impossible to animate every rain drop. This is where particle systems come in. They can be used to simulate rain, water, fire, sparks, and a whole host of other effects.

A few basic elements of a particle system are as follows:

Source

Particles are emitted from a specific source. This can be a point, a plane, or other geometry.

Number

You can determine the number of particles that are emitted. For example, is it raining softly or really pouring?

Geometry

What are the particles made of? Are they primitives? A specific geometry?

Color

Particles can be given a color. This color can be animated over time, if desired.

Rendering

Rendering is what the computer does when it takes all the information from a 3D scene and converts it into a 2D image. You can define the size or resolution of a render, the quality of the render, insert a background over which the render is composited, and so on. Most render menus have a wide range of options. Render your images in the desired final format; for example, video, film, or Quicktime format.

Summary

This chapter was a very basic introduction to 3D modeling and animation. The most important information to take away from this chapter is the process by which 3D animation is produced. Like most digital production processes, it has several distinct steps. If you follow these steps, you will end up with a much better product than by sitting down to the computer with an idea in your head and trying to get it out without a good plan.

We also covered all the basic elements of 3D theory. It is important to understand theory so that when you build your models and environments, the software will work in an efficient manner. Building models with too many polygons and lighting scenes with too many lights is not the proper way to work. If you are serious about 3D, refer to and study the books mentioned in the bibliography and learn the software inside out. Then work on your narrative and storytelling skills, so that your work has some meaning for those who watch it.

BIBLIOGRAPHY

Isaac Victor Kerlow, *The Art of 3-D Computer Animation and Imaging,* second edition, John Wiley & Sons, Inc., New York, NY, 2000. www.wiley.com

Isaac's book is becoming the standard text for 3D theory. It is very comprehensive and has an impressive collection of images. After reading this book, you will have a deeper understanding of 3D animation and imaging, and this will make your approach to this complex field much easier.

George Maestri, *Digital Character Animation 2, Volume I: Essential Techniques,* New Riders Publishing, Indianapolis, IN, 1999.

This is by far the best book on digital character animation. It is packed with easy-to-understand animation techniques. I have used this and Isaac's book as my two main textbooks for the Theory of Computer Animation classes I teach at the Hong Kong Arts Centre. If you buy only two books, these are the ones to buy.

Jeremy Birn, *Digital Lighting and Rendering,* New Riders Publishing, Indianapolis, IN, 2000.

This is a new book on this topic. It is part of a series edited by George Maestri and also highly recommended. The importance of lighting and rendering cannot be overempahsized in 3D. Although much attention is paid to animation, it is the lighting and rendering that makes your work look believable.

Jane Ashford and John Odam, *Getting Started with 3D: A Designer's Guide to 3D Graphics and Illustration,* Peachpit Press, Berkeley, CA, 1998.

This is a basic introduction to 3D from the still image and illustration viewpoint. If you are not concerned with animation, I highly recommend this book.

Terrence Masson, *CG 101: A Computer Graphics Industry Reference,* New Riders Publishing, Indianapolis, IN, 1999.

This is a reference book filled with definitions of all the terms you are likely to encounter with 3D. It also has a detailed history of the studios and a description of the different job categories. His Web site, www.cg101.com, is a good reference as well.

EXERCISES

1. **Create a 3D still life painting. Take some simple objects, add texture maps and work with the lighting carefully to create a high-resolution image reminiscent of the old masters. For example, a collection of fruit, or a wine bottle or glass. Refer to old paintings for ideas, but make it uniquely your own. Focus on composition, form and lighting.**

2. **Do a simple animation using an elongated sphere or other simple shape. Give it personality and character, and use a simple one joke situation. For example, a hot dog being chased by a bun, or an ice cube stuck in a rain shower.**

DIGITAL | Creativity

Joseph Nechvatal, Ph.D.

INTERVIEW

Digital Artist

Joseph Nechvatal has been an internationally exhibiting artist since the early 1980s. Before becoming involved with new media, his interests included drawing, writing, performance, video, and photo-mechanical activities. The symbolic power of new media is what attracted him to it. His one-person exhibitions have included Galerie Multimedia, Paris; Galerie Karin Sachs, Munich; and Universal Concepts Unlimited in New York. His work is in the collections of the Israel Museum, Museum of Modern Art, Museum of Contemporary Art, and the National Gallery of Art. He has been published in *Artforum, Unsound, New Observations* and *Real Life* magazines. He is the Parisian editor and correspondent for Rhizome Internet, Talkback!, The Thing, and Intelligent Agent. He has received grants from the National Endowment for the Arts and the New York Foundation for the Arts. He holds a Ph.D. from the University of Wales, and an MFA from Cornell University.

What aspect of your background have you found most helpful in your transition to new media?

My interdisciplinary (expanded) arts approach.

Who has influenced you most, within the field of new media art?

Georges Bataille.

What do you see as the important milestones in the development of new media?

Much of the disappearance, dedefinition and dematerialization of the art object that went beyond Modernism in search for a total art developed out of the visual spectator's participation called for in viewing Op Art: a hard-edge geometrical movement that flourished in the early-1960s (largely inspired by various optical experiments of Marcel Duchamp) in the work of Jesus-Rafael Soto, Bridget Riley, the GRAV group, Yayoi Kusama, Yaacov Agam, Pol Bury, Josef Albers, Marian Zazeela, and Victor Vasarely, among others.

Describe your creative process.

The basic premise behind my computer-robotic assisted paintings is the rhizomatic exploration of host/parasite omnijectivity (the metaphysical concept stemming from the discoveries of quantum physics, which teaches us that mind, previously considered the subjective realm, and matter, previously considered as the objective realm, are inextricably linked) under the influence of today's high-frequency, electronic, computerized environment.

Moreover, host/parasite viral encounters with the codes of computer simulation create the ribald opportunity for transgression of conventional limitations. In the viral rupture, thought detaches itself from the host/parasite order and authority of the old sign and topples down into the realm of the virtual, of imagination, of contradictory fantasy, and into sublime nonknowledge.

How do you begin a new media project?

For me, art is largely a matter of problemization. In its quintessence it is about dealing with differences within totalities.

How has the use of new media and the use of the computer affected this process?

Art is always a matter of inventing aesthetic sensations linked to concepts. Art is essentially a mental prosthetic then. The function of this prosthetic art is to create by extenuation different aesthetic sensations linked to concepts—what are called percepts. These percepts have affects that sway.

What are the major constraints you have encountered in working with new technology?

They are all related to traditional perspectivism being imposed in the tools. For me right now in the year 2000, art is about a personal investigation into perspectivism under the conditions of virtuality—conditions that are not quite historically conditioned yet. Technology is a rapidly changing and complex medium. Because of the diverse skill sets required to work in the field it is often necessary to collaborate. What effect does this have on the creative process? The collaborative act enmeshes and contravenes, alters, and disrupts the mundanity of communications in an inexorable, unrecognizable, and chimerical way.

Describe your most recent fine arts/personal project.

Satyricon 2000: A mingling of the virtual, the aesthetic, and the sexual. The work's general *fin-de-siècle* ornamental excess gives to us a metaphor for the current computational conditions of our seeing-and perhaps for our expansive conditions of parasite/host being. In the rising and collapsing of alternative visualizations and unordered revelations, the circuits of the mind find an occupation exactly congruent with my art's immanent structure.

What software do you use?

Director, Photoshop, Hyper-Card, Basic.

What hardware do you use?

Apple and painting machines.

What advice would you offer to people entering the field of new media and technology?

Learn everything about art because the non-knowledge of art is certainly the most erudite, the most aware, and the most conscious area of our consciousness.

Where they should focus their attention?

On learning everything about art.

What is most lacking in the education of design and new media students?

Philosophy.

What are the important elements of a new media portfolio?

Beauty and lack of cynicism.

Where do you see the Internet heading?

Toward an immersive VR-Net.

What are your favorite Web sites/URLs?

Rhizome Internet at http://www.rhizome.org
http://www.dom.de/

On-line Glossary of Theory and Criticism for the Visual Arts at
http://www.arts.ouc.bc.ca/fiar/glossary/gloshome.html
The Virtual Studios VR Worlds at
http://www.vrworlds.com/more-d~l/vssofar.html
Art+Com at http://www.artcom.de
Lacan Online at
http://www.hydra.umn.edu/lacan/gaze.html
Virtual Reality Applications WWW Virtual Library at
http://www.iao.fhg.de/Library/vr/applications-en.html
Glossary of Virtual Reality Terminology at
http://ijvr.uccs.edu/manetta.htm
Dictionary of Philosophy of Mind at
http://www.artsci.wustl.edu/~philos/MindDict/
The Catholic Encyclopedia at
http://www.csn.net/advent/cathen/cathen.html
ECIT: Electronic Compendium of Images and Technology
http://mondrian.princeton.edu/art430/art430.html
The Leonardo World Wide Web Site at
http://www-mitpress.mit.edu/Leonardo/home.html

What is your take on the development of interactivity?

Interactivity exploits the formal materiality of the immersive medium. Interactivity in synthetic-immersive applications is not solely the capability of navigating the virtual environment (VE) but is the capacity of the user to perform alterations in that environment. Moving the sensors and enjoying freedom of movement do not in themselves ensure an interactive alliance between a user and an environment; however, even if the user derives sufficient satisfaction from the exploration of the surrounding domain which is intended to "engulf." Full interactivity entails unrestricted movement at will within a virtual environment, but also, most importantly, when actions taken within the VE create momentarily enduring consequences.

The ability to randomly access any portion of an animation, or work, is unique to multimedia and allows interactivity. How has this changed your creative process, and what are the special considerations that this creates?

It makes art comparable to random access memory, which may or must undergo continual reconfigurations.

How important is programming in the work you do?

Very. Computational tools for transforming, combining, altering, and analyzing images are as essential to the digital artist as brushes and pigments are to a painter, and an understanding of them is the foundation of the craft of digital imaging.

What do you see as the most limiting aspects of the present technology, and how do you expect this to change in the future?

Nonimmersive VR, in a desktop virtual environment, is when you are looking at a 3D rendered image on a screen in front of you. Typically it is a conventional computer monitor onto which a 3D environment is rendered. It is the ability to perceive the environment from within which is the consequential property that immersive ontology brings to informational interchanges (along with its revised evaluations of self from bound to boundless) and which distinguishes immersive art from art graphics and from flat, 2D, window-like framed spatial representations.

What are your thoughts on digital fine art?

I very much like to work with the digital image in its ultimate elements, the immaterial abstract information of pixels, and I like very much the world-wide transportable dimension of the

Internet, where the digital data-stream travels at the speed of light—but I also like to see a large scaled iconic image just sitting still on a canvas so I can silently reflect on it and move within the work in natural light at my leisure with customary unrestrictions to my bodily movements.

Who are your favorite computer artists?

Victoria Vesna, Frank Gillete, Bill Seaman.

What is the future of digital fine art?

Recently, particularly interesting to me is the dialectic between theory and digital fine art practice, and between the symbolic and the imaginary. Can a digital artwork combine explicitly theoretical discourse with the intuitive practice? Can digital fine art show that the two are not "opposed"? The keyword here may be *explicit*. Without it, it seems that any discourse with pretensions of explanation is theoretical. In this sense, almost all conceptual art has reconciled theory and practice.

On the other hand, however, only discourses that situate themselves within a theoretical frame can claim to be "explicitly" theoretical. In other words, for a discourse to claim an explicitly theoretical status, it is necessary to hold a continuity through various rhetorical effects such as the use of certain jargon with other discourses of "recognized" theory. Since there is still no such framework within to place digital fine art alone, I think it is very hard for any digital fine art to play the role of explication. In other—very plain—words, digital fine art can do theory, but it cannot call it so. Because theory, as a practice, has defined itself in explicit exclusion, not so much of intuitive practice, but of art.

What is the outlook for the future of digital media?

There has always been an idea of the virtual, whether it was grounded in mysticism, abstract analytical thinking, or magical and romantic fantasy. All of these approaches have shaped and manipulated invisible worlds accessible only through the imagination, and in some cases these models have been given ontological privilege. What has made contemporary concepts and ideologies of the virtual possible is that these preexisting systems of thought have expanded out of the imagination, and manifested themselves in the development and understanding of technology. I expect more along these lines to follow.

What careers will be important?

Creative ones. For me, the theory of "virtuality" and "interactivity" is of extreme interest to the careers question because it is primarily in that theoretical generation of a space of action within a viewer's head where the link between exceptional moments and art can be established.

What emerging technologies will become important?

Immersive VR-Interneting ones because here we will have a virtual depth that enfolds the imaginative capacity into exceptional immersive moments.

Zach Schlappi

INTERVIEW

A Graduate Student's Perspective

All of the other interview subjects in this book are well-known professional artists and educators. Since many people will use this book as a textbook, I thought it would be valuable to get an honest statement from one of my former students, who is now working as a technical director at Blue Sky Studios. Zach came into my Open Studio class with all the enthusiasm and energy of a first-semester graduate student. We discussed and critiqued his work weekly in class, and I witnessed first-hand his trials and tribulations. Needless to say, he has made it, and I thought his reflections on his graduate school experience and a look at his work would be helpful and inspirational

I knew nothing about computer animation when I enrolled in the School of Visual Arts. Well, that's a lie. I knew a little. To increase my chances for acceptance, I took a six-month training course in Softimage and submitted a reel to supplement my appli-

cation package. It was, perhaps, the second smartest thing I ever did. The smartest thing I did was to choose not to have humans in my thesis. These two important decisions helped me considerably in achieving my goals, not only as an artist, but as a successful graduate student.

Many students, including myself, did not know the full consequences of taking a two-year graduate degree in computer animation. We considered computer animation a generic term. Within a few months, some of us realized how complex and absorbing computer animation really is. My first semester was spent understanding that principle. In spite of all the sundry courses offered, if I was going to be a successful student I had to focus.

Courtesy of Zachary Schlappi.

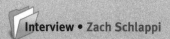

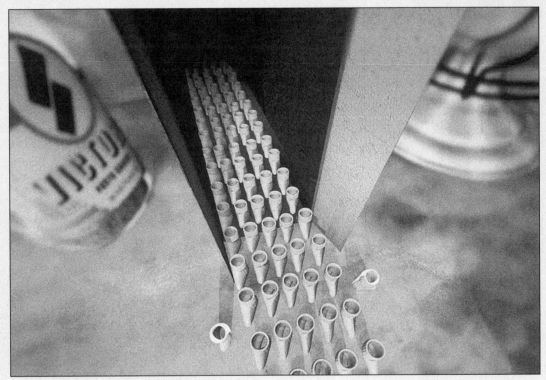

Courtesy of Zachary Schlappi.

When other students asked how I chose lighting, I replied, "I asked myself this, what do you want to be doing at four o'clock in the morning?" I also felt that lighting was the sole responsibility of the technical director, and that along with compositing and postprocessing, it was the icing on the cake. Animation and modeling and texturing were important, but it is lighting that fully realizes the image's potential. Without light, there is nothing to see.

At the time, my first love with lighting began with two moments. The first was in a technical director's issues course, when one of the instructors pointed me to a beautiful architectural Web site called lightscape. The second

was watching a former SVA teacher's first Oscar-winning film, *Bunny*. This film set a personal benchmark as to what I considered the new level of excellence. From that point, I sacrificed everything else to spend an entire semester learning how to light. Because I knew something about computer animation and Softimage before grad school, I could quickly build various simple environments to try out my lighting skills. However, I knew nothing about animation or complex modeling.

I was fortunate to eventually choose pasta as my main character, because it didn't require me to follow my colleagues along that torturous road of modeling a human being, rigging it,

DIGITAL|Creativity

Courtesy of Zachary Schlappi.

few controls, for it is just a cylinder, I could animate with ease and speed. I felt I was taking a gamble in not using humans, that the environmental models were simple and it wouldn't be in color, so I was forced to focus on the most important aspect of my thesis: the look and feel. In most cases, lighting ends up being an afterthought in many students' theses; in mine, it was the driving force.

and animating it. No human characters meant no expectations of human movement. I wasn't locked into imitating reality. Liberation. No one has ever seen pasta march, and with very

Pasta for War was not a great technical achievement. I used Softimage™ software (when most students had switched to the newer Maya™ software), animated with simple controls; I

Courtesy of Zachary Schlappi.

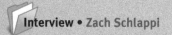

didn't even have sophisticated special effects. Due to time, I gave up depth-of-field, caustics, and radiosity; I had to fake it all in textures, sly lighting techniques, and postprocessing hacks. However, the single most important tool I did build for myself was my version of a distributed render. Few students cared to learn enough about C-shell scripting to achieve this, but for me, it was a necessity. In a matter of seconds, I could render up to 4 different scenes on 12 machines from a single shell. Although using so many machines at once did not make me the most popular student, many were impressed with my dedication. I had a very simple pipeline that involved burning all my frames at each production phase onto compact disks. This method not only allowed me to archive, but I could read my frames from any machine on the network, should it go down. Also, the collective local disk space for students could not possibly hold all my 1/4th film resolution frames at once, so I had to have 40% of my images on disc at any given time. To this day, I have a box of more than 500 compact disks sitting in my closet in Massachusetts.

By the fourth semester, I was so focused on lighting and technique that it nearly drove the spirit of graduate school out of my heart. The industry had drastically changed while we were in school, and I was willing to sacrifice everything for that first studio job. *Pasta for War* was becoming what it was about: heartlessness, advertising, and total consumption—technical skills can be learned by anyone, given enough time. I didn't learn to value myself as an artist until the last few months of school. This was the turning point of my graduate, if not my professional, career. At this time an instructor and a student forced me to come to terms with the fact that I was an artist. As painful as it was, I had to take an even bigger gamble and take my piece to an aesthetic place no one had gone before. When I started to take my rendered frames into postprocessing and write them to the Accom for the first time, I realized I was not here to just get a job, I was here to hone my artistry. I was here to become a better artist.

Although this principle is taught to us, it is something that we must find in ourselves, alone. Some may find it and others may think they found it, and still, others happily aren't worried by it. I found a will, meaning, and purpose, and as clichéd as that may sound, it has given my life momentum. Because I knew a little about 3D before entering graduate school and did not embark on a technical safari, I had more time to realize and focus on more important truths: that computers are just tools for the artist, and, like the graduate program at the School of Visual Arts, your art and life is not what get you out of it, but what you put into it.

✓ Resume

✓ Portfolio

✓ Exhibiting Your Personal Creative Work

✓ Maintaining a Personal Web Site

✓ Employment

✓ Professional Organizations

✓ Health

Chapter Twelve

DIGITAL | Creativity

Professional Issues

This chapter deals with the development of a professional career. Success is not measured by what software you know or how much money you make. Depending on the circles you travel in, success can be defined in a variety of ways. On a personal level, success should mean happiness and doing what you like for a career—and getting paid well for it. The digital media revolution has been a boon for creative people and artists with a knack for technology. The need for technically literate talent has never been so great. Digital tools are also pushing the creative envelope into new territory. Hopefully this book has inspired and directed you to being creative with digital tools. The next step is

to market your skills and to put you in the right place at the right time so that you can take advantage of it.

Resume

A resume serves as a brief introduction to your potential employers and clients. It should contain only the essential information about you, and often people have multiple resumes for different situations (e.g., freelancing, full-time employment, artist statements, different job roles). Your resume should be one page, faxable, and easily readable. The job titles should be in bold, followed by the company name and date. At the top of the resume should be your professional objective. State clearly what it is that you want to do. Be honest and realistic, and your professional experience below should support your moving into that role. Next, list your specific skills, both creative and with the software that you know. Many companies are looking for people to work with a particular area of their company and perhaps to work with a specific set of software tools. If those keywords are right at the top of your resume, you will have a better chance of getting an interview. Your job experience should be two or three sentences that describe exactly what you did on that job. You can list additional information at the bottom of your resume, such as relevant hobbies and language literacy.

Portfolio

Your portfolio should represent the best samples of your creative work. Portfolios can take many shapes (e.g., print, Web site, CD, DVD, etc.). However, you should always have a print portfolio to complement any other media. This is definitely a good idea, and it's a great idea when you do show up to an interview and they do not have any media devices handy. Although there are no hard and fast rules for portfolios, there are several recommendations.

It should have no more than 15 to 20 samples of your work. Always put the strongest work first. Decisions about your work are generally made during the first two minutes of a portfolio review. If you do survive the first few minutes, then there is some interest in your work. You should always try to tailor your portfolio to the particular interview. If your portfolio is not bound but contains individual laminated samples, this is easy to do. Some people do not use the ring binder portfolios for this reason. In a ring binder portfolio, you always have two images back to back. When using this type of portfolio, try to put images that complement each other, so that you do not have to keep changing the page. The general rule of thumb for a portfolio is that if the client sees what they want to buy in your portfolio, then you have the assignment or job. If your portfolio differs radically from their expectations, you will not get the assignment. Keep your portfolio up-to-date and always get samples of your work, if you can.

Exhibiting Your Personal Creative Work

This topic was put right after the portfolio and near the front of this chapter for a reason. Creativity is the most valued commodity in the new media business. Many people can learn the software and have the creative skills needed to produce commercial work, but the people who rise to the top are the most creative ones. Many educational institutions teach software but not creativity. Knowing the tools is not enough, and producing a creative body of work to earn a degree and then only focusing on commercial work is not enough. Enough of the soap box, but I hope I made my point extremely clear. Your creativity is the cornerstone around which your professional career is built. To neglect it is to weaken the foundation of the life you have built and to risk losing your enthusiasm and creative edge.

My creative interests are diverse and include digital art, music, poetry, photography, video, etc. Color plates 84 and 85 show my most recent creative work. I am now exploring interactive music. I am working with multi-channel music and audio in an interactive environment, allowing people to create different audio environments by interacting with sculpture. This approach combines my interest in art and music, as well as pushing me to break new ground in composing music. Most music is still stereo. Movies use surround sound, which has five channels. This approach gives me the freedom to use any number of channels depending on the environment and form of the sculpture. Even though I am well along in my career, the enjoyment I get from creative projects is just as great, maybe even more so, than when I was in graduate school.

The great thing about personal creative work is that it is completely your own, governed by no deadlines or commercial pressures, and it is relaxing, personally rewarding, and fun. Dedicate some time each week, or at least on a monthly basis, to continue your own work. It is a good idea to set some goals (e.g., one exhibition or show a year). This will give you something to work toward. By exhibiting your work, you will be gaining the self-satisfaction of being an artist and continuing your personal evolution and growth.

Maintaining a Personal Web Site

A personal Web site is a great way to exhibit your work. You are completely in control, have no restrictions, and you have a built-in worldwide audience. Personal Web sites are very easy to build and maintain. Your creative work can also be part of a more ambitious personal site. Typical personal sites have contact information, a resume, portfolio, and a wide range of other elements. As you complete your work, you can add it to your site.

Although a personal site can give you a lot of satisfaction, professional exhibition opportunities offer more. First of all, they build your professional reputation and public persona. Most professionals make a point of entering exhibitions and competitions, and it is expected of most creative academics. By putting your work in a public forum and getting recognition for it, you are further establishing yourself as a creative individual. This can come back to you in a number of ways. In a best-case scenario, you will sell your work and receive funds that can help you in any number of ways. Potential employers or headhunters may see your work and offer you a job or freelance work. Your current employer sees your work and knows that you are the type of person who takes their creative work seriously, thus gaining you points when raise time comes around. Finally, and to me the most important, you are expressing your soul. Creative self-expression is a gift that not everyone has, and if you have that gift you should use it.

Employment

There are generally two kinds of employment—staff positions and freelancing. Which one you choose depends on your personal preference and goals.

Staff Positions

Staff positions are by far the most common type of employment, particularly for people just coming out of school. The need for talented artists who are technically literate is huge, and the turn of the millenium is a great time to be graduating and to be a creative person. There are myriad staff positions available, and I will describe the process by which you can obtain one and keep it.

Job Searching

The first step in finding a job is obviously to start looking. Where do you look? Most colleges and universities have a placement office, and many companies come on campus near the end of the academic year to recruit. You can also do a lot of job searching on-line. Most large studios and a great percentage of small studios use on-line resume services or have a specific part of their Web sites dedicated to listing openings in their company and the type of people they are looking for. Once you do start some serious research on the Web, you will find that the digital media industry, although large, is actually a tight community. Although there are hundreds, if not thousands, of Web design firms, they generally break down into certain categories. There are the major firms, the midsized firms, and the smaller boutique studios. Depending on your personality, you will be attracted to one of these categories. If you like doing very specific tasks, you will be drawn to a large firm. If you like to do a little of everything, you will be drawn to a small company.

Freelancing

A typical description of a freelancer is a person who works on a per project basis for a wide range of different companies. This can vary greatly, depending on the person. Some people work what is called "full-time" freelance, where they work at one company and move from project to project. Other freelancers work for several clients. Others have a sales representative, or "rep," who contracts the work for the freelancer and takes usually takes a percentage fee from the work they give to the freelancer. Using a rep has its advantages and disadvantages. Reps generally handle the initial contact with the client and the selling. When a freelancer gets a job from the rep, they are generally quite clear as to the price and expectations. The rep can also act as an intermediary for the business aspects of the job. This gives the freelancer more time to focus on the creative issues. Some freelancers prefer this type of arrangement. In essence, a freelancer is running a small business, but generally freelancers remain individuals, rather than expand into small companies.

Freelancing can be quite lucrative. Freelancers generally fall under the "work for hire" category. That means you generally do not retain the copyright to your work, and the client also is not responsible for your benefits, taxes, and so on. Since the client is making money off of your labor and does not have to carry the other financial burdens, fees for freelance work tend to be much higher than if you were a staff artist, although remember that benefits can be worth as much as 30% above what your annual salary is. Security is always a concern with freelancers. Although the ideal situation is to have a

steady flow of work, it generally does not work out that way. Since you want to maximize your income, you generally will accept most assignments that come along. There will also be times when work is scarce, for example, during the summer vacation period and the year-end holidays. What ends up happening is that you might be working 12 to 24 hours a day for weeks on end and then go a month without any work. The key to this is to have faith and to market yourself constantly.

Professional Organizations

Being an active member of professional organizations is a critical component of any creative person's career. It puts you in an environment where you are in contact with people with similar goals and interests. It is also a way for you to keep your skills current and remain aware of what is happening in the professional world. There are many organizations for digital art and media. Some of the them are groups of professionals, while others cater to artists. This is a list of some well-known professional organizations. Check your local area for others, as well. This will introduce you to your colleagues and provide you with both professional growth and social activity with people who share your interests. Some of the better-known professional organizations are SIGGRAPH, National Association of Broadcasters (NAB), Audio Engineering Society (AES), Art and Science Collaborations (ASCI), International Society for Electronic Art (ISEA), Ars Electronica, Broadcast Designers Association (BDA), American Institute of Graphic Artists (AIGA), College Art Association (CAA). For an excellent reference on the Web, look at www.rhizome.org. It offers a comprehensive and current list of arts organizations, museums, art on the Web, and so on.

Health

Without good health, you will not be able to work or develop a professional career. Because working with computers involves a lot of sitting, looking at a monitor, and repetitive actions like clicking the mouse and typing on a keyboard, I want to make sure I talk about ergonomics. Figure 12.1 shows the proper way to sit at a computer. Be sure you have a comfortable chair that allows your back to be straight, your legs level, and your feet flat on the floor. Your eyes should be level with the monitor, so that you are looking directly at it or slightly downward. You should not be looking up at it. Adjust the chair and table height to get this balance. Also, I recommend

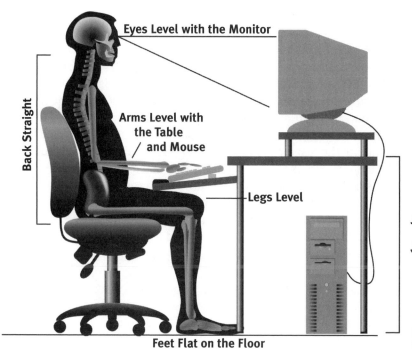

Eyes Level with the Monitor

Back Straight

Arms Level with the Table and Mouse

Legs Level

27" - 29"

Feet Flat on the Floor

[12.1] A diagram of the correct posture for using a computer. Please follow this guide.

using a mouse pad and keyboard with a wrist rest to prevent carpal tunnel syndrome. I use a mouse pad with a soft gel pad on it and a long soft gel pad in front of my keyboard. The important thing here is that your wrist stays level and is not bent. I had carpal tunnel syndrome in the early 1980s before it was widely recognized, and it can be devastating to your career if you cannot work on a computer. Fortunately, mine went away, but I always take precautions to prevent it. I spent hundreds of hours writing this book and took the measures to protect myself that I am recommending to you. Please take them seriously, as your health is one of the most important things you have.

Summary

The point of this chapter was to get you started on developing your professional career. If you have carefully read this book and done all of the exercises, you have a good start. As I mentioned early in the book, creativity is the most valuable talent and skill you can possess. Anyone can be taught how to use software. Those who use the soft-

ware to make art are the ones who succeed. This book is based on my seventeen years of teaching at the School of Visual Arts and my professional experience. My former students are now working at ILM, PDI/ Dreamworks, Disney, Warner Brothers, Digital Domain, Rhythm and Hues, Sony Imageworks, Blue Sky, MTV, Nickeodeon, and many other studios. What I taught them about creativity is in this book. The books in the bibliographies were carefully chosen by me during the research for this book and I own all of them, in addition to many others. As a reminder, I have listed the most helpful books first. Please add the ones that will help you to your personal library. A professional career takes hard work. With this book, the other references and the professional references cited in this chapter, you have all the information you need to begin your career. I wish you the best success.

Lois Swan Jones, *Art Information and the Internet: How to Find It, How to Use It,* Oryx Press, Phoenix, AZ, 1999.

This is an excellent, comprehensive book on exactly what the title says. If you are doing any Internet research related to art, this book is a must. It will pay for itself on your first project.

Anne Morgan Spalter, *The Computer in the Visual Arts,* Addison-Wesley, Reading, MA, 1999.

This book is a general introduction to computers in the visual arts. It has both a fine art and technical focus, and treats these subjects in a comprehensive manner.

Ray Kurzweil, *The Age of Spiritual Machines,* Penguin Books, New York, NY, 1999.

Ray Kurzweil is a visionary, and this book is a worthwhile read. He has many interesting, thought-provoking ideas.

---

1. Write a resume for yourself. Use the exact format recommended, with you name, phone number and e-mail at the top, followed by a one-sentence professional objective. Then list your software literacy. Next list your work experience with the title of the job you did first in bold, followed by the company name and location and a sentence or two describing your duties and responsibilities. Finally, list your education. If you are a student and have not had a lot of work experience, put your education first and list the courses that support your future goals. Finally, compose a 75- to 100- word biography of yourself.

2. Put together a personal Web site. Look to see if your name is available as a domain name. It is money well spent. Use the assignments in this book and your own portfolio to compose the site. Include your resume, bio, and samples of your artwork, photography, computer art, video, 2D and 3D animation, and so on, on it. Make a vow to update your site annually. Also, put together a print portfolio of your work. With this project done, you are well on your way to becoming a professional digital artist. Congratulations!

Bruce Wands

Chair, MFA Computer Art Department
Director of Computer Education
School of Visual Arts
209 E. 23 St.
New York, NY 10010

bruce@sva.edu
Web site: www.brucewands.com

Biography

Bruce Wands is the chair of the MFA Computer Art Department and the Director of Computer Education at the School of Visual Arts in New York. He has been a faculty member for seventeen years in the graduate, undergraduate, and continuing education programs in computer art. *Time Out New York* named Bruce as one of the "99 People to Watch in 1999." He has lectured and exhibited his creative work internationally, including Europe, Japan, Hong Kong, and Beijing, China. His computer art, photography, music, and writing explore the invention of new forms of narrative and the relationship between visual art and music. His Web site is www.brucewands.com. He is the director of the New York Digital Salon, an international computer art exhibition. Bruce is also an independent producer/ composer with his own company, Wands Studio, which has created award-winning design, video, animation, and music for AT&T, General Motors, United Technologies, Colgate Palmolive, and others. Bruce was the first musician to perform live over ISDN lines on the Internet in 1992. As an educational and corporate consultant, his clients have included the New York State Department of Education, the Center for Creative Studies, Buffalo State College, and Direct Gas Supply. He has a BA with honors from Lafayette College and an MS from Syracuse University, where he studied computer art and mass communication.

Awards and Honors

Time Out New York, "99 People to Watch in 1999"
3D Design Conference Advisory Board, 1999–2000
NY SIGGRAPH Board of Directors, 1991–2000
NCGA Educator's Scholarship
Gold Medal, Chicago Film Festival
AT & T "Dataphone II" Film
Silver Medal, New York International Film and TV Festival
Air Safety Foundation "Using the Airspace"
Silver Medal, New York Art Director's Club
"Quotron Foreign Exchange" Forex '92 videotape"
Poems of Light," computer-animated poetry
Spectacolor Billboard, Times Square, New York
8th place 2nd Annual Poetry Film Festival
National Safety Council Award for Excellence
"Stall/Spin: Myths and Facts," Air Safety Foundation
Academic Scholarship, Syracuse University
James Ellwood Jones Fellowship, Roanoke College

Academic Positions

Chair, MFA Computer Art Department, School of Visual Arts, New York, June 1998–Present

Responsibilities include overseeing the operation of a graduate Computer Art department with 100 full-time students, supervising 7 staff members, writing curriculum, managing a faculty of 40, supervising the operation of a computer graphics facility (35 Silicon Graphics computers, 25 Macintosh computers, 20 PC computers, digital and analog video editing and audio recording systems), planning and managing the budget, interacting with other departments, schools and companies, acting as the Chair of the New York Digital Salon (an international computer art exhibition), and promoting the department through professional activities and lectures.

Director of Computer Education, School of Visual Arts, New York, NY, 1992–Present

Responsibilities include writing computer art curriculum for academic departments, working with the Chairs of other departments to plan curriculum related to computer art, assisting the administration with the development and integration of new technology within the academic institution, meeting with students from other departments and continuing education students regarding curriculum, career planning, admission requirements and assisting faculty with the development of computer art skills.

**Computer Art Faculty,
School of Visual Arts, New York, NY, 1984–Present**

Teaching of graduate, undergraduate and continuing education classes. Classes taught include: MFA/BFA Thesis, 3D Modeling and Animation, Interactive Multimedia, Computer Video, Computers and Animation, Business Graphics, Graphic Design with a Computer, Desktop Publishing, MFA Studio I, Computers for Film and Video, Intermediate Computer Graphics Workshop, Principles and Practices of Computer Art, Storyboarding and Scripting with the Computer, Open Studio.

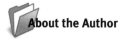

INDEX

10 base T, 34
100 base T, 34
24-bit color, 41
2D animation, 37, 241
    for the Internet, 260
    process, 245
32-bit color, 41
3D animation, 38, 273, 274
    cameras, 278
    lights, 289
    modeling, 281
    points, lines, curves, 279
    scanning, 283
    surface properties, 285
    world space, 274

A

Abacus and mathematics, 2
Acetate cels, 243
Acevedo, Victor, 269-272
ADC, 30
Adjusting a video monitor and signal, 192
Adobe® software:
    After Effects™, 39
    GoLive™, 39, 124
    Image Ready™, 39
    LiveMotion™, 132
    Premiere™, 38
Advanced animation techniques, 293
AES, 310
Aiff files, 219
AIGA, 310
Alias, 13
Alias/Wavefront Maya™, 38
Alignment, 109
Alpha state, 55
AltaVista™, 62
Ambient light, 289
American Institute of Graphic Artists, 310
Analog and digital audio theory, 216

Analog to digital converters, 30
Analog video formats, 192
Analog video signal, 190
Animatic, 87
Animation, 291
    animation drawing, 254
    field guide, 258
    photography, 257
    scriptwriting, 246
Animo, 38
Anticipation, 252
Appeal, 254
Apple computer, 10
Armstrong, Edwin, 7
ARPAnet (ARPA), 15
Artificial light, 172
Artists, 93
Art and Science Collaborations Inc. (ASCI), 310
ASCAP, 223
Ask Jeeves™, 62
Aspect ratio, 102
Asteroids, 9
Atari, 16
Audio, 94, 197, 215
    formats, 218
    on the Internet, 218
    input, 30
    Internet formats, 219
    locating sounds/music, 226
    MIDI, 11, 12, 218
    preproduction, 220
    production, 221
    recording process, 224
    sound and video, 133
    types of microphones, 224
Audio CD, 42
Audio Engineering Society, 310
AVID editing system, 31
AVID keyboard, 28

B

Babbage, Charles, 2
Bandwidth, 34, 260
Basics of digital media, 27
Bass, 216
BDA, 310
Benante, Catherine, 236-239
Bezier curve, 280
Bit depth, 217
Bit-mapped animation, 261
Bit-mapped programs, 37
Bit-mapping, 36,37
Black level, 191
Blinn, 285
BMI, 223
Books, 4
Borge, Rich, 142
Bounce flash, 173
Brainstorming, 57
Branching structures, 86
Bray Studios, 242
Breaking down a script, 248
Broadcast Designers Association, 310
B-spline, 280
Budgets, 88, 92
Bull's eye, 104
Bump maps, 288
Bus, 32

C

CAA, 310
Cable modem, 34
Camcorder microphones, 226
Camera:
    camera bag list, 167
    composition, 168
    covering a scene, 198
    digital camera, 162
    digital photography, 157
    equipment, 167
    exposure and shutter speed, 166
    lighting techniques, 290
    techniques, 194
Campbell, Joseph, 55
Cardinal spline, 280
Cardioid microphones, 225
Cartesian coordinate system, 275
Casio CZ 1000, 11
Cave paintings and drawings, 3
CCD, 163
CD-ROM, 13-14, 33, 42
Central processing unit, 32
CERN, 15
Character animation, 251, 293
Chinese language, 3
Choosing a microphone, 224
Choosing a typeface, 110
Choosing music, 223
Chroma, 191
Clean-ups, 255
Clipping plane, 277
CMYK, 41
College Art Association, 310
Color, 104, 106, 170, 285
    and images, 130
    depth, 41
    palettes, 42
    temperature, 196, 289
Compact flash memory, 164
Composition, 168
Computer animation, 94
Computer image, 40
Concept/idea, 123
Condensor microphones, 224
Contrast, 168
Covering a scene, 198
CPU, 31
Creating an animation for the Internet, 261
Creating and preparing content for the Web, 128
Creative photography, 168
Creative process for 2D animation, 245
Creative use of type, 110
Creativity, 51-52
Curves and arcs, 253

DIGITAL | Creativity

D

Defining the assignment, 160
Defining content and gathering
    information/resources, 123
Defining objectives, 160
Deforest, Lee, 7
Depth of focus, 164
Design, 102, 293
    bandwidth, 34, 260
    brainstorming, 57
    bull's eye, 104
    creative use of type, 110
    creativity, 51-52
    flow chart, 86
    four "I"s, 52
    grid system, 104
    layouts, 110
    metaphor and visual style, 127
    new considerations, 106
    rule of thirds, 102
    and typography, 101
    Web-safe palette, 42
    working with type, 111
Designers, 93
Desktop publishing, 10
Determining software for the Web site, 125
Development of personal computers, 10
Development of workstations, 9
Diffusion, 286
Digital 2D animation, 259
Digital audio production, 219-220
Digital camera, 162
Digital correction and editing, 161
Digital image, 178
    processing, 179
Digital methods, 59
Digital photographic production process, 159
Digital photography, 157
Digital subscriber lines, 35
Digital video
    formats, 193
    software, 204
Digitizing video, 198

Directional lights, 290
Director, 93
Disciplined creative process, 60
Discreet 3D Studio Max™, 38
Discreet Flame™, 39
Discreet Inferno™, 39
Disk drives, 33
Disney dozen, 252
Displacement maps, 288
Dolphin Productions, 9
Drawing and sketching, 63, 254
    animatic, 87
    brainstorming, 57
    bull's eye, 104
    painting and drawing, 36
    sketchbook, 59
    storyboards, 85, 247
DSL, 35
Duplicating, 229
DVD, 33, 42, 203
Dynamic microphones, 224
Dynamic range, 217

E

Early computer graphics, 8
Early Internet, 15
Ease in and ease out, 253
Edison, Thomas, 6
Editing, 199
Eight-bit color, 41
EISA, 32
Electricity, 5
Employment, 308
Ergonomics, 310
ERIC, 15
Ethernet, 34
Exaggeration, 253
Excite℠, 62
Exhibiting your personal creative work, 307
Exposure, 166
    and shutter speed, 166
Exposure sheet form, 248
Extrusion, 282
Eye point, 27

F

Farnsworth, Philo 7
Fill in flash, 173
Final preproduction materials, 88
Firewire, 31
Flash™, 172
Flat, 284
Flow chart, 86
Focal point, 103
Follow through and overlapping action, 253
Fonts, 130
Form, 169
Form follows function, 104
FORTRAN, 9
Four "I"s, 52
Freelancing, 309
Frequency range, 216
Fundamentals of motion, 251
Fundamentals of typography, 107
Future trends in digital video, 204

G

Games, 16
Gamma, 132
Genigraphics, 9
Gigabit ethernet, 34
Gloss, 285
Google, 62
GoTo™, 62
Gouraud, 285
Graphics tablet, 29
Grid system, 104
Gugliemo Marconi, 6

H

Hammer, Bonnie, 118-119
Harry Fox Agency, 223
Health, 310
Heller, Steven, 98-99
Hierarchical animation, 294
History of digital media, 1

Hobbs, Pamela, 146, 153
Hotbot, 62
Hovagimyan, G.H., 207
Hypertext markup language (HTML), 39, 129
    text and tags, 129

I

IBM, 8
    pc, 10
Idea/concept, 83
IEEE, 31
Ilink, 31
Image archiving, 161
Image file format, 131
Image maps, 287
Image plane, 276, 277
Image sequencing, 250
Immersion, 53
In-betweens, 255
Information architecture, 124
Infoseek, 62
Inking and painting, 256
Input, 28
Inspiration, 52
Intel, 32
Interlaced video, 190
International Society for Electronic Art (ISEA), 310
Internet, 14, 39
    search engines, 62
Inverse kinematics, 294
Irix, 36
ISA, 32
Isolation, 54
Iteration, 55

J

Job searching, 308
Johnson, Patricia, 233-235
Joint photographic experts group, 132
JPEG, 132

K

Kerlow, Isaac, 70-75
Kerning, 109
Keywords, 62

L

Lackow, Andy, 266-268
LaFarge, Antoinette, 210
Large studios, 89
Lavalier microphones, 226
Layout and camera composition, 292
Layouts, 110
Lenses, 164
Letterform, 107
Libraries and book stores, 62
Lighting, 172, 195
    contrast, 195
    fundamentals, 195
    intensity, 195
    lighting for 3D, 289
    techniques, 290
Lightwave, 38
Limited animation, 251
Linear lights, 290
Links, 133
Linux, 36
Locating sounds/music, 221
Location:
    lighting techniques, 197
    photography, 177
    sound, 226
    or studio shoot, 161
Long shot, 194
Lycos®, 62

M

Macintosh 512e, 10
Macintosh OS, 36
Macromedia:
    Director™, 38
    Dreamweaver™, 39, 124

Fireworks™, 39
Flash™, 132
Mainframes, 8
Maintaining a personal web site, 307
Making exposure sheets, 249
Manufacturing and distribution, 89
Mastering, 228
Medium shot, 194
Medline, 15
Meeting the client, 159
Memory, 32
Mesmer, Otto, 242
Metacreations Painter™, 38
Metaphor and visual style, 127
Microphone patterns, 225
Microphones, 30
    choosing, 224
Microsoft Windows™, 36
MIDI, 11, 12, 218
    parameters, 218
Midrange, 216
Mixing, 227
Modeling, 281
Modems, 34
Montiors, 40
Morris, David, 67
Mosaic, 15
Motherboard, 32
Motion pictures, 6
Motorola, 32
Mouse, 29
MP3, 219
Multimedia standard, 14
Multi-plane camera, 244
Music, 222
    choosing, 223

N

Narrators, 221
National Association of Broadcasters (NAB), 310
National Television Standards Committee (NTSC), 190
Nature of sound, 216
Navigation, 86
    and flow chart, 86

NCSA, 15
Nechvatal, Joseph, 297-300
Nessim, Barbara, 76-79
Netscape, 15
New design considerations, 106
Normal camera view, 278
Normal lens range, 165
NSFnet, 15
NTSC, 190
Nurb, 280
NYIT, 9

O

Omnidirectional microphones, 225
Ones, 255
Opacity maps, 288
Operating systems, 35
Oral history, 2
Output, 40, 180
Oxberry camera, 243-244

P

Page structure, 137
Painting and drawing, 36
Panopticon project proposal, 136
Particle systems, 204
Pattern, 172
Paul, Christiane, 20-25
PCI, 32
PCMIA card, 164
PDA, 35, 59
Peg registration system, 242
Peg systems, 243
Pentium, 32
Personal digital assistants, 35
Phase, 191
Phong, 285
Photographic production process, 159
Photographs, 5
Photography/video, 66
Photomation, 251
Pixel, 37
Planning animation, 291

PNG, 132
Point and shoots, 162
Point light, 290
Point, lines and curves, 279
Polygons, 282
Polyline, 280
Portable network graphic format, 132
Portfolio, 306
Portrait photography, 176
Ports, 33
Postproduction, 89
Practical concerns when digitizing footage, 199
Practical creative techniques, 58
Preparation of image in final form, 161
Preproduction, 82
Press release, 83
Previsualization, 87
Primitives, 282
Principles of design, 104
Printers, 43
Printing press, 4
Process of animation drawing, 254
Processing, 31
Producer, 92
Production, 88
    environments, 89
    pipeline, 81
    process, 83
    schedule, 91
    team, 92
Professional digital cameras, 162
Professional issues, 305
Professional organizations, 310
Programmed animation, 261
Programmers, 95
Programming, 39
Prosumer, 162
Pyramid of vision, 275-276

Q

Quantel paint box, 12
Quicktime, 219, 261
QWERTY, 28

DIGITAL Creativity

R

Radio, 6
RAM, 32
Raytracing, 288
Reader's Guide to Periodical Literature, 62
Reading a soundtrack, 249
RealAudio, 219
RealNetworks, 42
Recording process, 224
Red eye, 174
Reflection and environmental maps, 288
Reflectivity, 286
Rendering, 295
Research, 60
Research/sketching, 84
Resolution, 41
Resolution-independent software, 37
Resume, 306
Rhizome.org, 310
Role of the animation director, 246
Rotation, 277, 282
Rough mix, 228
Roughs, 254
Rule of thirds, 102

S

Sample rates, 217
Scaling, 277
Scanners, 29
Scanning and digitizing, 178
Scheduling, 90
Schlanger, Matthew, 182-188
Schlappi, Zach, 301-304
Script, 85
Scriptwriting for video, 193
Searching, 137
Secondary action, 253
Serial ports, 33
Shading models, 284
Shake, 39
Shape, 169
Shooting video, 197

Shotgun microphones, 226
SIGGRAPH, 310
Silicon Graphics Incorporated, 13
Site design and prototype, 126
Site structure, 137
Sketchbook, 59
Small studios, 90
SMPTE time code, 199
Software, 35
    applications, 36
Sound effects, 222
Sound and video, 133
Space invaders, 9
Spacing, 109
Specularity, 285
Spot lights, 290
Squash and stretch, 252
Staff positions, 308
Staging, 252
Stock music, 222
Storyboards, 85
    form, 86, 247
Storytelling, 2
Straight ahead and pose to pose animation, 252
Streaming media, 16, 203
Studio, 59
Studio lighting, 174
    techniques, 196
Sun and light, 172
Surface properties, 285
Surfaces, 283
SVA subway poster design, 113-115
System configuration, 43
Systems administrators, 95

T

Table-top photography, 175
Team, 122
Technical issues, 163
Telephone, 5
Telephoto camera view, 279
Telephoto lens, 165
Television, 7
Texture, 171, 287

Index

Timing, 253
  and exposure sheets, 291
Tours, 138
Transformations, 277
Translation, 277
Transparency, 286
  maps, 288
Treble, 216
Tripod, 167
Twist or roll, 279
Two-bit color, 41
Twos, 255
Typefaces, 107
  choosing, 110
Type size, 108
Types of microphones, 224
Type style, 109
Typewriter, 6
Typography, 107
  alignment, 109
  creative use of type, 110
  choosing a typeface, 110
  fundamentals of typography, 107
  kerning, 109
  letterform, 107
  size, 109
  typefaces, 107

U values, 287
Unidirectional microphones, 225
Unix, 36
US Animation software, 38
USB, 31, 33

V

V values, 287
Vector animation, 261
Vector-based painting and drawing programs, 36,37
Vector formats, 132
VGA, 12
Via Video, 9
Video, 42, 93

camera techniques, 194
editing and compositing, 38, 199
for the Internet, 202
input, 30
level, 191
lighting, 195
output, 202
production, 189
production process, 193
production techniques, 193
production team, 205
sync, 191
Viewpoint, 168

W

W3C, 16
Wacom tablet, 29
Wands, Bruce, 315
WAV files, 219
Web design and production, 121
Web design production process, 123
Web production, 94
Web-safe palette, 42
Webcrawler™, 62
Whitney, John, 9
Wide-angle camera view, 279
Wide-angle lens, 165
Windows media player, 219
Word spacing, 109
Working prototype, 87
Working with type, 111
Working with type and image, 112
World wide web, 15
Written language, 3
WWW, 15
www.pamorama.com, 146, 153

Yahoo®, 62
Zip drive, 33
Zoom, 195
Zoom lens, 165
Zworkin,Vladimir, 7

DIGITAL | Creativity

NOTES

NOTES

NOTES

NOTES

NOTES

NOTES